# Stopping 1. SS-Panzer Division during the Ardennes Offensive

# Stopping 1. SS-Panzer Division during the Ardennes Offensive

Hugues Wenkin and Christian Dujardin

Pen & Sword
MILITARY

First published in Great Britain in 2025 by
Pen & Sword Military
An imprint of Pen & Sword Books Limited
Yorkshire – Philadelphia



ISBN 978 1 03610 388 0



A CIP catalogue record for this book is available from the British Library.



Typeset by Mac Style
Printed in the UK by CPI Group (UK) Ltd, Croydon, CR0 4YY.

MIX
Paper | Supporting responsible forestry
FSC® C013604

The Publisher's authorised representative in the EU for product safety is Authorised Rep Compliance Ltd., Ground Floor, 71 Lower Baggot Street, Dublin D02 P593, Ireland.
www.arccompliance.com

For a complete list of Pen & Sword titles please contact

PEN & SWORD BOOKS LIMITED
47 Church Street, Barnsley, South Yorkshire, S70 2AS, England
E-mail: enquiries@pen-and-sword.co.uk
Website: www.pen-and-sword.co.uk
or
PEN AND SWORD BOOKS
1950 Lawrence Road, Havertown, PA 19083, USA
E-mail: uspen-and-sword@casematepublishers.com
Website: www.penandswordbooks.com

# Contents


*Introduction* vii

**Chapter 1 A Hangover for Peiper** 1
A Gloomy Tomorrow 1
Peiper Cut Off From the Main Body of 1. SS-Panzer Division 6
The Ruthless Counter-Attack Against Stavelot 10
The Beginnings of the Petit Spay Bridgehead 17
Meanwhile, On the Other Side of Amblève 21

**Chapter 2 The Elimination of KG Peiper Begins** 25
200 Children in Battle 25
Peiper Caught in the Trap 37
Pressure on La Gleize From the North 39
2/505th PIR Moves to Trois-Ponts 43
The Americans Seal Off the Front in the Stavelot Sector 48

**Chapter 3 Head-On Collision at Cheneux** 56
82nd Airborne Division Heads for Rahier 56
Cheneux Attack Ordered in Haste 62
The Bloody Assault 66
Cheneux Holds Out 71
The German Front Line Gives Way 76
Hand-to-Hand Combat in Cheneux 78
Close Support…From a Distance 82
504th PIR Loses Veterans 85

**Chapter 4 The Bloody Clean-up at Cheneux** 87
The SS Counter-Attack 87
The Capture of Monceau 91
Cheneux is Finally Safe 95
The Result of the Attack on Cheneux 96
Civilian Testimonies 100
A Critical Look at the Capture of Cheneux 101

**Chapter 5 The Battle to Reach Peiper** 103
1. SS-Panzer Division Completely Torn Apart 103
Hanging at Easy Company 106
KG Knittel Under Siege 112
KG Hansen Joins in the Dance 115
Consequences of a Collapsing Bridge 120
Fuel: the Eternal German Struggle of the Battle of the Bulge 123
The Pozit VT Proximity Fuze 127

**Chapter 6 A Fierce Battle for the Saint-Édouard Sanatorium** 129
Battling It Out in a Hospital Full of Children 129
New Unit Puts Pressure on Peiper 135
1/119th Attack Saint-Édouard 136
The Final Assault on Saint-Édouard 141
2/119 IR Attack 143
Peiper Retreats to La Gleize 145
The SS Evacuate Saint-Édouard 147

**Chapter 7 In the Cauldron of La Gleize** 154
Concern for the Injured 154
In the Cauldron of La Gleize 156
Pressure Builds on La Gleize 158
The Failure of Aerial Refuelling 161
The Americans Keep Up the Pressure 163

**Chapter 8 The End of the Stavelot Pocket** 166
West of Stavelot, Nothing New! 166
The Light Tanks Fall Back at Coo 167
Counter-Attack at Petit-Coo 172
The Fighting on Stavelot Ridge 175
CCB Withdrawn From the Stavelot Sector 178
The Remaining SS Evacuate the Bridgehead 184

**Chapter 9 Peiper Slips Away** 191
Understated Reports to OKW 191
Courage, Let's Go! 193
Start of the Nocturnal Odyssey 196
An American Front Undergoing Restructuring 200
Gavin Ignores the Runaways 203
KG Peiper Manages to Reach its Lines 205
A Watered-Down Vision of Peiper? 207
A Sympathetic Debriefing 212
Peiper's Self-Criticism 214
Epilogue 214

**The Violence of a Fiasco** 217
Equipment Lost by KG Peiper in the Stoumont – La Gleize Pocket 217
Deploying the Second Line of Defence 221
Pure Violence 222
The Key Point of the Offensive 223

*Appendix 1* 224
*Appendix 2: KG Peiper Order of Battle* 225
*Notes* 228
*Bibliography* 236

# Introduction

The failure of the last attempt to cross the Amblève at the Stoumont station marked a real turning point in the fighting in Kampfgruppe Peiper's sector, which is where our first volume (*The Breakthrough of Kampfgruppe Peiper in the Battle of the Bulge*) ended. Despite being on the verge of collapse, the American front had held, although SHAEF (Supreme Headquarters Allied Expeditionary Force) managed to bring back enough fresh units to block the German spearhead. On the morning of

Panther 221 of KG Peiper photographed by the US Army after its abandonment in La Gleize. The machine was equipped with steel-tired rollers (Stahlrollen). (*Nara*)

This Panther belonged to 130. Panzer Division and was photographed in the Neffe sector on 18 December while waiting for fuel. The wait was to cost 5. Panzer-Armee dearly by allowing 101st Airborne Division to move into Bastogne. (*Rockenbrod*)

The members of the Dachau Trial Tribunal, charged with judging the crimes committed by 1. SS-Panzer Division in the Ardennes, returned to Stoumont station to inspect the place where KG Peiper had been blocked. (*Nara*)

The US front line did not collapse without a fight; the GIs held out before being overwhelmed by their numbers. Their sacrifice, particularly in front of Saint-Vith, gave the US commanders an opportunity. (*Nara*)

19 December, two dangerous German salients had formed in the Ardennes. One had just been blocked at Stoumont and would not reach the Meuse, while the second failed to take Bastogne and decided to bypass the town, which was now a focal point thanks to the last-minute arrival of the 101st Airborne Division. This encirclement was to prove very costly for the 5. Panzer-Armee, which was to lose half of one of its two Panzerkorps.

At Stoumont, Peiper was faced with insoluble difficulties. After the losses he had suffered since the beginning of his breakthrough, the offensive potential of his Kampfgruppe was dulled. His fuel was running out and his lines of communication were threatened at Stavelot. The enemy had recovered from its surprise attack and was now up against fresh units. They were relatively well equipped, while his men were already tired after three days' fighting.

Half of Peiper's strike force was unable to reach him. Most of the Tiger IIs of the schwere SS-Panzer Abteilung 501 remained blocked in front of Stavelot; only twelve of these heavy machines had managed to cross the Amblève, three were stuck on the road between Stavelot and Trois-Ponts and two had broken down. The rest were struggling to reach La Gleize, where their gargantuan fuel consumption would bring them to a standstill. Their presence represented almost more disadvantages than advantages. Kampfgruppe Peiper could be regarded as a wounded animal caught in a trap, which was inexorably closing in.

In reality, the Americans' main asset was the terrain of the Ardennes. The Amblève valley represented the quintessence of what the Ardennes could offer to determined defenders. First, there is the winding course of the river, whose successive meanders needed to be crossed. There were several bridges on the road to Peiper, all of which were obstacles that the American combat engineers would transform into anti-tank ditches. The valley was very steep, so the presence of a ford and its capture were no guarantee of being able to cross beyond the crossing point. The height differences are also so great that without a road, it is impossible to get out of the valley.

The same observations also apply to Saint-Vith. On 19 December, this town, at the junction of the two Panzer-Armee positions, was still very solidly held; a resistance that would be key to the confrontation. First of all, this resistance meant that the German attack did not immediately form a broad-based salient, but two smaller salients. Here, as in other cases, size mattered. A small salient is easier to reduce than a large one, whose width would at least guarantee roads in its centre that would be safe from enemy artillery. Saint-Vith was also a railway terminal linking Germany to the string of small Belgian stations. The railway was an essential umbilical cord for the German salient in the Ardennes as it enabled the Germans to get away from the few roads they had and to make up for the endemic shortage of lorries that had plagued the Wehrmacht since the start of the war. However, Saint-Vith resisted and its railway station only fell into German hands once it was completely ruined. So, by holding the bridges and fortifying the major crossroads, Eisenhower's generals played their best trump card to perfection.

The historian needs to extract himself from these pragmatic realities in order to explain the facts correctly. It must also be said that the context in which the Battle of the Bulge was fought is essential in explaining the course of the battle in Kampfgruppe Peiper's sector. The situation of the two adversaries on 16 December is crucial to understanding the inevitable failure at *Wacht am Rhein*.[1]

At this stage, the Third Reich had been bled dry. Its recruitment services were scraping the bottom of the barrel to put together units that, in turn, they were struggling to train and equip. Poor quality substitutes became the rule. The soldiers were living in a demoralising wartime atmosphere. Defeats at the front, particularly in the East, followed the systematic destruction of Germany's most beautiful cities and industrial centres. No matter how perfect a system is when first put to the test, it can only survive adversity by rationalising its workings and stretching its components to the limit. This was the situation in Germany in the autumn of 1944. In this case, the lack of fuel on the eve of the fighting, the inexperience of the first waves, the impossibility of forming an entire Panzer Regiment equipped with medium tanks whose moderate size would have made it

The 82nd Airborne Division took part in Operation *Market Garden*, but despite their courage the operation was a failure. The German recovery had not been properly gauged by Allied intelligence. (*Nara*)

easier to manoeuvre in the sector than this substitute unit comprising two half-battalions of medium tanks and another of heavy tanks, all added up to Peiper's eventual downfall.

On the other side, the Allies had recovered from the setbacks they had suffered in the autumn in Arnhem, Lorraine and the Hürtgenwald, while the opening of the port of Antwerp considerably reduced the length of its communication routes. Eisenhower's force was also preparing to go on the offensive. The attack was planned for the north and south of the Ardennes shortly after the start of operation *Wacht am Rhein*. This planned attack explained the presence of a considerable strike force on the flanks of the German salient in the making. Eisenhower was going to rely on his two best generals to take over from the Bradley–Hodges duo, who had been knocked out of the running by the direct hit they had just received. Montgomery in the north was to play the role of anvil with the American troops placed under his command, while in the south, George Patton was

General Hodges was overwhelmed by the situation. His front collapsed under the final blow of the German offensive. He is photographed here in front of an audience of generals in spring 1945 at the presentation of the M26 Pershing. (*Nara*)

to be given a blank cheque to drive into the flank of the German position, the strength of which he unfortunately underestimated. The arrival of three fresh American divisions in Peiper's sector should be seen in this context, with the 82nd Airborne Division, 30th Infantry Division and 3rd Armored Division being sent to harden Monty's anvil.

The following lines will explain this process. We are not the first to talk about these key events in the Battle of the Bulge, yet we are certain that our approach is different. On the one hand, it is the result of our fierce determination to treat the products of the official American historiography with great circumspection. The army's historical services in Washington never lied, but they did often truncate the facts to hide the failings of the GIs and their officers, leading to holes in this disjointed version of the facts. We have filled these gaps by using new sources made possible by our collaboration with the Bastogne War Museum, which opened its documentation on the battle to us, as well as sources supplemented by our research in the major archive centres such as The National Archives at Kew, London, the Bundesarchiv in Freiburg and the NARA in Washington.

I have lost count of the number of times I have arranged for my friend Christian to meet me in front of the Tiger II at La Gleize to go back to a valley bottom indicated by a report in order to understand the influence of the topography of the area on the course of events. This systematic return to the field enabled us, on many occasions, to detect any untruths in the reports, which were sometimes written sparingly by officers who wanted to hide their mistakes. It would have been a mistake for local people from the Ardennes, like us, to have missed out. The result is an in-depth analysis, with a fresh look at the sources we used and our feedback from the field. Christian and I hope that the results will convince you of the usefulness of this approach.

I must also add that, as we touched those yellowed papers, we really got to grips with the conflict. Working with sources so close to the facts inevitably immersed us in the horror of war. We are veterans of this kind of historical essay and we had never experienced so much violence with such palpable acuity. Reading some of the reviews, I had the same suffocating sensation as the first time I saw the Omaha Beach landing scene in the film *Saving Private Ryan.* The difference here was that what I was reading was not fiction but had actually been experienced by young men in their twenties. I want to warn you, dear readers, that from the very first lines you, too, will be hit with this reality. We have chosen to show the war as it is, in all its horror. Be warned, you will not emerge unscathed from this journey through time. Some passages really are hard to read, but we hope that, like us, the more you learn about war, the more you will hate it!

Hugues Wenkin

Tiger II 213, now on display in front of the La Gleize museum. (*Hugues Wenkin*)

# Chapter 1

# A Hangover for Peiper

## A Gloomy Tomorrow

After the failure of the Stoumont station, Peiper quickly realised that his opponents were of a different calibre to those he had faced since the start of his breakthrough. Less than a year after the event, he told his US interrogators:

*At the time, we were confronted by elements of the 30th Infantry Division and the 82nd Airborne Division, who were fighting much more savagely than the 99th ID. We decided to hold the bridge south of La Gleize, as it could prove important later, while deciding to attack Stoumont. At dawn on 19 December we launched the assault with a Panzergrenadier Abteilung and a Fallschirmjäger-Kompanie attacking on either side of*

The remains of the Peiper armoured point in front of Targnon, photographed in spring 1945. (*Nara*)

*the road, all supported by Panzer fire. Once again, because of the terrain, the tanks were unable to leave the road. Heavy fire from Stoumont and heavy flanking fire from the north by your 30th Infantry Division prevented us from getting into Stoumont. However, using the same technique of sending up two or three tanks at full speed, we broke through and cleared the village. We then continued due west to the bridge west of Stoumont, which was all we could do with the fuel we had left.*[1]

*From there, events quickly began to turn against us. The officer commanding the Aufklärung-Abteilung informed us that Stavelot had been recaptured and that our infantry had been pushed back to the western edge of the town. I immediately ordered him to attack from the west and clear Stavelot.*[2] *On 19 December, three counter-attacks on Stoumont were repulsed. However, we began to realise that we no longer had enough fuel to cross the bridge west of Stoumont. As a result, we ordered the forces west of Stoumont to withdraw. On 20 December, we tried to attack again with little success. American troops were attacking from north-east of La Gleize and at the same time attacking Cheneux, where we had left a group to hold the bridge. Realising that we were too weak at La Gleize, Stoumont and Cheneux, and in danger at all three, we decided to abandon Stoumont overnight. A small counter-attack covered our withdrawal. After Cheneux was captured and recaptured twice, we abandoned it on 20 December to regroup at La Gleize.*[3]

In his account, Peiper talks about the problems caused by the American reinforcements dispatched to the area. To understand the circumstances of the problem, we have to go back two days to the Trois-Ponts sector. On 18 December, Colonel Wallis Anderson,

Stoumont station before the Second World War from positions held by the SS. It is immediately clear that the terrain favoured the defenders as it was difficult for armoured vehicles to get through. (*Nara*)

A Kettenkraftrad captured by an American engineer unit. This support troop proved to be very flexible and, in the end, its delaying action gave the SHAEF time to build a second line of defence. (*Nara*)

commanding the 1111th Engineer Combat Group, organised the defence of Trois-Ponts. The company of the 51st Engineer Combat Battalion (ECB) occupied the town. Lieutenant Fred Nabors' second section was at Aisomont on the Wanne road with two bazookas, while 3rd Platoon joined the twelve men manning the small anti-tank gun of the 526th Armored Infantry Battalion (AIB) on the Stavelot road. The rest of the company was deployed along the Salm and its confluence with the Amblève. The sappers of the second section set up a roadblock with a string of mines and two bazookas. At around 11:30 a vanguard of three Panzer IVs followed by around thirty vehicles approached the roadblock set up by Fred Nabors. The machine gun of the lead tank fired on the mines, causing them to explode, and the Panzer continued inexorably towards Trois-Ponts. The bazooka fire proved ineffective, and the sappers withdrew, losing only one bazooka. Near the station, a bridge over the Liège – Luxembourg railway line had been demolished in September 1944 by the Germans as they retreated. Although hastily repaired with wooden elements, it was not certain it could support the 25 tonnes of a Panzer IV. Nevertheless, the GIs dynamited it as a precaution.[4] Meanwhile, on the road to Stavelot, the 57-mm gun blocking the Peiper column's path was neutralised, the explosion giving the American engineers the signal to destroy the bridge over the Amblève.

The quickest route to the Meuse via Werbomont was blocked by 'those damned engineers'. In accordance with the instructions received before the operation, Peiper continued forward and did not concern himself with his flanks or with securing the passage of the troops that were supposed to follow him. On the US side, only one company of sappers defended Trois-Ponts. To impress the enemy and encourage them to be cautious, Lieutenant Colonel Fraser ordered several trucks to attach chains, remove their exhaust pipes and drive around the village to give the enemy the impression that tanks were arriving and occupying the town. In the early hours of 19 December, a

A mortar-carrying half-track from 3rd AD supported the unit's infantrymen. This armoured division, with fresh troops, was one of the reinforcements sent to hold the line. (*Nara*)

Sherman M4A3 (105mm) and M7B1 105mm self-propelled guns were part of 3rd AD divisional artillery available to Task Forces. (*Nara*)

reconnaissance platoon from 505th Parachute Infantry Regiment (PIR), 82nd Airborne Division, finally joined C Company of the 51st ECB on the road to Basse-Bodeux.

These were not the only US reinforcements sent to the sector. At 9 am on 19 December, Colonel John Welborn, head of the 33rd Armored Regiment (AR), called his officers to his headquarters. He had taken over 'ad interim' command of Combat Command B (CCB) of 3rd Armored Division (AD) in the absence of General Boudinot, and so gave instructions to his men.

The 1/33rd AR, under the command of Major Kenneth McGeorge, had arrived about 10 kilometres north of Stoumont, in the small village of La Reid, at around 11 pm to bivouac. The reinforced I/33rd AR was led with an iron fist by Lieutenant Colonel William Lovelady. The unit reached its destination at the hamlet of Marteau, 3 kilometres east of Spa, at 10 pm. The train and various administrative troops were left behind. The 3/33rd AR was then detached from the CCB and sent to reinforce troops near Hotton, a town much further south of La Gleize, where it came up against another armoured front, that of the 116. Panzer Division. The tanks were initially manned by the XVIII Airborne Corps under the orders of General Matthew Ridgway, before being attached to the Doughboys of the 30th ID 'Old Hickory', nicknamed 'Roosevelt's SS' because of their legendary fighting spirit.

The 30th ID was a veteran unit that fought in all the liberation campaigns. The members of this experienced unit earned the nickname 'Roosevelt's SS'. Here, two GIs inspect an abandoned Panther Ausf G in Normandy. They were used to fighting this type of equipment, which formed the backbone of KG Peiper. (*Nara*)

That same day, A Company, 743rd Tank Battalion (TB) was integrated into the third battalion of the 117th Infantry Regiment (3/117 IR), its objective being to surprise Kampfgruppe Peiper in its rear at La Gleize.[5] After securing Malmedy, the 3/117th IR was relieved of its mission as soon as the 120th IR arrived. The regimental command post was set up at Francorchamps at the Hôtel des Bruyères, in the same location as the divisional HQ. The battalion was sent to Ruy, 4 kilometres north-east of La Gleize, arriving at 11:15. Its L Company was sent to Roanne, K Company headed for Cour, while I Company remained in reserve at Ruy.[6] As a result of these American movements, Peiper's exposed northern flank came under threat from a powerful armoured element reinforced by an infantry battalion. To the south, from his position, the Obersturmbannführer found himself at odds with the paratroopers of the 82nd Airborne Division. A powerful vice had just been set up around the small village of La Gleize, occupied by the SS.

## Peiper Cut Off From the Main Body of 1. SS-Panzer Division

At dawn on Tuesday, 19 December, the ancient stone bridge spanning the Amblève at Stavelot was under US Army control thanks to the combined efforts of the small arms fire of first section and the 81-mm mortars of D Company, 2/117th IR. The heavy company of the 117th IR remained on the city's high ground. After many deviations, the

SS-Manners try to fight their way into the front line by taking advantage of a ditch. (*Nara*)

105-mm batteries of the 118th Field Artillery Battalion (FAB) took up position, a little late, at the place known as l'Eau Rouge, the low point of the legendary Le Raidillon bend, a legendary stretch of the famous Francorchamps circuit.[7] Rudolf Sandig, commander of the SS-Panzergrenadier Regiment 2 (SS-PzGr-Rgt 2), 1. SS-Panzer Division, was still trying to make his way through Stavelot. It, too, had seen its offensive potential dwindle over the previous days and now had only a third of its strength. Meanwhile, II/SS-PzGr-Rgt 2 was on its way to reinforce Kampfgruppe Peiper, which had already integrated Hauptsturmführer Josef Diefenthal's III/SS-PzGr-Rgt 2 via the Petit Spay bridge. Obersturmbannführer Rudi Sandig said of the action:

> *The deployment was discovered by the enemy to the west of the Amblève and it unleashed an incredible defensive fire consisting of light and heavy artillery, mortars, heavy machine guns, snipers and, later, even low-flying attack aircraft that dropped bombs on the whole surrounding area and fired their weapons on the battalion. There were very heavy casualties! It was impossible to advance any further. The men sought refuge in the basements to the right of the road. The distance separating our units was about 300 metres. Communications between the companies and the battalion command post*

> *were impossible. Only limited messaging traffic was possible the following night. Any movement was immediately met with artillery and mortar salvos. The enemy was particularly aggressive, and snipers, well hidden in the houses to the west of the Amblève, were particularly effective. This deadly defensive fire lasted all day. It was only as darkness fell that my remaining battalion commander, Sturmbannführer Richter, got a rough picture of the situation his men were in.*[8]

Untersturmführer Friedrich Pfeifer, commander of 2. Kompanie of Richter's battalion, was one of the Germans who managed to reach the houses on the right bank of the Amblève, which was swollen with water in that particularly wet winter:

> *We held our position on the other bank of the river for about eighteen hours, but we only had one MG42 machine gun and almost no ammunition left. We had no contact with the other bank. At dawn* [21 December] *we began our retreat across the river below the bridge under heavy fire. I remember that this action cost the lives of twenty-three men. If the 4th Company had been there and we had had reasonable fire support, it might have been different, but he* [Sandig] *had been too impatient.*[9]

Pfeifer stated categorically that his men had remained on the north side of the river until dawn on the 21st, whereas the American account indicated that they had been driven back at about 7:30 the previous morning. Whatever the details of Sandig's attack on the

The MG 42 could fire twenty rounds per second and could be deployed on a heavy carriage (photo) for sustained long-range fire, on an anti-aircraft carriage or simply with its light bipod to accompany the infantry in the assault. It considerably increased a squad's firepower. (*Nara*)

The Doughboys of 30th ID held out in Stavelot. Here, one of them is carrying a Garand with a rifle grenade attached. (*Nara*)

night of the 20th, he ordered I/SS-PzGr-Rgt 2 to withdraw and establish a defensive line.[10]

Despite several violent SS attacks, the Americans held firm, with the artillery playing a decisive role in the success of the Doughboys' fierce resistance. Every attempt to cross the Amblève at Stavelot was brutally and bloodily thwarted. At around 1:00 pm, at the Stavelot bridge, the Germans launched a new infantry assault supported by a Tiger II Ausf B. A well-placed M10 tank hunter, ambushed at the foot of the abbey, fired a 3-inch armour-piercing shell, hitting the huge beast below the turret and putting it out of action. The exploits of the crew, commanded by Sergeant Dudley, stopped any further attempts to cross the structure, and the area became an impassable no-man's-land.[11] As a result, the thin umbilical cord feeding the strike force at the head of the Leibstandarte was virtually cut off. At this point, only a small bridge still allowed the SS to cross the Amblève to join Peiper's forces. It was at a place called Petit Spay, near the 5-kilometre road between Stavelot and Trois-Ponts.

## The Ruthless Counter-Attack Against Stavelot

As far as the attackers were concerned, the guns preventing the recapture of Stavelot were operating directly from the northern heights of the town. After an impromptu meeting with Peiper at the end of the fighting at Stoumont, SS-Sturmbannführer Gustav Knittel, leader of the Schnelle Gruppe 'Knittel', which had emerged from SS-Aufklärungs-Abteilung 1, quickly ordered his subordinates to turn back and assemble at the Trois-Ponts viaducts. Knittel then took charge of the battalion. The order to retake and occupy Stavelot came from Wilhelm Mohnke, commander of the SS division. Kampfgruppe Sandig, which had remained on the left bank of the Amblève, had to force its way through and reoccupy Stavelot in order to re-establish the line of communication between Peiper's armoured fist and the rest of the division. Knittel quickly drew up an attack plan, bearing in mind that he did not have his entire Schnelle Gruppe at his disposal. SS-Aufklärungs-Abteilung 1, reinforced by half a dozen 105-mm howitzers and a company of pioneers, numbered around 1,200 men. Of the five organic companies planned, Knittel had only four at his disposal, the 1. SS-Kompanie having remained in Germany for lack of transport. Others were not fully manned, or had not arrived, the logistics route being cut off at the bridge over the Amblève by American fire. In addition,

The 105-mm guns of the American artillery wreaked havoc on the ranks of the SS attacking the heights of Stavelot. (*Nara*)

he had to leave his aide-de-camp with some of his troops to reinforce KG Peiper. A quick calculation gave him around 450 available soldiers. A reconnaissance patrol sent out urgently detected movements at the western end of Stavelot, and Knittel assumed that small numbers of American troops had occupied the town again during the night and morning.[12]

To carry out his mission, Knittel sent the 2. SS-Kompanie, commanded by Obersturmführer Manfred Coblenz, towards the town via the main road linking Trois-Ponts to Stavelot. The Stabskompanie,[13] led by Obersturmführer Goltz, had to climb to the northern heights of the town to annihilate the artillery or the observers who were supposed to be there. At the same time, its mission was to flank the 2. SS-Kompanie and was the first to arrive at the Trois-Ponts viaducts. Quickly disembarked from the troop carriers, the section leaders received their orders. Coblenz took with him the first and second sections, commanded respectively by Untersturmführers Hilbert and Farny. Their objective was to bypass the entrance to Stavelot from the north and take the shortest route to the bridge over the Amblève at the bottom of the town in order to renew contact with Sandig's SS men, who were trapped on the other bank. Mohnke was counting on this pincer attack to re-establish his lines of communication with his isolated troops on the other side of the tumultuous Amblève. The third section, led by Untersturmführer Siebert, launched its assault via the main road between Trois-Ponts and Stavelot, acting autonomously on the right of the road. Untersturmführer Jakob's 'heavy' section, meanwhile, provided the necessary support.[14]

Sturmbannführer Gustav Knittel commanded the Aufklärungs-Abteilung of 1. SS-Panzer Division. It was his unit that was responsible for most of the massacres of civilians around Stavelot and Trois-Ponts. (*Rights reserved*)

The Stabskompanie carriage soon arrived on the scene and the two railway viaducts towards Stavelot were crossed. SS-Untersturmführer Dröge, leading the first section, accompanied by around ten stray parachutists, reported to Knittel.[15] The officer gave him clear instructions: climb to the top of the hill to the north, then fall back towards Stavelot to the east and disable the enemy batteries. Dröge did just that and headed for the path leading to the top of the hill, where he came face to face with two civilians, brothers Oscar and Gustave Job, aged 57 and 59 respectively, who were shot down in cold blood. Ernst Malh, who was part of the Pionierzug, testified before his Belgian judges: '*We saw two elderly men walking towards us. Untersturmführer Dröge fired at the civilians with an American weapon. Then he turned to us and said, "This is what you have to do with all 'those'". I can't tell you whether he said, "including prisoners of war" at the time, but I think I heard him say it.*'[16] The move had barely begun when Obersturmführer Goltz arrived with the rest of his company. Urged on by his superior, he followed in Dröge's footsteps with the

Charges had to be carefully prepared to obtain optimum firing time. This gunner is preparing a 105-mm shell. (*Nara*)

Nachrichentenzug, led by SS-Oberscharführer Wieze.[17] Behind, on board GMCs, the Fahrradzug[18] was commanded by Untersturmführer Kolaschny. He received the same orders as his brothers in arms.

The procession of war leaves a trail of blood in its wake. Under cover of impunity, the depths of the human soul reveal their darkest side. For no apparent reason, the soldiers of the Schnelle Gruppe committed appalling atrocities against civilian men, women and

The Legaye house, where a large number of war crimes were committed. It is located at the western end of the town of Stavelot. The SS would not progress much further towards the town. (*Stavelot Library*)

children. The victims ranged in age from 9 months to 86 years old, from little Bruno Klein to old Ferdinand Bolette, both from Parfondruy. In all, ninety-seven people were murdered by Knittel's men on that tragic Tuesday, 19 December 1944 alone.[19]

Goltz joined his subordinate Dröge at the crossroads, where the small roads coming from Coo headed back towards Ster and Parfondruy. The pioneers continued to climb towards the hamlet of Ster, while the commander of the Stabskompanie, accompanied by the Nachrichentenzug, headed for the hamlet of Parfondruy. Dröge and his men occupied Ster without a fight. After their atrocities, they headed towards Renardmont, using civilians as shields before getting rid of them by massacring them in the shed in front of the Legrand farm.[20]

What follows is taken from the report of the Liège Military Prosecutor's Office at the end of the trial held to punish these war crimes:

Golz photographed crossing the Kaiserbarracke crossroads. He was formally recognised by witnesses at the Liège trial. (*Nara*)

*Dröge, who led the pioneer platoon, and Kolaschny, the cycling platoon, were escorted by a few tracked cars. Some immediately climbed the heights, while others followed the railway embankment, eventually crossing it and heading up the paths and meadows leading to the hamlets of Ster, Parfondruy and Renardmont. The first farms we came across were ignored, and we were only concerned to find out whether any American soldiers were hiding there, as was the case at Ferme des Maures, for example. A group arrived at the top of the hill and reached the hamlet of Ster. It was the Pioneer Platoon. Dröge gave the order to search the houses, gather all the civilians and have them march forward while being supervised. Around fifteen people, including two women, were arrested and taken away. They headed for the hamlet of Renardmont, in front of the American artillery position, which they had to locate and dislodge.*

*When they reached Renardmont, the situation became perilous; the Allies were some distance away; the patrols that had been sent forward realised that resistance was strong, that the American armies were holding the whole wood and that they had been assigned a difficult task. As the prisoners were a nuisance, Dröge planned to eliminate them. Three times, farms were explored, but no doubt not finding the right places, they continued on their way, persisting in stopping other inhabitants in their homes. Entering a small house, they found themselves in the presence of an invalid old man; they shot him without saying a word. Spotting another man fetching wood from a small shed in his garden, they shouldered their weapons in his direction and shot him; nor did they hesitate to fire in the direction of two young men who were trying to escape from the group of prisoners. Finally, this gloomy procession arrived near the Legrand farm. Using rifle butts and their boots, the twenty-three people, including the two women, were forced into a small wooden hut. Once everyone was inside, some merciless SS men machine-gunned the interior of the barn through the wooden walls. The bodies of the victims fell on top of each other, most of them killed instantly. Others, further back, were protected by the bodies falling on top of them.*

*Not yet satisfied, the SS entered the barn, examined the corpses and gave the coup de grâce to those they thought were still alive.*

*They continued to be relentless. However, the order was given to fetch wood and straw and set fire to the barn. When everything seemed to be over, a whistle sounded and the men set off again to attack the American positions.*[21]

The SS once again engaged in intolerable violence before moving down and regrouping in Parfondruy, which had already been sacked by Kolaschny's henchmen at around 2:00 pm. The three sections of Goltz's Stabskompanie returned empty-handed; not a single enemy battery had been spotted, let alone deactivated. Worse still, the artillery they were supposed to be muzzling began to target them: the 81-mm mortars of D Company, which had arrived on 18 December with the 1/117th IR. Although placed in battery above the Erlinchamps, on the northern edge of Stavelot, their range was sufficient to reach German infantrymen in the Ster – Renardmont – Parfondruy area.

Allied press correspondents photograph German atrocities. (*Nara*)

Charles Corbin was an artillery observer with the 391st Armored Field Artillery Battalion and remembers the horrific sight of the SS massacre when he arrived at Renardmont:

> *The next morning, as I was watching our position, I went into a house and saw an elderly couple dead, bullets in their heads, throats cut, lying in blood. In another house, two women and a baby in a cradle were dead. One of the women was naked, with a bullet in her head and part of her left arm torn off. I was in a corner of a courtyard when two children appeared as if out of the mist and said to me: 'Long live America'. One of our soldiers stopped them and told them not to go into the house because the people were dead. They said they were looking for their parents and relatives and went in. I returned to our CP in a daze. William Whitten and I had just turned 20 less than a fortnight ago. It was hard to get back into the war.*[22]

## The Beginnings of the Petit Spay Bridgehead

Elements of the 2. SS-Kompanie, the 1. and 2. Züge under Hilbert and Farny, were commanded by Manfred Coblenz. After following the main road, the SS headed towards the town along the railway towards Stavelot. After a few hundred metres, they came under fire from the machine guns and 60-mm mortars of the GIs stationed in a nearby villa. Coblenz decided that the objective should be taken by his subordinate Siebert with his platoon, and that it would be too costly for his group to support him. He logically diverted towards higher ground to avoid the obstacle. Arriving on the heights to the east of Renardmont on the edge of the Borzée wood, Coblenz wanted to assess the possibilities of attacking the town. Unfortunately, his group was spotted and immediately bludgeoned by the artillerymen, who were not sparing with their projectiles. At around 2 pm, Knittel set up his HQ at the Antoine farm, along the main road between Stavelot and Trois-Ponts, where he found the crews of three Tiger IIs. Tiger 008 was damaged and could hardly move, while Tigers 132 and 133 were simply bivouacked. The commander of the Schnelle Gruppe asked for their help. As no marching orders or missions had been given to the tank commanders, they agreed.

Tiger II 008 was plagued by mechanical problems and its mobility was reduced. It would later be used as a bunker to protect Knittell's HQ. (*Nara*)

Despite its mobility problems, Tiger 008 managed to position itself to face the enemy coming from Stavelot, using it as a bunker. Meanwhile, Tiger 132 took up position at the outlet of the viaducts at Petit Spay, blocking all incoming traffic from Trois-Ponts. Finally, Tiger 133 would support the troops attacking the city to be reconquered.[23] The 105-mm howitzers and the three Pak 40 75-mm anti-tank guns took up positions on the left bank of the Amblève at Petit Spay, reinforcing the presence of Tiger 132. Uncle Sam's artillery rolled up its sleeves; any movement in the martyred hamlets became impossible, and the SS had to wait for darkness to allow them to set off again. Obersturmführer Goltz took refuge at the Loffet farm on the edge of the forest,[24] where he stayed until midday on 21 December.[25]

At around 5 pm, Siebert's formation, supported by elements of the heavy section, launched an assault with the 3. Zug. The assault was directly thwarted by guns from the 118th FAB, but shortly afterwards, the GIs began to run out of ammunition and decided it would be wiser to abandon their position and reconstitute a solid line of defence 300 metres to the rear.[26] At around 9 pm, Siebert reached the extreme point of his assault, 500 metres from Stavelot town centre. The darkness of the night allowed the leaders of 2. SS-Kompanie to report back to their commander, and Sturmbannführer Knittel sent the two officers back to the front line to force their way through the town. The evening and night of 19–20 December were relatively quiet, with only a few shots reported around 9 pm by A Company, 117th IR. An additional macabre detail here is that the shots heard by Uncle Sam's sentries were fired by Sibert's SS, who were murdering twenty-three civilians aged between 4 and 68 at the Legaye house.[27]

What follows is the interrogation of Régine Grégoire, a survivor of this massacre, on 1 June 1946, recorded at the Dachau trial. Like many people from the region, she spoke German, a skill that was to save her:

Question from the accuser, Lieutenant Colonel Crawford.

*Q: What is your name?*
*A: Régine Grégoire.*
*Q: Where do you live?*
*A: In Stavelot.*
*Q: In which country is Stavelot located?*
*A: In Belgium*
*Q: What do you do for a living?*
*A: Housewife.*
*Q: Are you of Belgian nationality?*
*A: Yes.*
*Q: Where were you on 19 December 1944?*
*A: In the cellar of the house next door.*
*Q: Were there other people in the cellar?*
*A: Yes.*

SS victims shot near the hedge of the Legaye house. (*Public domain*)

A mother and her little daughter were mercilessly shot dead by Knittel's SS. (*Public domain*)

*Q: Who?*
*A: There were twenty-six of us in all.*
*Q: Were there any other members of your family in the cellar apart from yourself?*
*A: Yes, my two children.*
*Q: How old were they?*
*A: They were 3 and 6 and a half.*
*Q: Was the house on the Trois-Ponts road?*
*A: On the right-hand side.*
*Q: In which part of Stavelot is the house located?*
*A: At the top.*
*Q: Was it on the outskirts of Stavelot in the direction of Trois-Ponts?*
*A: Yes.*
*Q: What happened on the evening of 19 December?*
*A: Shortly before 9 pm, a German threw a grenade into the cellar. Shortly afterwards, the Germans shouted at us to get out. I went out first with my two children, the others followed me. One of them told me we had to get out of the cellar. He told me to look and see if everyone was there. I did, and then he told me to go back into the cellar to see if anyone had stayed. I told him there was nobody left. He told us to sit down and said that the woman who spoke German should come towards him with her two children, which I did, and I saw one of the soldiers take his revolver and shoot at the people, and from what I could hear on the other side, there were SS men shouting and firing rifles.*
*Q: Did you see the flames coming out of the guns when they shot at people?*
*A: No.*
*Q: How many Germans were shooting at people?*
*A: Two as far as I know.*
*Q: How far away were you from the group?*
*A: Two metres.*
*Q: How long did the shooting last?*
*A: Ten minutes.*
*Q: After the shooting stopped, did you hear any shouting from the group?*
*A: No.*
*Q: How many people were in the group?*
*A: Twenty-three.*
*Q: How many men were there?*
*A: Two*
*Q: How many women were there?*
*A: Eight, I think.*
*Q: Who made up the rest of the group?*
*A: Young girls and children.*
*Q: After the shooting, were the bodies left behind?*
*A: Yes, on Friday they were still there.*
*Q: They were still in the same place where they had been shot on the 19th?*

*A: Yes.*
*Q: Where did you go once the shooting was over?*
*A: I asked what was going to happen to me and a soldier told me that it would be better if I took refuge somewhere else.*
*Q: Where did you go?*
*A: I took refuge in a cellar.*[28]

## Meanwhile, On the Other Side of Amblève

Stavelot was also attacked from the west by KG Knittel. On the afternoon of 19 December, we take up the testimony of Friedrich Pfeifer, commander of an SS-Panzergrenadiere company, who recounted his fight for the bridge:

The last island of SS resistance of KG Sandig, on the bank held by the Americans (right bank of the Amblève), was located downstream of the bridge in former tanneries. (*Stavelot Library*)

*Without having had any direct contact with the enemy, my company, which was the spearhead of our regiment, reached the southern part of Stavelot on the Amblève. At the time, this part of the town was not occupied by the Americans. However, we were bombarded by American artillery throughout our approach to Stavelot. Just in front of the bridge was a destroyed tank. It belonged to our Panzer Regiment. An arch on the bridge had also been blown up just before we arrived. We concluded that the northern part of the town, the largest, must be in American hands. In order to lead my men in a victorious attack, I needed the support of a heavy company. But my regimental commander gave me the order to attack immediately, ignoring my request. All this happened thirty minutes after our arrival near the bridge over the Amblève on the afternoon of the 19th. After placing two sections on either side of the bridge as cover, I set off with two other sections.*

*I reached the north bank of the Amblève with great difficulty, having walked along the destroyed arches of the bridge. Suddenly, we were shelled by enemy artillery. We were also hit by grenades thrown from the old abbey and nearby houses. On the roof of the abbey were large flags with red crosses, indicating that the building had been used as a hospital. We did not manage to pick it up. We gathered in the undergrowth by the river to defend ourselves as best we could. We ran out of grenades and ammunition for our machine guns. Waiting for help from anyone was out of the question. The enemy launched flares as soon as daylight fell. Any forward movement became impossible. We were forced to abandon*

A water-cooled .30-calibre machine gun from Dog Company, 1/117th IR, 30th ID, firmly entrenched behind the thick walls of Stavelot Abbey. (*Nara*)

Tiger II 222 was put out of action by a TD M10 embossed on the right bank at the foot of the abbey. (*Stavelot Library*)

> *the north bank of the Amblève at dawn on 20 December. Still under American fire, we marched through the icy waters of the river to reach our rear. We lost twenty-three men. My liaison officer, Biedenkamp, can testify to the truth of this report.*[29]

After reading these accounts, it is clear that attempts to retake the town to the west and south of Stavelot had failed. For the time being, however, the full effects of this noxious situation had yet to be felt. The Petit Spay light bridge, located halfway between Trois-Ponts and Stavelot, was still able to bring reinforcements and supplies to Peiper, and although its load-bearing capacity was limited, it did allow relatively light vehicles to cross.

Tiger II 105 would remain stuck in the Rue du Haut Rivage, its engine muffled by the rubble. (*Stavelot Library*)

This Schwimmwagen was abandoned on the hotly contested Stavelot bridge. (*Stavelot Library*)

## Chapter 2

# The Elimination of KG Peiper Begins

### 200 Children in Battle

The 20 December marked the end of KG Peiper's success after it was caught in a trap that was gradually closing in on it. At 4 am, the first battalion of the CCB of the 3rd Armored Division, which had just arrived in its rest zone, divided into three Task Forces, two of which were made up as follows:

Task Force McGeorge took over I Company, comprising of around fifteen Shermans, accompanied by the second section of D Company, 36th Armored Infantry Regiment

SS-Panzergrenadier move to reinforce the Festung Saint-Édouard. (*Nara*)

SS-Panzergrenadier, Fallschirmjäger and Luftwaffe anti-aircraft artillerymen fought together in the La Gleize – Stoumont sector. (*Nara*)

(AIR), i.e. infantry support composed of infantrymen, reinforced by the first squad of D Company, 23rd Engineers (twelve sappers). Four self-propelled 10-mm Priest M7 howitzers and six 81-mm mortars completed the tactical unit.

The second Task Force was entrusted to Captain John Jordan and its strike force consisted of two sections of M5A1 light tanks totalling ten vehicles, F Company, 33rd Armored Regiment (AR), with around fifteen Shermans, and F Company, 36th AIR, with around 160 infantrymen. All this was supported by six 81-mm mortars and two 105-mm M7 Priest howitzers.

The third Task Force was the most powerful and came under the command of Lieutenant Colonel Lovelady. It was made up of two companies of M4 Shermans, i.e. thirty-four medium armoured vehicles and the rest of the M5A1s from D Company. A platoon of sappers and an infantry company completed the strike force.[1]

At 8 am, with the first light of dawn, the first two tactical groups headed for their respective objectives. Task Force Jordan raced towards Stoumont via the road from Spa, attacking the village conquered the previous day by Peiper. Meanwhile, Task Force McGeorge had to invade the village of La Gleize. As he had been held up at Stoumont station on 19 December, Peiper gave the order to withdraw to the village invaded that morning, located 4 kilometres upstream from the station. At the crack of dawn on 20 December, the 1/119th IR followed the retreating SS and advanced from the Halte de Lorcé towards Stoumont via the hamlet of Targnon. The SS troops had laid strings of mines across the road as it wound its way up the hillside towards Stoumont. Which

The Saint-Édouard Sanatorium took in children to improve their health, but was to become one of the most hotly contested areas of the battle. It is shown here before the fighting. The land around the thickly walled building is open and the configuration of the site explains why it became the keystone of the German defence at Targnon. (*Rights reserved*)

were further covered by snipers to delay the inexorable advance of the 'Ike Jackets' for as long as possible. Five minefields were laid to delay the GIs' advance with some success. In order to make the most effective progress, C Company advanced along the road and two Doughboys were mortally wounded by German sniper fire. B Company advanced to the left of the main axis on the northern flank, while A Company followed slightly behind on the right. The infantrymen were supported by tanks from 740th TB but one of the tanks hit a mine, while a man lost a leg stepping on another well-concealed explosive.

At 3:30 pm, the 'Olive Drabs' were at the entrance to Stoumont when the lead tank hit a mine. Its track was broken and it had to wait for the maintenance echelon to repair it. At 4 pm, despite the gathering darkness, an imperative order came down: '*continue the attack and take Stoumont.*' The II/119th IR remained in reserve at Targnon, which had been emptied the previous day, with the inhabitants having been forced to leave their homes by the Germans. Georgette Harquemanne was 7 years old at the time and has strong memories of the event:

Armoured infantrymen, such as these of Task Force Jordan, were transported on M3A1 half-tracks. (*Nara*)

*It happened in the afternoon, the soldiers made us leave our houses and grouped us in the small square in the centre of the village. A polite German officer, who seemed kind, told us in excellent French that no harm would come to us, but that we had thirty minutes to leave, after which anyone found in the village would be shot. We hurried back to the house with Mum, while Dad went to feed the cows and left the stable door open so they could escape if need be. We mostly took warm clothes, and with Blanche, my big sister, Mum, Dad and Toby the farm dog, we headed for Lorcé, via the wooden bridge that spanned the*

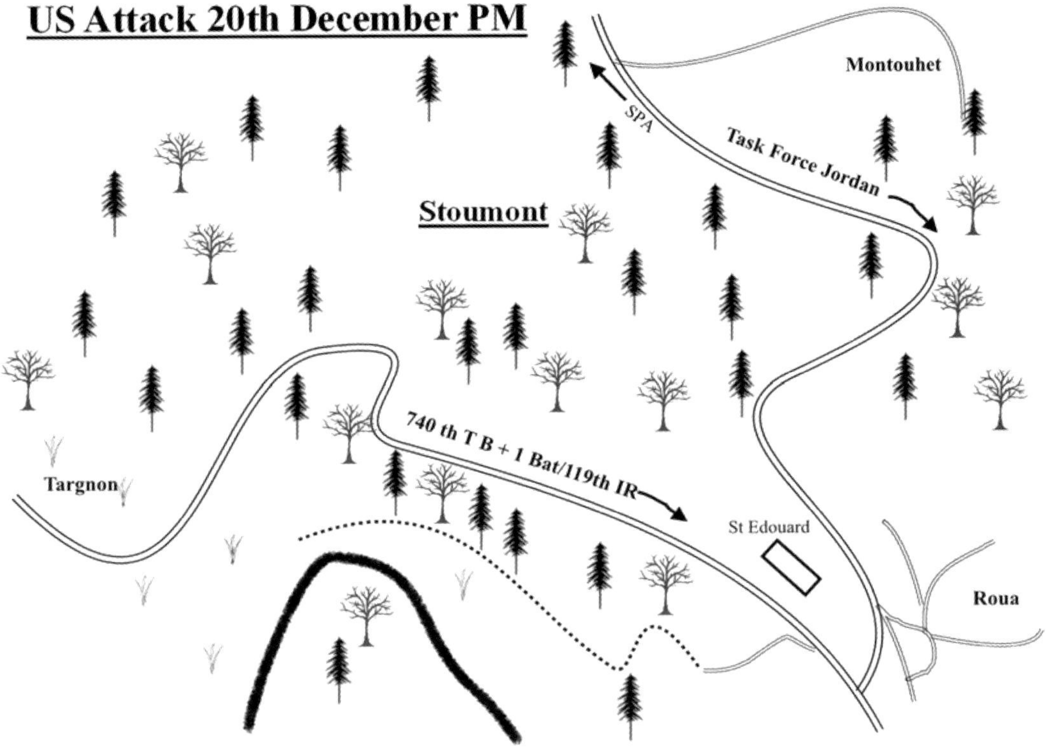


The attack on Saint-Édouard on 20 December was designed as a pincer movement. (*Christian Dujardin*)

> *Amblève, heading for Naze farm along the forest paths on the left bank of the river. We hardly slept at all, as shells kept flying over the farm. The next day, we went to stay with our family in a hamlet near Louveigné.*[2]

The GIs' first target was the Saint-Édouard Sanatorium, located at the western end of the village between the road linking Stoumont to Spa in the north and Stoumont to Liège in the south. Its imposing mass jutted out like a promontory towards the Amblève valley and the building occupied a prime tactical position, being able to hold all accesses to the village under its fire. Its thick stone walls protected the occupants from fire and its many rooms and maze of corridors meant it was a veritable bastion, which is why it became the keystone of the German defences in front of Stoumont. The GIs called the sanatorium 'Le Château' (Castle), while the Germans called it the 'Festung (Fortress) Saint-Edouard'.[3]

The sanatorium housed around 200 children and around fifty German-speaking refugees who had been evacuated from the Elsenborn region. These 250 or so refugees were crammed into a corridor in a cellar with large skylights. It is hard to describe the anguish of these practically walled-in unfortunates faced with the deluge of steel and fire from the incessant artillery shelling. Try to imagine this dark, foul-smelling passageway, 3 metres wide and 30 metres long. An atmosphere filled with dust; the gases from the blasts exploding everywhere amid the screams and cries of terrified children.[4]

A quadruple anti-aircraft gun on a Panzer IV Ausf H 'Wirbelwind' chassis was destroyed during the first attack on the sanatorium. It was fitted with four 20-mm guns that could have done a lot of damage to the GIs. (*Nara*)

Two artillery observers direct a barrage; an operation that was vital to the success of an assault. (*Nara*)

The road alongside the sanatorium was mined and the mines themselves were connected to hand grenades. The aim was to detonate them so that they felled trees, which would then obstruct the road. The US artillery began its work of weakening the enemy defences and as night fell, US infantrymen advanced towards the building.

Unterscharführer Karl Wortmann was one of the defenders of 'Festung Saint-Édouard', and was able to see for himself the growing American pressure on the German positions:

> *We saw the American tanks approaching while a barrage of heavy artillery advanced along another road. The sanatorium came under heavy shelling. A large number of disabled children, several nuns and a priest took refuge in the cellars. No enemy movement was visible to the naked eye. The Americans continued to approach and the shelling intensified. With its massive construction, the sanatorium resembled a fortress. Nevertheless, the walls were dismantled by enemy tank shells, anti-tank guns and artillery. In the end, it was nothing but ruins, with the roof threatening to collapse. The few Panzergrenadiere who weren't wounded didn't want to surrender. They were still fighting hard. It was clear*

The American artillery considerably hampered the SS movements. This Schwimmwagen paid the price. (*Stavelot Library*)

Successive assaults finally drove the defenders back. The American artillery never stopped supporting them. These artillerymen, in well-concealed positions, are preparing shells for the next salvo. (*Nara*)

> *to all the men. The sanatorium was becoming a decisive stronghold. If it was taken, the Americans could easily approach La Gleize. The Americans stormed the ground floor. The SS climbed to the upper floors. There was merciless close combat, man against man, hand to hand. Our comrades threw grenades down the stairs and fired pistols and rifles to clear a way out of the fortress.*[5]

After terrible hand-to-hand combat with grenades and knives, the 'Château' fell to the Americans. Some of the troops occupied the large building while the other GIs dug in their foxholes to await a predictable counter-attack, which began at around 11 pm. B Company received it head-on as the pioneers of Franz Sievers' 3. Kompanie (Gep) SS-Panzer Pionner Battalion with elements of the 9. (Pi) SS-Panzer Regiment and some Fallschirmjäger Regiment 9 rushed towards the Festung and the GIs' positions. Sievers and his men regained a foothold in the sanatorium as the Germans occupied the ground floor while Uncle Sam's men took refuge upstairs. The adversaries were now so close that the GIs could hear the Germans' radio communications.

Abbé Hanlet was a key witness to the tragic events that took place at the sanatorium:

> *On 19 December at around 9 am* [during the German attack on the village], *the Germans burst into Saint-Édouard and captured around twenty American soldiers without ammunition. You can imagine how distressing it was to see these enemies again who had occupied the country for more than four years and from whom we thought we had been definitively liberated. Alas! For three days and three nights, they occupied us like never before. The soldiers set up camp on the ground floor, in the kitchen, in the visiting room, in the community room, in both halls and even in our cellars. Cannons, machine guns and tanks were positioned in front of the buildings and in the surrounding meadows. The peaceful retreat for children and young girls was transformed into a fortress. The soldiers entrenched themselves in each room as if in a fortress and, sheltered by thick stone walls, fired through the windows at our allies.*

After fighting in the ruins, these GIs are recovering from the stress of hand-to-hand combat. (*Nara*)

General view of Saint-Édouard overlooking the valley. The day ended with the capture of the area by 1/119th IR. The SS counter-attacked during the night of 20–21 December. The fighting lasted all night. (*Nara*)

*On the first evening, Tuesday, the Germans, who were still in control of the area, descended into our cellar. They said they were the vanguard of a division that was to march on Liège, where they would be before Christmas. Tomorrow, reinforcements would arrive that would allow them to advance. 'You have nothing to fear from us,' they said, 'if you don't do anything to us. We had to shoot people from Stavelot who were firing at our troops from the windows of the houses.' It was the old legend of the francs-tireurs that served as a pretext for the terrorist methods of the German war.*

*In the cellars of Saint-Édouard, the first night on the battlefield was organised. Mattresses were laid out along the walls: we all recited the last rosary together – it was the day's date! Then, rolled up in a blanket, we went to bed, wishing our neighbours a good night that no one dared hope for themselves. During the night, the battle continued. At regular intervals, the deepest silence was pierced by the cannon fire exchanged between a large German tank standing guard in front of the great hall and the American artillery established at Nonceveux.*

*On the morning of Wednesday, 20 December, we woke up in the catacombs. In the middle of the dark underground passage, an improvised altar stood, lit by a large Paschal*

The damage caused to the Saint-Édouard building testifies to the determination of the combatants to capture this tactically important position. (*Rights reserved*)

*candle, and the Chaplain, assisted by another priest, celebrated the Holy Mysteries before a crowd of 200 people, kneeling or sitting on their mattresses in the most pious contemplation.*

*Every morning there was a truce, or rather a lull, which the inmates took advantage of to wash and have breakfast. They were emboldened to go up to the ground floor, and even upstairs, to pick up useful objects and clothes, and to look around with curiosity.*

*That Wednesday morning, the damage was still minimal, except in the chapel where a few shell holes pierced the vault; in the choir, on the right, a large opening half a metre square pierced the ceiling showing the sky.*

*The fighting resumed in the morning, proceeded by a violent bombardment from the American artillery. Throughout the afternoon there was a terrible fusillade, which increased in intensity until the evening: the house was shelled and machine-gunned from all sides. Bullets crackled relentlessly and clattered against the walls like hail. In the long, dark cellar, another battle was being waged by young girls and children at prayer. While the battle raged around us and over our heads, the attackers had stormed the house and were now fighting in the halls and bedrooms, chasing each other with machine-gun fire. As night fell, the gunfire became less frequent and more distant.*

The 250 refugees were now in a shelter that was becoming increasingly precarious. Abbé Hanlet continues his account:

An M36 Jackson recovered from the Sprimont depot by the 740th TB. It had taken part in the assault on Saint-Édouard, with its 90-mm shells used to fire at points of resistance. (*Nara*)

*Above us, we were walking in the great hall. Isolated shots were still being fired here and there in the house. For a long time, we waited with the greatest anxiety for the outcome of this terrible day. Suddenly, a cellar door opened and a few shots rang out on the staircase, followed immediately by heart-rending cries: 'Civilians, civilians!'*

*American soldiers were arriving: we were saved! What joy, what relief!*

*To calm the crowd's fever, Sister Superior had a dozen rosaries recited in thanksgiving and for the eternal repose of those who had fallen in battle.*

*Then, in the cellar, supper was being prepared. People were talking, laughing, singing: there was joy.*

*The Americans settled into the rooms on the ground floor, and in the kitchen we hurried to get them hot water for tea, coffee and chocolate. Our liberators were as happy as we were. 'It's been a hard day,' they said, 'but the enemy's losses are severe. Tomorrow we leave for Stavelot, Malmedy and ... Germany.'*[6]

Meanwhile, at 12 noon on 20 December, Task Force Jordan joined the roadblock set up at Chefna by survivors of the III/119th IR and two 90-mm guns. These elements were to join Task Force Jordan and advance towards the village and the Saint-Édouard Sanatorium, but the group was quickly halted by a mine barrage shortly before the hamlet of Monthouet. The Germans were ambushed and held the barrage under sniper fire. At around 1:15 pm, the snipers and the minefield were put out of action, and Task Force Jordan then slowly continued its advance in the hostile environment. The road was lined with heavily wooded embankments and the steep slope made lateral deployment of the tanks simply impossible. Its flanks were terribly exposed to any Panzer-armed fighters who might be hiding in the woods, and soon Jordan once again found himself halted by another roadblock as he approached Stoumont.

## Peiper Caught in the Trap

With no news from KG Knittel, which had gone to the rear to retake Stavelot and re-establish the logistics line, Peiper decided in the morning to send a patrol towards Stavelot.[7] The small troop arrived at the Roanne Coo railway bridge and was stopped by Hauptscharführer Nüske, a staff non-commissioned officer, who reported that the road to Stavelot was under the control of an imposing armoured column, which was, in fact, Task Force Lovelady. For the Germans, it was no longer possible to continue and so the unit decided to take up a defensive position at the Moulin Maréchal, 800 metres towards La Gleize. In addition to Tiger II 221, commanded by Untersturmführer Hantusch, the roadblock consisted of a Panzer IV, from 7. Kompanie, commanded by Hauptsturmführer Oskar Klingelhöfer, the only Panzer IV from 7. Kompanie to follow the Peiper column, the others having failed to cross the Amblève at Stavelot. An Sd.Kfz. 234/3 Puma equipped with a short 75-mm gun and a platoon of tank breakers completed the group, which all took up positions on either side of the road to be defended, at the end of a bend in the hillside. If the position was ideal for an ambush, it was imperative

Panzer IV Ausf J equipped 6. and 7. Kompanien of SS-Panzer Regiment 1. They were equipped with Tomas schurtzen, which detonated shaped charges before impact. They no longer had a two-stroke engine to turn the turret, which was operated manually. (*Nara*)

that the Germans were able to hold it, because if they failed, the road would be caught under counter-slope fire.

The staff officer proposed the following plan of attack:

> *The Panzer IV is positioned on the left of the mill, the Tiger on the right. When a sufficient number of American machines are in the open, the Tiger will destroy the leading machine and we will destroy the last. Then we can clear the column from the ends towards the middle. The 'Amis' won't be able to deploy because the road is too narrow there. We have the element of surprise and home advantage. If things go wrong, we can fall back into the valley.*[8]

The Sd.Kfz. 234/3 had a short 75-mm gun similar to this one. (*NAC*)

However, the Panzerführer of the heavy tank rejected the plan: *'Shoot up the hill?! I'm not going to kill myself; I've only got 30 mm of armour on the roof.'* In reality it was 40mm of steel that protected the horizontal upper parts of the Tiger II, not 30, but such detail obviously does not change much in the tank commander's reasoning. However, this discussion highlights one of the weaknesses of the machine's armour, which limited its medium-range interdiction capability on steep slopes.

Pressure from the Shermans from A Company, 743rd TB, accompanied by the Doughboys of the 117th IR was about to materialise. In the end, the engagement did not take place, as a broken track on the enemy side halted the column for the night. The following day, 21 December, the Sperrgruppe was back in line and took up position at Wérimont farm on the heights north-east of La Gleize.[9] This was an important event as it meant that Peiper's withdrawal line towards Stavelot was irretrievably cut off. The KG was practically out of fuel and its imposing Tiger and Panther aircraft were of no use unless they were refuelled. The alternative would be for the bulk of 1. SS-Panzer Division to get through the American bottleneck at Stavelot and join the surrounded KG.

## Pressure on La Gleize From the North

As we saw in the previous volume, the 1/117th IR was relieved of its defensive mission at Malmedy on the morning of 19 December by the 1/ and 3/120th IR of the 30th ID. The 3/117th's new mission was to block the exits from La Gleize to the north and north-east.

The Shermans of 743rd TB and GIs from 117th IR preparing for the assault. (*Nara*)

The battalion was commanded by Lieutenant Colonel Samuel McDowell, who gave K Company the task of blocking the secondary road running north along the ridge to Spa, and the company took up defensive positions at Cour that afternoon without incident.

The Doughboys were joined in the courtyard by elements of A Company, 743rd TB. Floyd Jenkin's 2nd Platoon and Anthony Couri's 3rd Platoon of the 743rd TB reached the objective without encountering any resistance. However, they did drive off some Panzergrenadiere, who had attacked the large fuel depot at Le Rosier, now completely evacuated. The 1st Platoon remained in Roanne before moving towards the Stoumont – Trois-Ponts road. One of the Shermans stopped and fired at a stationary target at the junction of the RN33 road and the Roannay footpath. Tiger 223 was out of action because of a broken track, and the trajectory of the shells was clearly visible with their red tracer as they bounced off the thick frame of the heavy tank. There was no reaction, the crew having left the now harmless steel monster.

A Sherman made a half-turn in search of a better firing point and when it reached a meadow, the tank stopped. The tank commander and his gunner got out to interview some of the civilians there and while the conversation was going on, a Tiger lurking on the heights in the centre of La Gleize adjusted the Sherman in its crosshairs. The firing distance was 2,200 metres and hitting a target at such a distance was a real challenge, but the Tiger's commander was Rolf Möbius, an ace of German aces. As the thick fog suddenly lifted, allowing the Tiger to aim at the US tank, a single shot was fired and the immobile Sherman was easily pierced by the 88-mm shell, which caught fire and trapped the rest of the crew, leaving them to perish in the inferno.[10]

At 1 pm, the men from 743rd TB in Roanne saw a long column of armoured vehicles pass by, as Task Force Lovelady headed towards Stavelot. Meanwhile, Task Force McGeorge arrived in the hamlet of Cour, and added K Company, 117th IR, and the Shermans of 743rd TB to its strike force. Despite its tactical power, Task Force McGeorge was not at its best. On the way to La Gleize, between the hamlet of Borgoumont and its objective, the unit had been targeted by the enemy at 2 pm, with the Germans firing and

Tiger 223 was immobilised when its track broke. It came under fire, but to no avail, from the Shermans of 743rd TB attacking on the heights of La Gleize in the direction of the Moulin Maréchal. (*Nara*)

destroying a Sherman. What McGeorge did not know was that he was dealing with 9. Kompanie (Pi) under the command of Obersturmführer Rumpf, supported by a Panther, four Panzer IVs and Tiger 334.[11]

With time to regroup its forces, Task Force McGeorge launched a second assault at 2:40 pm, consisting of an enveloping movement from the right by the infantry, which forced the SS to retreat about 300 metres and dig in solidly at the Nabonru stream. This time, the terrain at this point made it possible to repeat an overrun manoeuvre, and as night fell, at around 8:20 pm, the SS launched a violent counter-attack. The GIs had to give ground and retreat to the hamlet of Borgoumont, where they set up a solid roadblock. Lieutenant Wanmaker from I Company, 36th AIR, was killed in action.[12]

Doctor Bastin was a privileged witness to the events and provides further details of the unit's After Action Report:

> *Wednesday, 20 December 1944: The Americans arrived opposite Borgoumont; first five tanks rolled down from the Cour, at 10 am. At midday I found them on guard at the edge of the hamlet. As I'd seen a lot in the last three days, the men asked a lot of questions: how many German tanks? Calibres of guns? SS or Wehrmacht? The officer was less demanding: he was mainly interested in identifying on the map the places outside*

The GIs retreated into the woods towards Borgoumont. (*Nara*)

*the village from which the Germans had fired machine guns. The officer told me that Stavelot and Trois-Ponts were in American hands and that the German tanks were cut off from their base. When I got home, I learned that a German soldier had dragged my sister out of the house. She came home all muddy. She screamed despite her fear: the Kraut hid immediately and she fled into the fog. I had no trouble convincing my family of the need to leave the house, which was now between the two camps, and to take shelter in Borgoumont or the Sanatorium. At around 2 am, the Americans, determined to enter La Gleize, set off. I was invited to join the column, to show the soldiers where the terrain was rough: paths, streams and, above all, machine-gun nests. There were twenty-five tanks, 200 men and a dozen resistance fighters from Spa led by Decerf, known as 'Mickey'. These poorly armed young men marched in front of the first tank along the fences. After an hour, we were approaching the village; just a few metres away in the thick fog there was the Villa Closset; we lay down and the leading tank fired a cannonball into the façade. I thought it prudent to drop back 10 metres to the level of the second tank. We soon got up and resumed our march. Then we stopped again and a machine gun fired in the fog. A soldier was wounded in the knee. Dead leaves fluttered above our heads. Two steps from my left shoulder, the earth was shaken by bullets as if by a mole. I knew enough. I wouldn't go any further. But everyone had had enough as far as I could see and the word got out 'We go back'.*

*There was an explosion at the front of the tank I was still lying next to, but I didn't immediately understand that it was a mine; the Sherman hadn't moved a muscle and was moving off again straight away. As I moved back towards the Nononruy, the lead tank, which was also moving backwards, a second mine detonated in the same place; the rubber on the tracks burned; the men lifted the covers, not angry, and left…the tank burst into flames and exploded. The soldiers looked terrible. They were going to have to do some reconnaissance. Mickey and his men were at ease and disappeared into the undergrowth. The tanks scattered under the trees between the Nononruy bridge and the Tchéoux hotel. All were hidden in the mist. But in the evening a gust of wind swept through the air and the German I could see from my window fired a cannonball and burnt up in the tank that remains abandoned to this day 100 metres from Les Tchéoux at the top of the meadow.*[13]

## 2/505th PIR Moves to Trois-Ponts

Around noon, the main body of troops from 82nd Airborne Division's vanguard unit arrived in the village, with Lieutenant Colonel Vandervoort, commander of 2/505th PIR in the lead. The officer would later be immortalised by John Wayne in the film *The Longest Day*. Vandervoort was appreciated and respected by his men for the leadership he had shown in the previous two campaigns when, during the first days of the Battle of Normandy, he commanded his battalion with one foot in plaster.

The colonel deployed his three companies, sending D Company along the Grand Halleux road towards Vielsalm, and E Company to the crest of the Aisomont road,

Lieutenant Colonel Benjamin Vandervoort became legendary for commanding his battalion in Normandy with one foot in plaster. He was a man of great experience and was greatly appreciated by his men. (*Nara*)

which had recently been abandoned by the sappers. Finally, F Company was ordered to set up solid positions at Trois-Ponts, behind the River Salm. Vandervoort recalled:

*In December 1944, the war was taking place in the worst possible conditions. The Belgian Ardennes were heavily wooded, hilly and mountainous. The ground was frozen. Night-time temperatures were below zero. The cold alone incapacitated many soldiers of the 2/505th PIR, who had contracted malaria in Sicily. Like most airborne units in the Ardennes, the 2/505th PIR was plunged into a vacuum miles from any other element of the 82nd Airborne Division. On 20 December 1944, the battalion landed, deployed and marched cautiously along a dual carriageway to a place called Trois-Ponts.*

*There was no information on enemy or friendly forces in the area. Trois-Ponts was a small rural village of two-storey stone houses and shops. The town lay in a narrow valley, dominated by mountains, at the confluence of the Salm and Amblève rivers. At Trois-Ponts, the Salm, with its steep banks, formed a permanent barrier to vehicles, but its shallow headwaters were easily forded by infantry willing to risk their frozen feet.*

*A few women and children were the only civilian occupants when we entered the town. A handful of combat engineers were setting up a defensive position on the bridge over the River Salm to prevent anyone from crossing. These sappers were happy to see the parachute battalion.*

*Due to the wide dispersal of airborne forces, the II/505th was placed under the direct command of the 82nd Airborne Division, which established a forward command post at Werbomont, 16 kilometres west of Trois-Ponts.*

*Holding Trois-Ponts was the cornerstone of General Courtney Hodges' plan for the First US Army to halt, repel and destroy the German winter offensive. Brigadier General Ira P. Swift, deputy commander of the 82nd Airborne Division, newly assigned to the paratroopers, took a personal interest in Trois-Ponts. He ordered my battalion to establish a bridgehead with a single company on the heights east of the Salm River. The rest of the battalion was deployed on the west bank of the river to prevent the enemy from crossing. At the foot of the town, the road crossed the Salm eastwards on a heavy wooden bridge. Immediately after the bridge, the road ended at the foot of a cliff. It then split into two parts, one to the north and the other to the south. The northern road led to two bridges spanning the nearby Amblève. Hence the name of the town: Trois-Ponts. The southern road climbed gently for a few hundred metres, then turned left 180 degrees northwards, over the railway tracks running parallel to the river. The narrow two-lane road climbed steeply up the side of a 100-foot-high cliff, split by a long steep road and a railway line. At a point opposite the bridge, now well below ground level, the road turned 90 degrees to the east, then sloped gently back down to ground level. No vehicle could enter Trois-Ponts from the east along this road without exposing itself to 2.36-inch bazooka fire at close range as it negotiated a hairpin bend for 300 metres.*

*E Company was sent across the Salm to block the cliff road where it stabilised. The men dug in, their left flank slightly straddling the road. Facing east, the bulk of the company chose positions on the edge of a dense wood at the top of the cliff. The wood stretched to the*

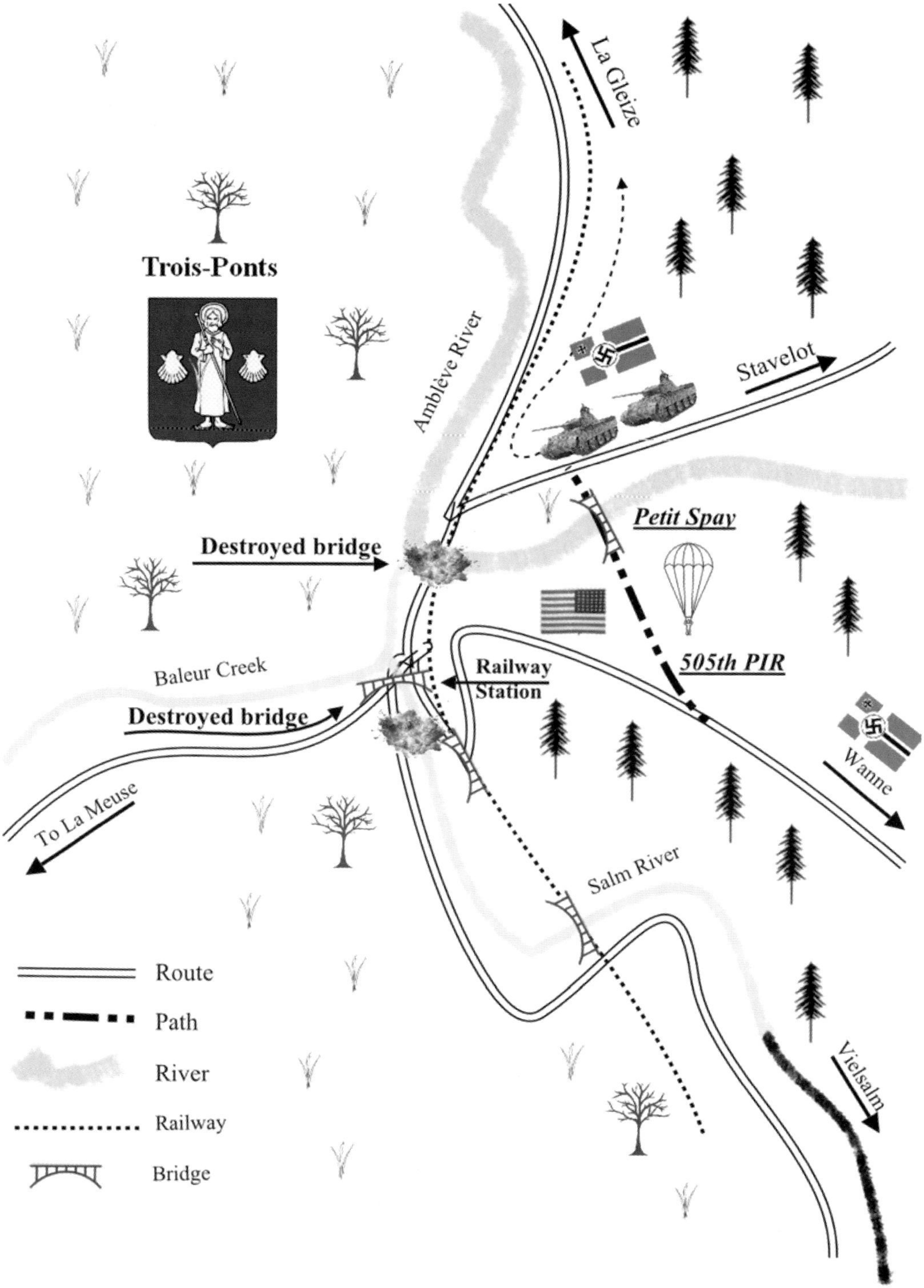


The layout of the Trois-Ponts site prompted Vandervoort to take one of his companies to the heights overlooking the town. (*Christian Dujardin*)

*right, gradually turning into a forest. In front of them, the left side of the road was dense woodland. The right side of the road was a large open field with little vegetation other than pasture-like stubble. From their position inside the tree line, the paratroopers had an ideal field of fire across the road and across the open area. Anti-tank mines were scattered along their front. E Company's command post was located a short distance to the right of the road with the front-line platoons. A 57-mm anti-tank gun was buried in the right-hand shoulder of the road, 20 or 30 metres behind the riflemen. Lieutenant William J. 'Bill' Meddaugh, the company commander, placed a battery of six bazooka teams just in front of the position, in the woods to the left of the road. Behind the bazooka ambush, they placed anti-tank mines across the road. Before nightfall, they were solidly entrenched and*

The paras settle in for the night. Those on higher ground did not benefit from the cosy warmth of a fire (these men are in a barn). (*Nara*)

*settled down to wait in the freezing cold. No fire. No light. No smoke. It was an excellent position for an ambush, but inherently a weak one.*

*It is not possible to defend against armoured vehicles accompanied by infantry. But on the cliff, it was the best position available. The thick woods to the left of the road provided a natural approach for infantry, and the open area to the right of the road was good ground for tanks. The River Salm separated the company from the rest of the battalion and prevented mutual support. On the west side of the River Salm, F Company and the battalion headquarters company, in particular the light machine gun platoon and the bazookas, established a main line of resistance among and in the houses on the riverbank. Machine guns were spotted providing flanking fire on both sides of the bridge. A few more US Army engineers came down from the hills towards the town. We were happy to welcome these lost children. They were dispersed in the main line of resistance so that they could use their 50-calibre machine guns to provide a final overlapping line of protective fire. D Company was sent south on the riverside road to defend the nearest still intact bridge across the Salm. It was to destroy the bridge if attacked in force. The 2nd Battalion was usually teamed up with a platoon from B Company of the 307th Airborne Engineer Battalion. They were sent with D Company to carry out demolitions. D Company and F Company were in contact 24 hours a day with the foot patrols on the west bank of the Salm.*

*Our 81-mm mortar section found a nice observation post on the north sloping mountainside above Trois-Ponts. From here they could see the road network to the east, the bottom of the two rivers and the open field to the east of E Company's position.*[14]

The paratroopers of Vandervoort's E Company were unaware that they had landed in a hornet's nest; they were on the last line of communication of 1. SS-Panzer Division, enabling Peiper to be resupplied.

## The Americans Seal Off the Front in the Stavelot Sector

A little further on, in Stavelot, during the night of 19–20 December, anti-tank mines were laid by sappers from the 30th ID in front of the entrance to the road leading to the Château des Rochettes, where Captain Kent, leader of A Company, had set up his HQ. Although the night had passed calmly, the early morning was restless as the Germans launched a new attack from the Trois-Ponts road towards the centre of Stavelot with the support of one of the three Tiger IIs caught in the trap, in this case No. 133. Arriving at the Legaye house, the tank commander, Unterscharführer Werner Wendt, refused to continue, as the accompanying infantry was unable to clear the mines blocking the road a few dozen metres in front of his tank. Unable to move forward, Tiger 133 stayed put and blocked the road by acting as a bunker; the thickness of its frontal armour making it invulnerable to Allied gunfire.

A Sherman of the 743rd TB managed to approach the monster via the GI-held Stavelot station. When it came within sight of the steel monster, the US tank fired four

Little by little, 30th ID fighters secured their hold on Stavelot. (*Nara*)

anti-tank shells at it but to no avail, as the shells bounced off the thick armour. Following this setback, the Sherman quickly took cover from the German tank's retaliation.[15] The presence of the Panzer prevented any counter-attack by the GIs on 20 December. Despite being pounded by howitzers, a few SS men reached the sawmill on the right of the road and infiltrated towards the company HQ at the Château des Rochettes. Lieutenant Theodore Foote, leader of the section holding the position, immediately asked for fire support from 118th FAB, just under 7 kilometres away. The battery commander advised him that the shells would land on his head and asked him to correct the landmarks. Foote replied that he had not made a mistake and repeated his request to fire on his positions, as his Doughboys had been forewarned and had consequently dug their foxholes deep. The result was not long in coming: the attackers were literally hacked to pieces and not a single GI was wounded.[16] At the end of the night, Schnelle's II/SS-PzGr-Rgt 2 crossed the Petit Spay bridge and headed for La Gleize to reinforce Peiper's troops.

As explained earlier, Combat Command B (CCB), commanded by General Boudinot, was seconded to support 30th ID, which was responsible for blocking the advance of 1. SS-Panzer Division. The CCB was divided into three Task Forces, tactical battle groups: two Task Forces were sent to destroy the Peiper column that was halted at Stoumont and La Gleize. Task Force Lovelady was attached to the 117th IR, which received additional support from E Company, 120th IR, which had remained in Malmedy, who accompanied the tanks and went into battle with Lovelady's tankers.

As his instructions obliged him to do, Peiper did not concern himself with his flanks during his advance. Instead, stopped at Stoumont, he took care to protect his rear as he

General Boudinot commanded the CCB of 3rd AD. In this capacity, he led the assaults on Task Forces Jordan, McGeorge and Lovelady. (*Nara*)

The crew of the M10 that destroyed Tiger 222, which was stopped on the far bank of the Amblève, continued to support the defenders of Stavelot. Since the Normandy campaign, the American command had not hesitated to use them in this way. (*Nara*)

knew he was isolated from the rest of his division. Four Tigers, armed with the formidable 88-mm gun, were in fighting order. Peiper placed them in the village of La Gleize to protect his battle group. The village was strongly defended by the Panthers and Panzer IVs, which had been able to follow Peiper and had dug in.

In the Ardennes, fog is often present at the beginning of winter. In the early hours of 19 December, it protected the infiltration of Panzergrenadiere and Fallschirmjäger into Stoumont. Taking advantage of the pea soup, they advanced undetected, which helped them destroy most of the US Army's anti-tank guns, enabling the Panthers to attack afterwards without too many casualties. In the late morning of 20 December, the same thick smog hid the Lovelady tanks from German armour on the main road between La Gleize and Trois-Ponts below the promontory. Without this providential mist, the American armoured column would have been annihilated by the Panzer tanks, which were ideally positioned to counter any intrusion to the rear of the Kampfgruppe. Lovelady's objectives were twofold. Firstly, he wanted to isolate Peiper's armoured force in the Stoumont – La Gleize sector. Secondly, he wanted to reach Stavelot. Covered by fog, Lovelady's elements raced down the Roanne road towards the main road leading to Trois-Ponts.[17] Once there, a solid roadblock was set up to cover Lovelady's rear. The

The divisional headquarters of 30th ID 'Old Hickory' was in Francorchamp. The building was just a stone's throw from the famous motor racing circuit. (*Nara*)

rope was now firmly around the neck of KG Peiper. As soon as the roadblock was set up, the Shermans and infantrymen set off again towards Stavelot, the column being led by a Sherman whose platoon leader was Lieutenant Hope.

Although the German line of communication passing through the centre of Stavelot was irretrievably cut off, there was still the possibility of reaching the combatants halted at Stoumont via a bridge that crossed the river at a place called Petit Spay, and it was this route that still allowed precious fuel and reinforcements to be transported to KG Peiper. A column of supplies had recently passed over this bridge on its way to La Gleize, where it soon came face to face with the Lovelady column. Lieutenant Hope's lead Sherman reacted quickly. Faced with the Shermans, the German trucks, armed only with light weapons, were quickly put out of action. The passage of troops from the main body of the Leibstandarte to Peiper via Stavelot now became increasingly complicated.

A Hummel, a 150-mm self-propelled gun belonging to SS-Panzer-Artillerie Regiment 1, was destroyed by the leading Sherman of Task Force Lovelady's column on the outskirts of Petit-Coo. The railway line seen here linked Liège to Luxembourg, and its capture would have provided an excellent logistical bypass in the salient. (*Jean Collignon*)

A second roadblock was set up by Task Force Lovelady at the entrance to Coo, a third at the bridge over the railway line in the village. Continuing on its way, Lieutenant Hope's Sherman came face to face with a fearsome Tiger II as it exited a bend. Fortunately, the beast was abandoned when its crew ran out of petrol. The gunner's reflexes were quick; the incendiary shell in the breech went off, and the Tiger II was hit in the right front without suffering any damage. Phosphorus splattered the front of the house alongside which the Panzer had been abandoned. The fire soon spread to the building, completely destroying it.[18] Lieutenant Hope continued on towards Stavelot and once again came up against an enemy column. The Germans took a heavy toll: two trucks, a liaison car, two Pak 40s,[19] a 150-mm Hummel self-propelled artillery gun, five trucks of ammunition and an unknown number of enemy infantrymen were neutralised.[20] An amount of equipment that never reached Peiper.

The direct route from Trois-Ponts to Stavelot was held by Tiger II 132 and the heavy weapons of the Schnelle Gruppe Knittel. As it passed the viaducts towards Stavelot, the US tank platoon was ambushed, and its four leading Shermans quickly put out of action.

The GIs of 30th ID were masters of cleaning up in urban combat. While one of the men covered a room from the window, the second is seen about to enter. (*Nara*)

During the skirmish, a Pak 40 was destroyed; the wreckage cluttered the roadway and Lieutenant Hope was killed.[21] Afterwards, an imposing roadblock was set up to block any German attack towards the Trois-Ponts viaducts. After the violent clash, Lovelady quickly regained its bite: the next charge was scheduled for 8:30 am the following day and would leave Coo for Stavelot by the dirt road via Parfondruy. In the afternoon, Obersturmführer Goltz, who had remained on the heights at the Loffet farm, gathered as many soldiers as he could to launch an assault on the town. Running into the open, the attackers were once again massacred by US artillery: it was the last assault that the exhausted and decimated Germans attempted against Stavelot.[22]

American forces were now in force on the right bank of the Amblève, in addition to the 30th ID. It was necessary, for reasons of efficiency, to bring everyone under a single command, and so Brigadier General William Kelly Harrison Jr., second-in-command of the Old Hickory, took charge. Harrison was responsible for organising and training the 30th ID. He was a man of the field, always close to the front lines, who was well liked by the GIs.

## Chapter 3

# Head-On Collision at Cheneux

### 82nd Airborne Division Heads for Rahier

When 82nd Airborne Division arrived at the Werbomont crossroads, the first thing to do was to ensure the deployment of its paratroopers along the left bank of the Amblève was to clear the German bridgehead at Cheneux. From there, the SS could effectively turn back any American positions along the banks of the river. Colonel Reuben Tucker's 504th PIR was assigned this difficult mission, and its success was the key to securing the defensive line. The parachute regiment was ordered

The battle of Cheneux inaugurated a long campaign for 82nd Airborne Division and was to end in polar conditions. On 20 December, at the beginning of the battle, there was still not a single snowflake on the battlefield. (*Nara*)

When the German attack began, General Ridgway, commanding VXIII Airborne Corps, was in England and so responsibility fell to General Gavin, with General Taylor in Washington. (*Nara*)

to take Rahier, with the 2/504th in the lead, followed by the 1/504th.[1] The paratroopers set off at around 6 pm on 19 December and after a long six-hour march through steep forests, the paratroopers reached Rahier, which they found to be free of the enemy. The recapture of Cheneux was the next logical step.

The diary of paratrooper Corporal George D. Graves gives details of the events leading up to the capture of this village on Wednesday, 20 and Thursday, 21 December 1944. Graves was posted to the S-1 section of 504th PIR headquarters and was responsible for the official record of its daily activities. He also kept a personalised version of the unit diary and this first-hand source is an exceptionally valuable document. Graves describes with masterly accuracy the build-up to the battle, with all the ups and downs and emotions that went with it:

Colonel Reuben Tucker commanded 504th PIR and was a veteran of previous campaigns. (*Rights reserved*)

*The regiment was going to try and take the village of Rahier about 13 kilometres north-east of Werbomont. It was not clear whether the enemy occupied the village or not. The 1st and 2nd battalions were due to move at 6 pm. The 2nd Battalion would take the lead, followed by the Headquarters Company and the 1st Battalion. Captain Hauptfleisch, Sergeant Griffin and I were to move forward, leaving the rest of the S-1 section at Werbomont until the situation at Rahier had stabilised. The night was pitch black as we silently formed up on the road in front of the command post. A thick fog had fallen and the air was damp and very chilly. Captain Hauptfleisch, Griffin and I were at the head of the company column which moved forward in two lines, one on each side of the road. It was 7.30 pm when the last of the 2nd Battalion passed us. We took up a position behind their column for what my fertile imagination led me to believe was our last march. We set off at a fairly brisk pace and, despite the damp cool of the night, I was soon sweating. The country was rugged and heavily wooded. It was during this walk that I saw my first flying bomb. Suddenly I saw a series of lightning bolts streaking across the sky at terrifying speed. A few seconds later, I heard a curious, jerky engine gasp that sounded like two or three large diesel trucks climbing a steep hill. The 'thing' was moving so fast that it was out of sight before we even heard it. After the first one had passed, I heard many more, but they were hidden in the clouds.*

*After walking about 3 kilometres, we started to hear the rumble of artillery: the first I'd heard since we arrived in Werbomont. It was coming from the north, not too far from where we were. Several times we turned in the direction of the impact zone as the road wound around the hills. I was very nervous and expected to be bombed at any moment. To calm my nerves, I said a little prayer asking God to guide us all through the night.*

*We were directly behind D Company in the order of march. When it turned off the dirt road, we naturally followed. This led us down a narrow cow path. We waded knee deep in mud for about a quarter of an hour before the company in front stopped. Lieutenant Colonel Harrison, commanding the first battalion, who was behind our company, ran up and made a hell of a scene.*

Paratroopers arriving at Rahier. Note the British 6-pounder anti-tank gun issued to parachute units. Less bulky than the US 57mm, it could be transported by air. (*Nara*)

Willard Harrison had reached the rank of captain in the regiment during the jump on Sicily. Small in stature, he was promoted several times and became one of the most decorated officers in the regiment; what he lacked in physical size he made up for in courage. After the battle of Cheneux, Sergeant Michael Jalowey said: '*We had a hell of a fight, but our colonel stayed up there with us. He's beaming in battle, but he's the best guy in the world.*'[2]

Meanwhile, Graves' diary continued his account:

*It was obvious we'd taken a wrong turn somewhere. We had to turn the column around from the inside, causing great confusion, swearing and apprehension. Medical jeeps from the 1st and 2nd battalions with trailers loaded with stretchers and valuable medical equipment were following us. The road was too narrow for them to turn in place. If we'd needed them straight away, the situation would have been serious. At this point, I thought Colonel Harrison was going to burst one of his blood vessels. We ended up turning around and returning to the main road, our boots heavy with mud. That was the only mishap of the march; we arrived at the village of Rahier in the middle of the night. There was a*

Jeeps patrolled the length of the column and went up the line. (*Nara*)

> *great deal of firing of all kinds to the north and east of where we were. When the moon came out, it was possible to make out the houses in the village. There was not a living soul outside us, not a ray of light shone anywhere. This deathly stillness in the village itself was unearthly, to say the least. I arrived at the advanced S-1 detachment to act as an interpreter for Captain Hauptfleisch. My task was to find a headquarters for the regiment.*[3]

In the early hours of 20 December, General Gavin was still looking for information from the front lines. He visited Tucker's HQ in the village of Rahier where he learned, independently of any information from XVIII Airborne Corps, of the presence of the enemy at Cheneux, a small village between Rahier and the stone bridge over the Amblève. Colonel Tucker informed him that he had just received information from civilians that about 125 German vehicles, including about thirty tanks, had moved through Rahier on the afternoon of 19 December, in the direction of Cheneux. The information seemed reliable to the commander of the airborne division and shed some light on the enemy's intentions. Gavin assumed the Germans had given up all hope of crossing the Lienne at Neufmoulin, the bridge there having been destroyed. Peiper had also moved to the right bank of the river, leaving a bridgehead on the left bank, holding Cheneux and its precious

General James Gavin was the youngest divisional commander in the US Army. He is pictured here in September 1944 checking his equipment before boarding his C47 to be dropped into Holland. (*Nara*)

strategic bridge. For the moment, he was awaiting reinforcements before continuing his drive towards La Meuse.

Gavin was not mistaken. Before the attack on Stoumont, on his return from the Lienne valley, Peiper had left Major Wolff's anti-aircraft guns to hold the bridgehead. On the afternoon of 19 December, the Panzergrenadiere of the II/SS-PzGr-Rgt 2, commanded by Sturmbannführer Schnelle, arrived in Cheneux as reinforcements. This battalion was part of KG Sandig, which was blocked at the Stavelot bridge. The Schnelle battalion set off on foot from Stavelot towards Wanne, crossed the Amblève at the Petit Spay bridge, then reached La Gleize and finally Cheneux, a journey of around 20 kilometres.[4]

Schnelle's SS quickly organised the Ardennes hamlet into a defensive bastion using the 5., 6. and 7. Kompanien. The commander of 7. Kompanie, Hauptsturmführer Leopold, was killed in the fighting. The Panzergrenadiere companies each had four sections of around twenty-five to thirty men, and each section had impressive firepower. Sixteen MG 42 machine guns gave them incredible support as this type of weapon could fire twenty rounds per second. 11. Kompanie (Gep) of Hauptsturmführer Josef Diefenthal's PzGr-Rgt 2 was also present and was commanded by SS-Obersturmführer Heinz Tomhardt. In theory, this company had three sections of Panzergrenadiere carried by half-tracks. However, only two sections were present at Cheneux, with the third remaining in Germany due to a lack of equipment. The fourth section was a heavy unit equipped with two Sd.Kfz. 251/9 armed with a short 75-mm gun. Only one of the two vehicles was in Cheneux, the other having been blown up by a mine. There were therefore 400 elite infantrymen in Cheneux supported by sixty-four MG 42s, all waiting with bated breath for the enemy. In addition to the Panzergrenadiere, there were also four 105-mm Feldhaubitze from the SS-Panzer-Artillerie Regiment 1, commanded by SS-Obersturmführer Fritz Butschek. Normally, a battery had six howitzers, but the two missing ones had been destroyed in an air attack. These SS units were supported by two light Flak batteries belonging to the Luftwaffe which, when fully manned, numbered twenty-four anti-aircraft self-propelled guns armed with multiple or single 20-mm cannons, and others with multiple 15-mm machine guns.[5]

## Cheneux Attack Ordered in Haste

Although a reconnaissance had been ordered, Gavin and Tucker were unaware of the size of the German forces in Cheneux. Tucker, however, was eager for a fight and managed to convince 'Slim Jim'[6] to attack immediately, playing down the mortal danger posed by the presence of any Panzers because he knew his men were motivated and because he was also counting on a lorry full of Panzerfauste. This German anti-tank weapon had been captured during the fighting in Holland and was far more effective than the American bazooka, so Tucker felt his paratroopers would be up to the task.[7]

Colonel Tucker decided to keep the 2/504th on the defensive around the village, while the 1/504th, minus A Company, which had been sent towards Brume, had the difficult task of gaining a foothold on the left bank of the Amblève. The two remaining companies, B and C, headed for the hamlet of Cheneux at 1 pm on 20 December. The objective was clearly defined: to take Cheneux and the bridge over the Amblève and drive the 'Jerries' off the left bank of the river, while 30th ID 'Old Hickory' was to dislodge them from the right bank.

In his memoirs, Corporal Graves also recalls the departure of the young soldiers for the front: '*At about 1 pm, the first battalion passed our HQ on the road to Cheneux, which we*

82nd Airborne Division arrived on the Ardennes battlefield with a cargo of Panzerfauste captured in Holland. It was not the only American unit to adopt this practice: these infantrymen here have done the same. (*Nara*)

*heard was the battalion's objective. The lads were in high spirits and I heard one man shouting, "Four more days of shopping before Christmas, pass it on" – it sounded like a bloody good joke and the men burst out laughing.'*

One of the weak points of an American airborne division was its lack of anti-tank and anti-aircraft weapons. To remedy these shortcomings, an airborne anti-aircraft battalion reinforced the support provided to infantrymen. In addition to anti-aircraft weapons, the unit was equipped with three anti-tank batteries, with each battery having two sections (the anti-aircraft batteries had three). The paratroopers' anti-tank gun was the British 6-pounder, a gun very similar to Uncle Sam's 57-mm. American airborne units were equipped with this gun because it could be carried in the standard American F CG-4A glider, whereas the US 57-mm's bulk did not allow this.[8]

Lieutenant Marschall W. Stark's section of four anti-tank guns from the 80th Airborne Anti-Aircraft Battalion (AAAB) was attached to 1/504th PIR. The section was initially sent to Xhierfomont, a hamlet that lay between the bridge over the Amblève and the confluence of the Lienne and was the only possible route for German armour to reach the regiment's headquarters at Rahier.

The US 57-mm gun was different from the one used by paratroopers, who opted for the British version with a muzzle brake. (*Nara*)

After setting up his guns, Lieutenant Stark returned to report back to HQ. On the way, barely 500 metres from his positions, he discovered that a minefield had been laid after his section had passed through. Arriving at Lieutenant Colonel Harrison's HQ, he convinced his superior to move two of his guns to the rear of the minefield, where infantry fire support would be available. The request was granted and two guns were hastily brought back about 200 metres from the Rahier exit in the direction of Cheneux.[9]

Like Corporal Graves, Sergeant Ross S. Carter and his brothers in arms in C Company, 504th PIR, were very apprehensive before the fighting at Cheneux:

> *Our company, C Company, followed B Company along a winding road that wound through the branches of the fir trees. We could hear sporadic machine-gun fire ahead of us. Aydelot, who was leading the battalion's reconnaissance element, soon came across us, coming down to the rear with a big SS devil he had taken prisoner. The fire soon became so intense that B Company found itself pinned down. We took cover behind the trees to avoid the machine gun fire, with the occasional 20-mm shell smashing the branches over our heads, and waited for night.*

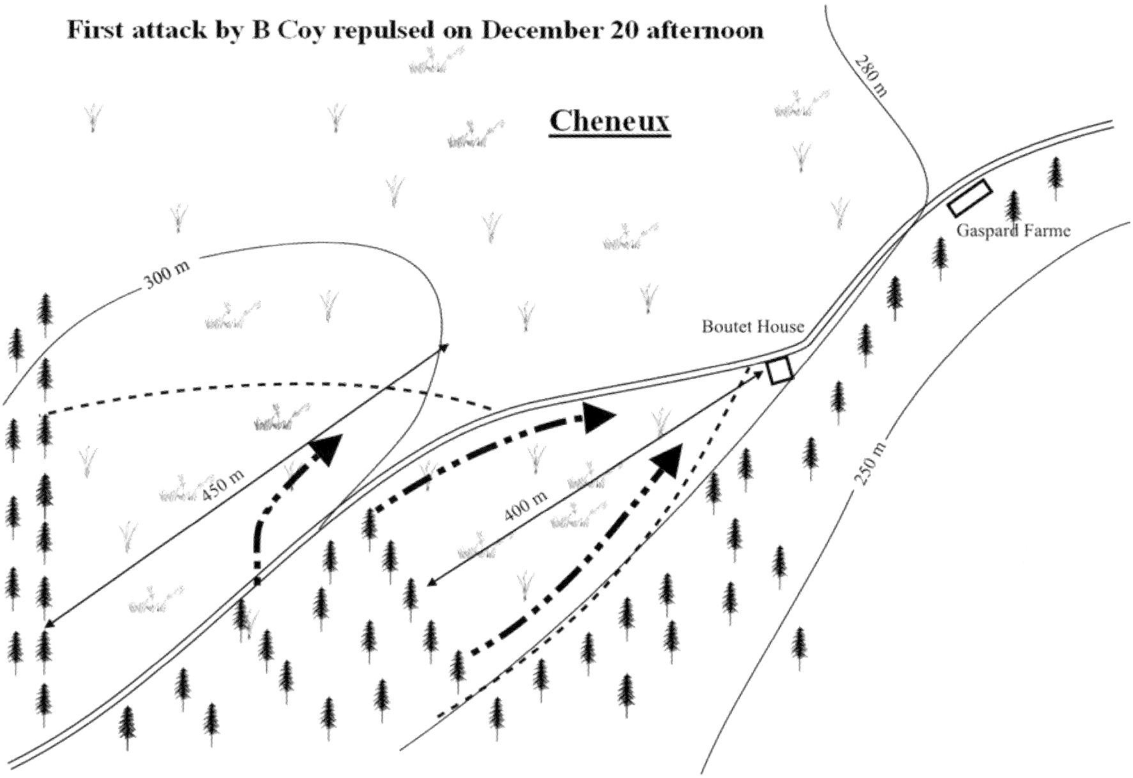


Diagram of the first daylight attack by B Company, 504th PIR. (*Christian Dujardin*)

*The Arbi observed with the interest of a professional psychologist the reactions of our new lieutenant, who was getting his baptism of fire. Turning to Casey and me, he remarked: 'No experience, but probably up to the job.' Larkin and Sheraton joined us. Larkin looked at Casey, who shook his head wearily. The taciturn giant said sadly: 'There's something about this story that gives me the blues. I don't know what, I've had this feeling before. The day an Oregon stallion nearly kicked me in the gut at the Pendelton rodeo.' A glint of warm camaraderie lit up Casey's usually cold eyes. It was a bad sign. Never in our previous fights had I sensed such despondency, such resignation. I felt uneasy; the jokes and boasts that had once masked the prelude to battle had given us a kind of unshakeable optimism. Casey was right. This time we were going into battle as glum as if we were going to a funeral. I won't say anything about it, but I too was plagued by painful forebodings.*

*At dusk C Company moved to the left and stopped in the heart of a dense forest to await orders. They were not long in coming. Orders always came in the end. Lieutenant Freisinger called his NCOs together: 'Lads, there's a roadblock blocking the road a few hundred metres along the edge of open ground, just opposite this wood. Behind this roadblock is a hamlet called Cheneux. At 7:30 pm, our platoon will spearhead the advance in front of C Company, with the rest of B Company attacking at the same time on the other side of the road. The 1st Battalion will support us with its 81-mm mortars and machine guns.... That's all.'* [...]

The first daylight attack was violently repulsed. (*Nara*)

> *The promised barrage came whistling over our heads, aimed at the enemy lines. There was still no sign of the two tank destroyers, armed with 90-mm guns, whose mission was to precede us on the road and destroy any German armoured vehicles that might oppose our advance.*[10]

## The Bloody Assault

Before launching the attack, Lieutenant Colonel Harrison took care to send out patrols to ensure his flanks were clear. Those sent out towards Xhierfomont and Meuville indicated that the ground was free of the enemy and the attack could therefore begin without fear of being caught from the rear. However, reconnaissance by D Company, heading for Cheneux, 800 metres to the east of the town, encountered a German sortie flanked by a handful of SS. After a brief exchange of fire, the squad leader, Sergeant Venable, was wounded in the hip.[11]

The battalion commander, Harrison, had developed the habit of recovering as much enemy equipment as possible in order to use it against him. He had learned his paratroopers from 2/504th PIR had captured an intact German half-track, abandoned

A Sd.Kfz. 251/9 Ausf D belonging to 1. SS-Panzer Division recovered intact from the Neufmoulin bridge was returned to its former owners. (*Nara*)

during the abortive attempt to cross the Lienne at Neufmoulin,[12] and the recovered vehicle was an Sd.Kfz. 251/9 nicknamed 'Stummel',[13] its nickname deriving from its short 75-mm .24-calibre gun. This type of gun was present on the first Panzer IV models during the invasion of May 1940[14] and was perfect for supporting an infantry attack, which was the reason the weapon was designed in this way.

Harrison temporarily suspended the start of the assault by B and C companies towards Cheneux, as he wanted to use the German machine gun to support his paratroopers. Lieutenant Stark recalls:

The short 75-mm gun earned the machine the nickname Stummel (butt). The American stars were hastily added to avoid any misunderstanding. (*Nara*)

> *The battalion commander asked me to provide two artillerymen to operate the German 75-mm semi-track*[15] *that had been abandoned somewhere in the vicinity. I chose two of the best men in the section, Pfc Harold Kelly and Pfc Harry Koprowski. At that point the column was ready to leave, but my two men didn't know how the armoured vehicle worked, so I asked for a short learning period for the crew. Personally, I'd never seen this type of weapon other than during theory lessons. Harrison gave me just five minutes to explain what little I knew to Kelly and Koprowski. During this short time Pfc Snow, secretary to the S-1, offered to drive the machine while Captain Helgeson, commander of B Coy, appointed two parachute infantrymen, Pvt Thomas R. Holliday and Pvt Buland Hoover of the first section to cover the gunners and the driver, both of whom were armed with BARs. My men managed to fire a few shells, all appearing to be in good condition.*[16]

As the troops set off, Helgeson's B Company was at the front of the column, followed by Anderson's C Company. The third section led B Company, commanded by Lieutenant

Padre Kosak comforting the men of 2/504th PIR before they are sent to reinforce those who had been badly beaten at Cheneux. (*Nara*)

William Meerman, followed by Lieutenant Thomas' second section, the Company Staff section and Lieutenant Ralph S. Bird's first section. The requisitioned Sd.Kfz. 251/9 started off and inserted itself between B and C companies. Third section advanced on the right of the causeway, second on the left, while first section was held in reserve. The formation had advanced 500 metres when it was halted by an enemy force estimated at one squad: around ten SS supported by an MG 42. The paratroopers dislodged the SS and slowly pushed them back along the road leading to Cheneux. The elite German troops retreated step by step, inflicting the first casualties on the battalion of 504th PIR. After advancing about 1,000 metres, the company arrived in front of the first enemy defensive lines, who were strongly entrenched in Cheneux.

The nervous tension is clearly visible in this paratrooper as he moves under enemy fire. (*Nara*)

Without waiting, Captain Helgeson launched his men into the attack. Third section deployed on the left to provide fire support and serve as a firing base for second section, which had to reach the first German line 450 metres from its starting point. The regiment's intelligence service had not anticipated the presence of an enemy force of this size, and Lieutenant Colonel Harrison's paratroopers were to pay the price for this underestimation of the enemy. The men of II/SS-PzGr-Rgt 2, exhausted by the fighting at Stoumont station the previous day, dug in to strong defensive positions. The anti-aircraft guns of the 84. Flak Abteilung of the Luftwaffe had already been in position since 19 December. After the arrival of II/SS-PzGr-Rgt 2 under Sturmbannführer Schnelle, a company of this battalion was sent to Cheneux. The SS-Panzergrenadiere were partly installed above the village, where there was an unobstructed view from which an attack could be launched. At the highest point, near the intersection of the Rahier road and the path leading to the oak wood, several armed vehicles had set up camp and were eagerly awaiting the GIs. In the middle of the road was an Sd.Kfz. 251/9 Stummel and its cannon. Behind it, an Sd.Kfz. 251/2 with an 80-mm mortar, a 105-mm howitzer and the vehicle used to tow the howitzer, probably an Opel Maultier. Three Sd.Kfz. 10/5 Leichter Zugkraftwagen 1 t D7 armed with 20-mm Flak 38 anti-aircraft guns completed the firepower of the KG Peiper elements facing Gavin's men. Anti-aircraft weapons used against infantrymen could prove deadly against infantry with seasoned servicemen.

On their right flank, the airborne also came under fire from another Sd.Kfz. 251/9 and its 75-mm gun, which was set up about 400 metres on the other side of the hill in the direction of Monceau. All these armoured support vehicles were supported by several MG 42s, which had an unobstructed view and were ideally placed to crossfire.[17]

Second section advanced about 100 metres before being pinned down by the crossfire from the semi-tracks, machine guns and mortars, while a shell landed on the company radio, knocking out six men in the squad. Protective fire from third section made no difference and the attack became bogged down. The Sd.Kfz. 251/9 took up position to support the attack, but thick fog and the crew's lack of experience meant they were of little help to the attackers they were supposed to be supporting. Shrapnel hit Private First Class Kelly in the lower lip and chin, and the driver, Snow, came to the wounded man's aid and carried him to the shelter of the vehicle's rear and took his place. When the half-track had to move to engage new targets, Snow returned to his driver's seat. Having used up all its ammunition, the vehicle turned around and was abandoned after unloading soldiers Holliday and Hoover to allow them to rejoin their unit.[18]

Seeing his two assault sections blocked, Captain Helgeson decided to send first section forward in an attempt to flank the defenders, with Lieutenant Ralph S. Bird's airborne being held in reserve. The men went deep into the woods and crossed the Cheneux stream to reach a forest road leading to the first building in the village, the Boutet house. The enemy crossfire was once again merciless, and this second attempt was a failure.

The paratroopers regrouped on the outskirts of Rahier before attacking again. (*Nara*)

## Cheneux Holds Out

With the company radio out of action, the commander of B Company, Captain Helgeson, was unable to contact C Company and so Harrison, commander of 1/504th PIR, decided to retreat to the edge of the woods, considering the position he had been given untenable. On 20 December, the supporting artillery moved up to Habiémont, about 200 metres from the Werbomont – Basse-Bodeux road. The battalion fired 145 shells in the fog,[19] but its fire proved ineffective due to a lack of radio links to correct trajectories. Dispatchers were sent to give the order to withdraw, and the sections pulled back one by one, covering each other as they did so. The return to the American lines at the edge of the forest was made easier by the fog,[20] but the affair had turned into a head-on clash, as Gavin witnessed the ferocity of the engagement:

> *I was there during the attack, and the German firepower was impressive. They used a lot of 20-mm anti-aircraft guns. A weapon that infantry consider the most uncomfortable to face. Colonel Tucker had deployed his 1/504th against the Germans trying to get out of Cheneux. It was a tough fight when darkness fell on the battlefield, C and B companies were under tremendous fire from the village.*[21]

The airborne division had no armoured vehicles for its operations and so help was requested. However, the 1st US Army was in dire straits in the early days of Hitler's offensive and had to scrape the bottom of its barrels. The 703rd Tank Destroyer Battalion (TDB) was currently serving with the 1st ID at Sourbrodt, and its transfer order to the

The columns descend on Cheneux. (*Nara*)

The paratroopers left for Cheneux carrying their sleeping bags, not expecting to have to fight a furious battle. The bags were abandoned on the edge of the wood before the second attack, many of them being later found by civilians. Their former owners had been were put out of action. (*Nara*)

82nd Airborne Division arrived on 19 December. The next day a self-propelled section commanded by Lieutenant Roberts set off at 8 am, and was expected to be at Werbomont by around 1:30 pm. The 703rd TDB was equipped with M36s, which were tank fighters on Sherman chassis. They were armed with a 90-mm gun that was particularly effective both against German armoured vehicles and in support of infantrymen. The US Army's manning tables specify that a Tank Destroyer section is theoretically equipped with four guns, but unfortunately for Gavin and his men, only two were available for the support mission as the other two were being repaired.[22] Lieutenant Roberts received the password for his two tanks at 5:15 pm[23] and Harrison, the battalion commander, called a meeting, attended by his two company commanders who were engaged at Cheneux. After taking stock of the situation, Colonel Reuben H. Tucker was informed of the new attack plan that had been rapidly drawn up. The time of the assault was set for 7:30 pm and was to be preceded by ten minutes of artillery fire. C Company would attack from the left, and B Company from the right. The assault would consist of four waves spaced 50 metres apart,

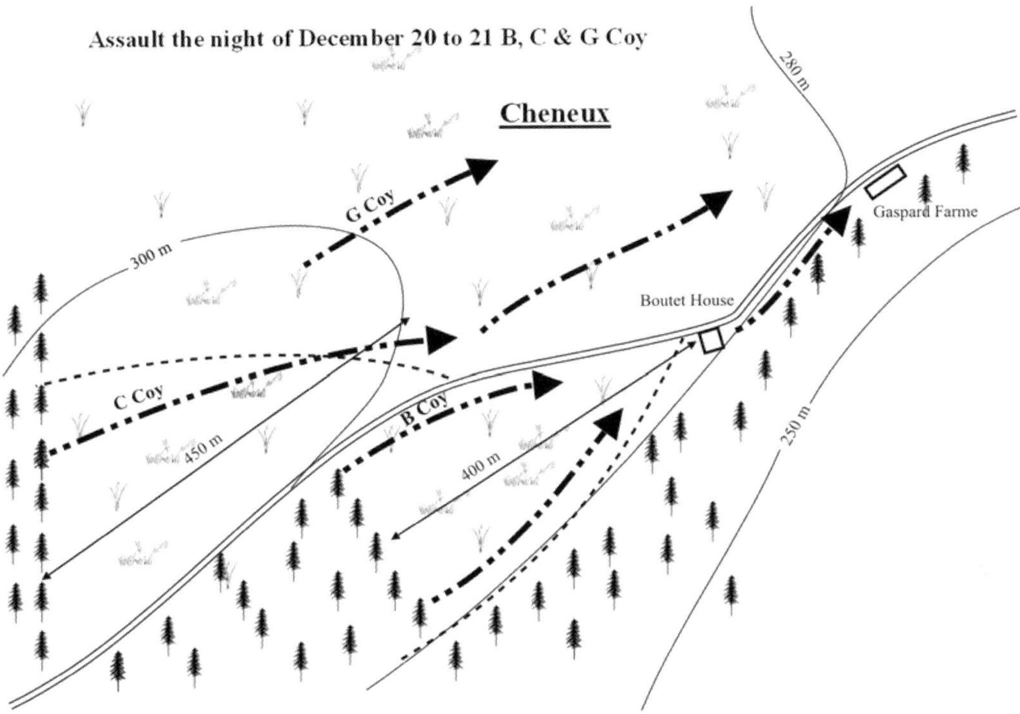


Diagram of the second attack, which took place on the night of 20–21 December. (*Christian Dujardin*)

with the two M36 Jackson Tank Destroyers providing support to counter the heavy fire and charge across the 400 metres of open ground.

The Germans bombarded the troops gathered in the woods and at 7:30 pm, the two American companies attacked at about 50-metre intervals. Just as the main American assault waves were spotted in the darkness, the SS opened up with intense and precise fire. As the first two waves began to suffer heavy casualties, yawning holes opened up in their ranks, which were almost completely decimated. On the left side of the road, Sergeant Frank L. Dietrich and Staff Sergeant George W. McAllister of C Company were in the first wave. They were the only ones in the section with pliers to cut the barbed wire in the pastures, which otherwise caught on the soldiers' jackets and injured them. The only way through was to climb over it or crawl under it, so Sergeant Dietrich created a gap in a fence and the men took advantage of it to get through. Some rows of barbed wire were no more than 20 metres apart, and Dietrich continued his work as unobtrusively as possible, hoping that the thick fog and the darkness of a moonless night would hide their approach to the German positions. Visibility was limited to 3 metres as they left the woods, and the Americans had no idea what awaited them on the open ground. Arriving at yet another fence, the wave of paratroopers found themselves in hell.

On the right of the road, Private First Class Holmstock recalled:

*It was dark and foggy. You couldn't see more than 3 metres in front of you. We didn't know what was in front of us. There was total darkness in this completely open field. I came to*

The Germans also used an Sd.Kfz. 251/9. They knew how to use it better than the paratroopers and took a heavy toll on 504th PIR. With it out of action, the paratroopers broke through the first line of German defence. (*Nara*)

> *a barbed wire fence and stepped over it. We walked a bit further, and I came to another barbed wire fence, and I moaned: 'What's all this b…?' There was someone with a box of machine gun ammunition. He said, 'Hold this for me.' I got down on the ground and pushed the box in front of me and started crawling under this barbed wire fence. Then I heard screams in German. All hell broke loose. We were trapped and we could see the tracers, which fortunately didn't reach us, the road to my left was elevated and we were on the slope of the field. We must have been about 3 metres below the level of the road. The Germans were firing over our heads. However, in addition to the 20-mm anti-aircraft fire from the half-trackers on our left, we were taking low-level machine gun fire on our right. We were paralysed, it looked like a hundred machine guns were firing at once. I could see the tracer bullets passing a few centimetres above my head. I was frightened by this unleashing of iron and fire. I lay as flat as I could and prayed. It was the longest minute of my life.*[24]

At the rear of the village of Rahier, Corporal Graves also witnessed the violence of the fighting:

*It was 7 pm when I was woken by the sound of a terrible battle just north of us. We imagined that the 1st Battalion had come across something very hard. Tracer bullets were flying in all directions over the field across the road from the house where the 2nd Battalion was entrenched. Heavy artillery shells were crashing down below us. All hell was breaking loose; to top it all off, the air was filled with the jerky backfire of the robots*[25] *that passed in great numbers over our heads. Captain Hauptfleisch had returned from HQ where he had seen our first SS prisoner who told our men that Antwerp had been recaptured by the Germans! I ate a tin of C ration and drank a glass of milk. As I was still exhausted from lack of sleep, I went back to bed on the wooden bench. The heavy artillery bombardment was so close that it made me nervous for the first time since we had arrived in Rahier. The thatched roof over our heads was not strong enough to blow up even a heavy mortar shell. I lay there with my eyes open, listening to the cracking explosions of the 20-mm shells around the house with great trepidation. When Lieutenant Madruga, with whom I had spoken earlier in the day, burst into the house, he was bleeding profusely from two wounds. He said they needed extra ambulances in a hurry in the First Battalion area. Moments later Captain Duncan (S-3 of the battalion), an old soldier who had seen a lot of action as a company commander and was not one to get worked up in the heat of battle, came in saying that the 1st Battalion was being cut to pieces. He had come back to report the situation to the colonel. Coming from Captain Duncan, the news was most serious. The situation being what it was, I again prepared to stay up all night.*[26]

The Boutet house (on the right) was the first Cheneux house to be captured. It was to serve as Tucker's headquarters. On the left is a Ford V 3000 Maultier that was destroyed during the assault. It was probably used to mobilise the 105mm FH. (*Nara*)

## The German Front Line Gives Way

The paratroopers were immobilised by the crossfire. Most were wounded. Sergeant William P. Walsh, affectionately called 'Knobby' by his men[27] (he owed his nickname to his small size, which was more than compensated for by his courage), saw his men pinned down when the devastating German fire began. The whole company came to a halt as the list of dead and wounded grew longer. It was at this crucial moment that Sergeant Walsh stood up in defiance of the tracer shells that lit him up. Private First Class Morris Holmstock was nearby and heard him shout: '*Come on, let's go and get those sons of bitches! If you stay here, they'll kill you.*' The NCO started running towards the village and everyone who could move followed him, charging and shouting angrily.[28] In the first two waves, Walsh's signal had effect like an electric shock, as all the officers and NCOs also urged their men forward. They were joined by the third wave and in their rush, the GIs actually overran the first line of German defences.

Madame Boutet occupied the first house on the road to the airborne, but had retreated to the wooden hut below the road behind her house, which was normally used as a small workshop and chicken coop. She was deafened by the sawing noise of an MG 42 set up in front of the door, as the machine gun held the dirt road coming up to her property under its fire. Soon, the wooden partition of the precarious shelter became a sieve, as the

The house on the right, in front of which stand three survivors of the fighting, was captured during the night during the final advance. (*Nara*)

hail of bullets hit everything in the vicinity, smashing a series of objects inside. Suddenly, the machine gun fell silent. Curious, Madame Boutet opened the door to her henhouse. The German soldier was still there, grumbling. She remembered:

> *We were thirsty in our hut, dying to die, so I decided, without knowing what time it was – it was Thursday morning – to go and get some drinks from the cellar.*[29] *I opened the door and my astonishment was shared by a dozen Americans who were taking care of themselves, eating or servicing their weapons. Armed with food and drink, I returned to the hut, where the fight continued, bitterly tragic. I heard sounds of fighting inside the house, and the same sounds of fighting on the ground floor could be heard at Gaspard's house.*[30]

By 10 pm, the first house in the village was in the hands of the American soldiers. The roadblock was crushed under shellfire as the SS began to move back towards the centre of the village. Sergeant Walsh carried on as his comrade Sergeant Boyd reported:

> *Walsh continued to lead the platoon. I could see he was beginning to wear himself out. Eventually he fell to the ground, completely exhausted, but despite his weakness he got to his feet and said, 'Somebody come and take the pin out of the grenade.' He then went towards an enemy anti-aircraft semi-track and threw a grenade at it from a distance of about 3 metres. He neutralised the whole crew, I got close to him and saw that he had been hit in the left arm and leg, I suggested that he treat his wounds, but he replied curtly: 'Later' and continued down towards the village. One of Walsh's soldiers, Private Edward Focht, was overtaking the anti-aircraft. He told me that every German in the vehicle was killed or wounded, and we didn't get any more fire from that particular vehicle.*[31]

After Walsh's act of bravery, a mad rush to the village began, although the fighting still continued on the outskirts. Private First Class Holmstock and his brothers in arms Clements and Hudson arrived at one of the first houses on the right-hand side of the road. Clements and Hudson rudely opened the door, shouting '*Komm Raus! Hände hoch!*' Receiving no response, they threw a grenade into the cellar, before going down themselves. On inspection, they found they had killed around four or five sheep huddling there. After clearing the room of the sheeps' remains, the room became a first-aid post, where the medics began to round up and treat the wounded. After this incident, in the intensity of the fighting, Holmstock found himself separated from Clements and Hudson. Holmstock swung to the right and found a ditch along the tree line behind a house, which gave him a clear line of fire on a German anti-aircraft semi-track in position on the road. The paratrooper recalled:

> *At the back of the house, where I had come down, the ground was steep, I crawled to the foot of a tree and started firing at the Flak Wagon. The German gunner spotted my position, turned his gun on me and fired. I ducked quickly and the bullets hit the tree above*

*me. The deadly splinters from the trunk and branches, mixed with the shrapnel from the 20-mm shells, surrounded me. As I reached the shelter, I felt a warm liquid dripping down my face, tasted it and thought 'Oh shit! I've been hit!' I realised my wound was only slight, so I headed for the stable where the nurses had set up a first-aid centre. I was treated. The wound stopped bleeding and I went back into action.*[32]

## Hand-to-Hand Combat in Cheneux

At 9:05 pm, Lieutenant Colonel Harrison's battalion requested emergency medical reinforcements.[33] On the left-hand side of the road, C Company was also experiencing major difficulties. As Carter continues his story, which in itself is worthy of the best action novels, his account plunges us right into the heart of the fighting for Cheneux. The atmosphere is chilling, full of adrenaline, and gives us an idea of what a combatant can feel in the midst of such a fight to the death, where it is a question of killing or being killed:

*After looking at our watches, I don't know how many times, we finally saw the time had come for the attack. We stood up and slowly fanned out. Lieutenant Freisinger, accompanied by Berkely, both gigantic in the shadows, surveyed our line. Then the order to advance was passed from man to man. The thirty-three lads in our platoon led the march of the other two platoons, fanning out. They advanced noisily, breaking the branches under their feet. From one second to the next, we expected a hail of burning steel to rain down on us. The silence continued, broken only by the trampling of men making their way through the forest. A few reams of wood separating us from the field forced us to form a single file. When we reached the edge of the field, intersected every 40 or 50 metres by barbed wire, we deployed again. In terrain like this, a fan-shaped formation provides an ideal target for machine guns. I felt a strange numbness come over all my senses. Beside me, I heard Duquesne whisper to Gruening: 'This time we're in the clear!'*

*We were in the open now. The deadly machine-gun fire we had expected to scour the plain was not yet unleashed. We couldn't avoid making a noise as we slipped through the barbed wire. The comforting explosions from our artillery, which was pounding the German lines, didn't make up for the absence of the two tank destroyers.*

*Our men, now deployed somewhat haphazardly because of the difficulties of crossing the barbed wire, were almost in the middle of the field and were tackling a new barrage when the great game began. Suddenly, thousands of tracer bullets, strangely beautiful despite the mortal danger they represented, drew trajectories above our heads whose arabesques intertwined. Their flamboyant striations lit up the night and made us perfectly distinct targets. The air was filled with the whistle of 20-mm shells preceded by a yellow glow, the crackle of machine guns and the roar of mortar shells raining down on the comrades behind us. I was in the process of stepping over a roll of barbed wire when little Finkelstein, who had just passed by and was a few paces away from me, was hit by a 20-mm shell, which exploded his grenades and burnt him instantly. He ran a few more steps and collapsed in the barbed wire.*

*Stunned by the first shock of enemy fire, our soldiers flinched. I heard Berkely's bass voice faintly: 'Forward, lads! Shoot the bastards who killed Finkelstein.'.*

*I continued forward in a kind of fog. Two metres away from me, a series of tracer bullets seemed to be looking for me and 20-mm shells were systematically spraying the field, exploding in deadly little fireworks. A field gun methodically cannoned the centre of our formation. Mortar shells continued to decimate the ranks of the 2nd and 3rd platoons. The machine guns wove a web of bullets in front of us. It was worse than a Dante nightmare. It was a man-made, mechanised hell. It seemed like years had passed since I'd left little Finkelstein on the barbed wire to keep moving towards the guns. Gradually, the din of battle faded, as had the past and the future and all my thoughts except this one: I know I'm going to die because I'm lost, but I hope I can hold out long enough not to go empty-handed.*

*I was still walking, unloading my rifle, but I couldn't hear it go off anymore.*

*'This time I've had enough.' It was the weakened voice of L'Arbi lying in a pool of blood right in front of me. I knelt down beside my old comrade and prepared to give him first aid: 'There's no need.' Any hint of cunning had disappeared from his eyes to make way for the gentleness I had once seen in Carlton's gaze: 'Tell my mates, if there are any left, that I was hoping to do better.' He tried to say something else, but he was too weak. As I left, I put my foot on his book of Homer, all blood-stained and almost torn in two by the machine-gun fire. I put it on his chest and felt his heart. It wasn't beating any more. I crossed his arms over his beloved book and ran off.*

*For a few minutes, apart from a brief encounter with Kong, I found myself isolated in my little piece of hell. I was lurking at the foot of a barbed-wire fence, cleaning my jammed rifle, when he slithered past me like a snake, his white teeth gleaming in his swarthy face, his machine gun pointed in front of him. 'Kong,' I asked him, 'where are you going? Shoot the bastards, shoot the bastards!' He disappeared to my left. I continued to run down the field, firing until my rifle burnt my hands, swearing like a madman and getting closer and closer to the place where the bullets that had killed Finkelstein, L'Arbi and probably most of my other comrades. I noticed that my bayonet was loose and wondered if it would swing too much for me to use it. In the shadows, three shapes appeared next to a machine gun. I reloaded my rifle and charged at them. The smoke from a burst grazed me. I was just a few metres from the Germans. When they ran off, I got down on one knee and fired eight bullets at point-blank range. Then I let myself roll to the ground to avoid a burst of machine-gun fire.*[34]

During this phase, the company commander, Captain Roy Anderson, was wounded and replaced by his second-in-command. The attack proved to be very deadly: the officers were killed and there were only twenty-six survivors from the ranks. As a result, B Company was put out of action. However, even though their officers and non-commissioned officers were neutralised, the paratroopers continued to attack. Those who had run out of ammunition continued their savage charge with trench knives or used their rifles as clubs. A soldier from the company crawled up to an anti-aircraft unit where, armed only with a knife, he climbed aboard to slit the gunner's throat.[35]

The battalion commander, Lieutenant Colonel Harrison, established his new HQ at the Boutet house after occupying a destroyed enemy half-track. The surviving officers reorganised the decimated B and C companies to form a solid defensive line, expecting a violent SS counter-attack. At 11 pm, Colonel Tucker went to Harrison's HQ and after analysing the situation, he gave the order to send G Company, 2/504th PIR, as reinforcements.

During this time, the fighting above the village continued to rage, as Carter reported:

*As the area ahead of me was calmer, I walked another 10 metres or so. I found Casey, riddled with MG-42 bullets, a few metres from a machine gun nest where the bodies of four SS men lay. I screamed with rage and hatred and moved to the right where B Company seemed to be in trouble. At that moment Berkely popped out of the shadows, his little finger bleeding; he had been hit there by shrapnel and his hand was paralysed. He had shot two machine-gunners, thrown his rifle at a third and was about to jump at his throat to strangle him when the soldier in front of him had saved him the trouble with his submachine gun. Unable to hold a gun, he went to help the medics, 'Casey is in the hole over there,' I said. 'L'Arbi is dead too. Duquesne is wounded in the head and Gruening in the stomach. Both seriously.'*

*We slapped each other on the shoulder and went our separate ways into the night. A hundred metres away, I met a sergeant from B Company, William Walsh. He was trying to reform his platoon under the deadly Flak fire, formed into a roadblock in the middle of the road. 'Let's go, lads!' he shouted. 'We've got to take this town. We can't stop now!' He didn't realise that most of his men were dead or wounded. He thought, it seemed, that they were letting him down.*

*'I'm going with you, Knobby.'*

*Together we rushed towards a monstrous shape that spat flames in the dark and whose metal sides made our bullets ineffective. Diving into the ditch on the right I spotted six more similar monsters in a circle spewing an endless stream of machine gun bullets and small shells. I heard Sergeant Walsh in a nearby ditch trying to dominate the screams of the wounded and rally the survivors.*

*Three metres away, on the other side of the road, was another armoured vehicle and I noticed that its 20-mm gun was no longer firing. I concluded that it must have jammed. A pair of hands lifted the turret hatch and unloaded a machine gun onto the road. I pulled the pin on a grenade and said to myself: 'Next time you go out with your gun, I'll make you taste bread!'*

*Then I crawled towards the armoured vehicle and stood still. Without hearing a sound, I felt the hatch being opened and half rose to throw my grenade. But before I could make a move, an egg-shaped grenade fell limply between my shoulders and bounced off, leaving behind it a bluish trail of burning powder. I crossed the road again and went to sprawl in the middle of the barbed wire. Unable to get out of the mess I'd got myself into, my*

The M36s of 703rd Tank Destroyer M36 Jackson were sent to support the attack on Cheneux. They are seen here on their arrival at Werbomont. (*Nara*)

*face and hands bleeding, I waited humbly for the projectile to explode. When it exploded, I felt something hit my back and shoulder and numb that whole area. The idea that I was wounded didn't stop me from freeing myself from the barbed wire and diving into a ditch filled with water, right on the buttocks of a paratrooper who was wounded and who let out a bellow of pain. I moved away quickly, far too preoccupied by the presence of the armoured vehicle whose engine was rumbling, to ask him if he needed treatment, let alone to apologise. I was seized with panic as the machine backed up and stopped right in front of me.*

*'He must have seen me,' I thought, 'otherwise he wouldn't have thrown his grenade.' Just as I was thinking that everything was cooked this time, the engine stopped, the hatch lifted and three men emerged in disorder. I aimed my rifle and fired until they fell, either wounded or trying to take cover. Sergeant William Walsh and his men seemed to have disappeared.*

*I decided to cut off to the left to see how my company's battle was going. On my hands and knees, I crawled behind the abandoned armoured car and followed the road until I came across another tank that also looked abandoned. I crawled in front of it and examined the terrain carefully. I stood up to get a better look when the horrible roar of an automatic cannon erupted behind me. I leapt up and suddenly felt a red-hot splinter rip through my right arm. At the same moment, a violent shock tore my rifle from my right hand, the weight of which, now resting entirely on my left hand, sent me stumbling out of the gun's line of fire, towards an enemy lorry. As I staggered back to my feet, Sergeant Walsh, also wounded, ran past me and into Cheneux, where he was awarded the Distinguished Service Cross. Blood the size of my thumb trickled down my arm. I started calling frantically for help. I hadn't gone a hundred yards when I began to feel a delicious weakness come over me. Red and purple lights danced before my eyes. I collapsed to the ground. When I regained consciousness, Ciconte was kneeling beside me. He took off my bonnet and jacket, unbuckled my belt and put a tourniquet round my arm. At that moment, he picked up his rifle and fired a shot: 'There's a German who won't be playing any more dirty tricks on my staff.'*

*Then he knelt down beside me again, gave me a shot of morphine and tightened the tourniquet.*

*I think I must have fainted every 50 metres or so on the way to the first-aid post. On one occasion, I was slumped against some barbed wire, unable to move and not caring, when I heard Winters' sarcastic voice ringing in my ears. 'I don't want to bother you, Ross, but are you really planning to spend the night in that barbed wire?' So Winters was still alive. A wave of comfort came over me and I smiled at his question. 'No, Winters, I don't want to sleep there, but I don't think I could get through their barbed wire.' He helped me through and asked Esman to escort me.*[36]

## Close Support…From a Distance

In his lengthy testimony Carter states he did not see the M36 Jackson Tank Destroyers and their 90-mm guns in action. However, we found confirmation of their intervention in the report by 1/504th PIR, which states:

*After 10 pm, both companies had suffered heavy losses, and although our airborne were fighting fiercely, there could be no coordinated combat until we had fire support from the M 36 Jackson 90-mm Tank Destroyers. Our lads couldn't disable a 20-mm Flak Wagon, there weren't enough men left fit to fight and what's more, ammunition was becoming scarce. The Flak Wagon was opposite the Gaspard house and was wreaking havoc and preventing any progress towards the centre of the village.*

*Because of the intensity of the enemy fire, the two Jackson Tank Destroyers were unwilling or unable to advance. As the Tank Destroyers had not yet intervened, Harrison sent in the heavy weapons section of the headquarters company, armed with .30 calibre machine guns. A new joint attack by the surviving men of the two companies B and C and the heavy section advanced as far as was humanly possible. Most of the eight machine guns and their crew were neutralised. It was no longer possible to advance without the support of an armoured vehicle. Lieutenant-Colonel Harrison ordered the tanks to attack.*[37]

The M36 was not designed for close support, being too lightly armoured and its turret having an open superstructure. This was why the Tank Destroyers of 703rd TD stayed back during the attack. (*Nara*)

Lieutenant Roberts, section leader of the two 90-mm Tank Destroyers, gives us his impressions of the moment:

> *Our two Tank Destroyers were the only armoured force, the other two were being repaired. Our mission was to support the infantry and make as much noise as possible by firing at anything that moved to give the impression of a large strike force. Visibility was very limited and we could see very little as we moved towards the village. One tank moved forward while the other stayed back to cover the advance of the first. The lead destroyer moved forward but ran into a German tracked vehicle on the right side of the road; the gunner swung the gun and the barrel hit the other vehicle. The driver immediately rammed the small enemy armoured vehicle and the German crew began to abandon it. I took over and got to a good spot to aim, lock on and take out the Flak wagon and a tracked tractor. With this resistance eliminated, the infantry resumed their advance towards the centre of the village, until they were again held up by another anti-aircraft wagon. It was hidden near a stone house and the gunner had no way of manoeuvring into a good firing position. We then used plan B: eliminate the protection, then neutralise the enemy vehicle. Using APDS ammunition,*[38] *the gunner fired directly at the building, blowing up the wall and then destroying the exposed anti-aircraft wagon. A few moments later, two*

An Sd.Kfz. 10/5 1-tonne anti-aircraft gun with a 20-mm Flak 38 was a weapon feared by the M36. This one is photographed after the fighting. (*Nara*)

> *semi-tracked vehicles left their hiding places behind the buildings in front of us. They were destroyed as they tried to retreat along the road. This concluded the action of the destroyers for the rest of the night, and the infantry consolidated the gains they had made so far.*[39]

The timid attitude of the Tank Destroyer crews is understandable. In fact, the 90-mm M36 Jackson was designed on the basis of a Sherman chassis onto which was grafted a turret fitted with an excellent 90-mm anti-aircraft gun. The self-propelled Tank Destroyer was originally designed as a tank fighter, and as it gained experience throughout the conflict, the self-propelled anti-tank took part in front-line fighting, quality of its tense fire making it a tool of choice for destroying enemy strongpoints, bunkers and machine gun nests. During an assault in an urban area, the tank would first fire into the upper storey to drive enemy soldiers down into the cellars, after which the infantry would enter the building.[40] However, the vehicle had a major design flaw for front-line use: its body was poorly armoured, its designers preferring to sacrifice protection for mobility. While the armour was thick enough for the scrap metal of the battlefield, 20-mm anti-aircraft fire could still put it out of action. What is more, its turret had an open superstructure, so grenades, mortar fire and sniper fire were mortal enemies for the crew occupying the turret.

## 504th PIR Loses Veterans

Let us look back at the final moments of the night attack on 20–21 December, as Carter, who was now seriously wounded, continues his account:

> *As I was coming down the 'via Dolorosa', I met Nixon, who had shrapnel in his back, and Sokal, who had a serious head wound. I asked Nixon what had become of Larkin and Sheraton. 'Dead...And O'Connel, too.' Of all the old-timers, only Berkely, Winters and I remained, and even then I was in danger of bleeding to death. Finkelstein was charred on the barbed wire, L'Arbi had his hands folded over his Homer, Casey was lying in front of his four victims, Duquesne and Gruening were mortally wounded, and now I was told that Larkin and Sheraton, two other old-timers, had fallen too. I thought about what the platoon was like when we had left the United States. A sweet weariness came over me again. The instinct for self-preservation that had set my wobbly legs in motion seemed to dissolve into nostalgic regret. I slumped to the floor. What was the point of living when better people than me were dead? What was the point? For three years, my comrades had been the best in my life. More than 300 days spent in front-line fighting had given our camaraderie a reality that made the memories of civilian life pale. Deprived of the company of all those brave men, I could no longer see any purpose in my life. The prospect of seeing new faces in the platoon revolted me and filled me with bitterness. A feeling of unfathomable loneliness brought tears to my eyes.*[41]

Ross Carter never recovered from his serious injuries and died in hospital on 18 April 1947, aged 28.

Despite or because of the loss of comrades in battle, the paratroopers were consequently unleashed. Blood calls for blood. When two experienced elite units clash, expect nothing less. Everyone knows that the side that flinches first will suffer the most casualties. Holmstock recalled:

The Flak Wagons were platforms topped by MG 151/15s. The fire from these 15-mm machine guns, combined with that from the 20-mm guns, wreaked havoc in the ranks of the attackers. (*La Gleize Museum*)

> *At that moment, I stopped being afraid. There was still a lot of shooting, but I got up and threw a grenade at a Flak Wagon. I took cover and then it exploded. I continued to advance along the road. There was shouting and shooting. The tumult of battle is something difficult to describe. I climbed into one of the anti-*

Carcass of an Sd.Kfz. 251/21 Ausf D armed with a Flakdrilling MG 151/15 anti-aircraft gun. The open superstructure made it highly vulnerable to grenade attacks. (*La Gleize Museum*)

> *aircraft wagons. I remember sticking my rifle in the cab and firing the eight rounds from my Garand. With these metal vehicles, you don't need to aim at anyone, the bullets will bounce off and kill everyone inside.*[42]

Scenes of extreme savagery and madness came together. Lieutenant Richard Smith and his men attacked two Luftwaffe anti-aircraft vehicles and two MG 42 positions. On the outskirts of the village, Smith had reorganised his platoon, now down to eleven soldiers, and was killed attacking another anti-aircraft semi-track and two houses on the edge of the village. One of the orderlies, Private Theodore S. Watson, did not hesitate to brave the furnace to go to the aid of the wounded, and evacuated five men to safety. Despite the dangers, ambulance drivers at the front came to the aid of the wounded and dying, saving many lives. Acts of incredible heroism became the norm.[43] Soldiers were enraged after seeing so many of their brothers in arms struck down. They fought individually or in small, closed groups against an enemy with very strong firepower. Semi-armoured anti-aircraft guns, armoured SPWs specialising in infantry support and reconnaissance vehicles took a heavy toll. When they got close, the paratroopers took no mercy with their occupants.

Chapter 4

# The Bloody Clean-up at Cheneux

## The SS Counter-Attack

At 1:45 am, Colonel Tucker returned to his regimental command post and at 2:30, he was informed that seven half-tracks, a truck and an 88-mm gun had been destroyed by 1/504th PIR. After a lull in the fighting, G Company took over the assault on Cheneux, which was launched at 2:45. Although pushed back by the airborne troops, the German troops reacted quickly and strongly, with the 75-mm guns, 20-mm Flak guns and the MG 42s grouped together in crossfire forming an impenetrable wall of fire and steel. G Company had no choice but to withdraw and integrate back into the defensive system.[1] After this, the night was relatively quiet, with only sporadic firing.

The SS counter-attacked on the morning of 21 December. It was a costly affair, as the paratroopers were solidly entrenched. (*Nara*)

The barbed wire demarcating the numerous pastures was used by both sides to set up positions. This machine gun is well buried, with only the gunner's head sticking out. (*Nara*)

Further north, towards La Gleize, the Germans still held the bridge over the Amblève at the bottom of Cheneux, allowing them to send reinforcements into Cheneux, and at dawn on 21 December, a counter-attack was launched to retake the village. A rare testimony from the German side comes from Feldwebel Karl Laun, who did not belong to the SS but to the Luftwaffe. He recalls that few people were motivated to go into contact with the Americans, and that a Tiger was mobilised for the attempt to retake the village:

> *On 21 December, one of our counter-attacks at dawn was smothered by enemy fire. No one showed the slightest inclination to fight – not even the SS. In fact, they were the first to withdraw. Suddenly, one of our tanks appeared near the bridge. Another frantic demand for petrol. Emptying all the vehicles, including the Volkswagen, and the destroyed engines, we scraped together 150 litres. The Tiger continues towards Cheneux. I'm bloody glad I didn't have to go through the hell in that village.*[2]

At 7:45 am on 21 December, the SS-Panzergrenadiere, preceded by a thirty-minute artillery barrage, tried to retake the ground that had been hard won the previous night

Two eyewitness accounts agree that Tiger 104 supported the German counter-attack at Cheneux. On its return to La Gleize, it broke its track in a sunken path behind the village church and the paratroopers used it as a target for bazooka training. (*Nara*)

by the parachutists of the 1/504th PIR. The German attack was supported by direct fire from tanks and 20-mm anti-aircraft guns. With only light weapons at their disposal, the GIs managed to halt the assault thanks to fire from the battalion's mortars. A Flak Wagon was destroyed by mortar fire, and SS casualties were heavy.[3]

Lieutenant Stark's anti-tank section had been attached to the 1/504th PIR since 4 am when the early morning German attack began, and his four 6-pounder guns were still on the road between Rahier and Cheneux. The guns were, in fact, the original British version of the 57-mm in service with American conventional infantry units. The battalion commander called for them to be deployed to oppose the counter-attack Peiper's troops had just launched. The anti-tank platoon set off but stopped at the end of the forest, as Lieutenant Stark refused to move the trucks towing the guns forward without a minimum guarantee of safety for his men and equipment. After a hundred metres or so, Stark saw the 81-mm mortars firing non-stop towards the village, and asked the gunners where the command post was through the bushes about 300 metres away. The men told him they were firing at 350 metres to contain the German thrust, and so Stark began moving along the ditches lining the road. Halfway along he met Lieutenant Colonel Harrison, who had gone to meet him, and the two men returned together to the command post to take stock of the situation. The anti-tank arrangements were clarified: two 57-mm guns were to be positioned to counter any armoured breakthrough coming from Cheneux along the road, while the other two were to be placed to the north. To the south of the position, no special arrangements were envisaged, as the wooded terrain sloped steeply and no motorised breakthrough was possible from that direction. After reconnoitring the future locations of his anti-tank artillery pieces, Stark rejoined his section.

Each man in the anti-tank platoon received his instructions but at 8:45 am, a fog fell over the battlefield. The mist reduced visibility to less than 100 metres, covering the deployment zone. The two guns that were to embark towards Cheneux were pushed towards their positions by attaching them to the front of the trucks so that they could clear the area as quickly as possible in the event of danger. The hitches moved very slowly, making as little noise as possible. Then the barrels were quickly disconnected, so that the vehicle could reverse a short distance and be relatively safe from direct fire. The other two vehicles and guns, using the standard towing procedure, took up position on open ground in a scrolling area. Only two men plus the driver set up the anti-tank guns; the other members of the section stayed back at the edge of the woods and dug foxholes.

The paratroopers dug in to await the counter-attack, which was to be synchronised with an attack from Monceau by 3/504th PIR (minus G Company, which was already committed to Cheneux). (*Nara*)

The move was completed quickly and the guns carefully camouflaged. The position was reinforced with bags to give them extra protection. Taking advantage of the misty cover, the artillerymen left their foxholes at the edge of the forest and took up position close to their guns, ready for action. By 10 am, visibility had returned to normal. The commander of 1/504th PIR feared that the Germans were gathering their armour and forces for a brutal attack on his positions, but this was apparently not the case. The numerous vehicle movements that had been heard were becoming increasingly distant. Not a single enemy vehicle was seen during the day. The situation in front of Cheneux seemed to have temporarily stabilised.

At 9 am, General James Gavin went to the 504th PIR command post and gave the order to liquidate the Cheneux pocket once and for all. All the regiment's available forces were to be deployed to finish off this Peiper bridgehead on the left bank of the Amblève.

## The Capture of Monceau

The 3/504th PIR was in position at Froidville, a hamlet 1 kilometre south-west of Rahier. Lieutenant Colonel Cook, the battalion commander, had only two companies left, I and H companies, while G Company was already under fire at Cheneux. The plan of attack was to cut off the enemy's rear, and to prevent any reinforcements from arriving

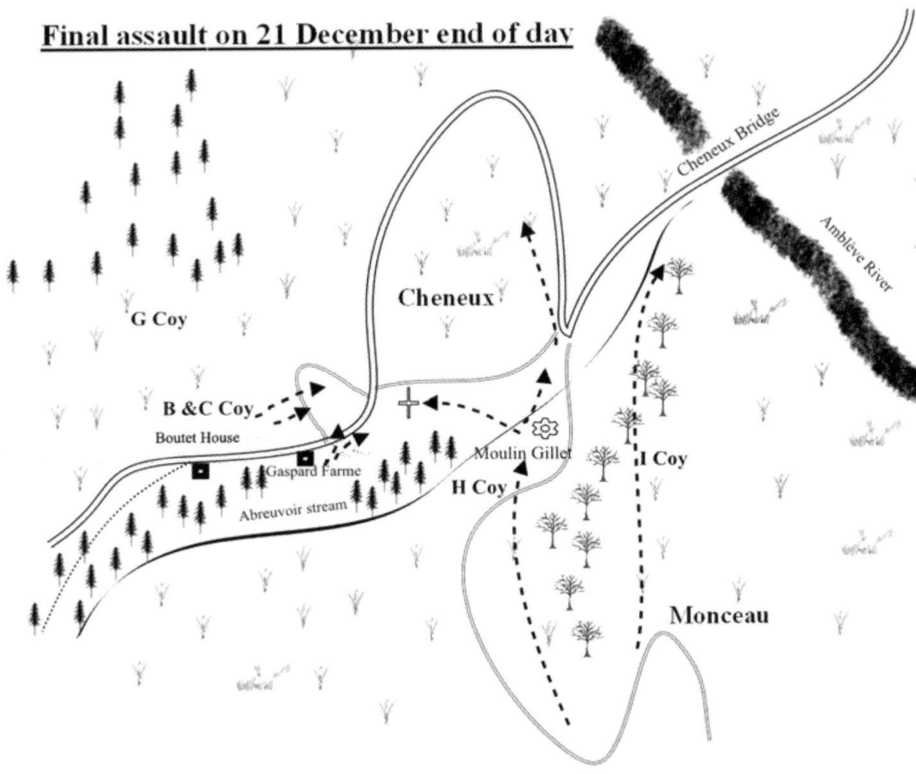


With the previous day's attacks having failed, the Americans launched a pincer attack via the village of Monceau. (*Christian Dujardin*)

by advancing to the bridge over the Amblève and setting up a roadblock there. Then they would envelop the village from the north and a joint assault would be launched by 1/504th PIR and 3/504th PIR to definitively annihilate the Peiper bridgehead south of the river.[4]

At Cheneux, the day passed almost calmly until the two companies of the 3/504th PIR were ready to launch the final assault. Cook's first objective was to take the hamlet of Monceau. Although the distance between the hamlet of Froidville, where I and H companies were located, and Monceau was less than 5 kilometres via forest tracks, the airborne attack only began from the heights overlooking Monceau at 4 pm. Captain Kappel's H Company was in the lead, followed by Captain Burriss' I Company, with the Staff Company bringing up the rear. The leading elements came under fire from MG 42s and 20-mm anti-aircraft guns, but by around 4:30 pm, Monceau had been taken. Civilians confirmed that the Germans had not occupied the hamlet, but one or two armoured semi-tracks were covering the banks of the Abreuvoir stream, which ran in the talweg between Cheneux and Monceau. H Company arrived at the bottom of the valley at the old Gillet mill, not far from the bunker in which Peiper had taken refuge during the attack by US fighter-bombers. Now, the Americans began the assault on Cheneux from the south, running as the 20-mm fire began to surround them. Sergeant Bill Hannigan led his team as they returned German fire. During the run, he saw one

Companies H and I of 504th PIR regrouped before attacking Cheneux via Monceau. (*Nara*)

A photograph taken in the centre of Cheneux after the fighting. The l. FH 105mm is visible in the foreground, and to the rear is the Sd.Kfz. 10/4 with its deadly 20-mm Flak mounted on its platform. (*Nara*)

of his airborne men hit in the shin by a 20-mm anti-aircraft shell. The man tore off his trousers to assess the extent of the damage, but the leg was in tatters. Hannigan, his squad leader, stopped to lend the medic a hand, exclaiming, '*Well, the leg will fall off by itself*'. The medic replied, '*No, we're going to give it a facelift*'. The wounded man was evacuated and sent to England for treatment.

After the fighting, the first news Sergeant Bill Hannigan received from his team member was that his former protégé had undergone successful surgery. However, during his convalescence, the drunk soldier fell down and the surgeons had to start work all over again.

Sergeant Ray Walker also took his boys to the shelter of a hedge a few hundred metres from Cheneux. Robert DeVinney cautiously crawled out into the open to 'lock on' to his target, an anti-aircraft gun that was giving them a hard time. As he fired towards the enemy vehicle, the enemy gunner spotted the source of the shot and swung his weapon towards DeVinney. He quickly returned to the shelter of the hedge, which the tracer shells set on fire. One of the buildings behind them was a house with a small barn attached, known as the Gillet mill. The medics drove the horses out of it and turned it into a first-aid post. Joseph Barnard, the veteran parachutist who was the young DeVinney's partner, was wounded in the head by shrapnel from a 20-mm German gun. He remembers: '*Jo put his hand to his forehead to stop the haemorrhaging, the blood was so thick it was coming out of his sleeve. White as a sheet, he went into the first-aid post and was quickly treated. A few*

The Sd.Kfz. 10/5 which hindered the paratroopers in their attack on Cheneux from Monceau photographed after its destruction. (*Rights reserved via Lemaire*)

*minutes later he reappeared with a large bandage around his forehead and came straight away to join me in the fight.*[5]

The Luftwaffe's anti-aircraft guns continued to wreak havoc on the paratroopers' ranks. To reach safety, they had no choice but to climb the steep slope behind the Cheneux cemetery. Corporal George Graves of section S1[6] was on the heights of Cheneux in the late morning of 22 December. His mission was to estimate the provisional casualties of the fighting. He said:

*B Company had lost its eight officers and first sergeant. Only one staff sergeant commanded what was left of the company, which he estimated at around 30 men. C Company had lost 5 officers, had about 55 men wounded and about 15 killed. First Battalion Headquarters had 2 officers killed, 2 or 3 conscripts killed and about 30 wounded. G Company, who had come in as reinforcements, had their first sergeant killed and about 25 men wounded. In reality no one knew exactly who had been killed and who was still alive. Colonel Harrison, already holder of the Distinguished Service Cross and Silver Star, was sitting leaning against a pile of hay in the barn. He stared blankly at the floor, fiddling with a piece of straw between his fingers. He told us that the assault across the top of the hill had had to cross many barbed wire fences, worse than any nightmare he had imagined, as a solid curtain of 20-mm Flak and machine gun fire swept the assault waves from three sides. That morning, they had repelled a powerful counter-attack and wondered if they would have the strength to repel another. Houses were being occupied in the village, which had not yet been completely cleared. We made a rough estimate of what we thought the remaining strength of each company was and left for our S1 CP. On the way back I looked at some of the bodies in the ditches to see if I recognised any of them – the same boys who had been shouting with laughter the previous afternoon, 'Four more days of shopping before Christmas'. I didn't recognise any of them personally, but I could see what they must have been going through. There was at least one place in that German offensive where the rampaging Huns had been stopped, perhaps temporarily. Only time will tell.*[7]

## Cheneux is Finally Safe

As night fell, Colonel Tucker was at 3/504th PIR's HQ in Monceau and gave the order at 5 pm to sound the death knell.[8] At Cheneux, the surviving men of B and C companies raced towards the village, while G Company was held in reserve. This time, Lieutenant Roberts' two Tank Destroyers took part, with its leader recalling:

*Throughout the day, the All Americans remained on the defensive. As dusk set in, the final assault began. The Germans put up fierce resistance and it was clear that they would not give up easily. Our frontal attack was backed up by an assault on the enemy's rear. We followed our boys. Glesring, the gunner, was firing at anything that moved. Right from the start we destroyed a 105-mm gun and its tractor. We moved cautiously through the village, continuing to fire. By 9 pm enemy resistance was over. We then moved to the edge of the village, our position overlooking the approaches to Cheneux. Late at night*

> *we spotted a Flak Wagon that had remained hidden and was moving towards Vaulx-Renard. We destroyed it.*[9]

For the airborne, the fighting was merciless. Twenty hours of hand-to-hand combat for every house, every room. The paratroopers were sometimes driven out of a house, only to return with even more rage. Corpses were everywhere and many soldiers came out of the action in a state of shock.[10] Nevertheless, Cheneux finally fell into American hands at around 7:30 pm.

On 21 December, the Luftwaffe's 84. Flak Sturmabteilung became part of KG Peiper's air shield. Feldwebel Karl Laun kept a diary, and one of the passages gives us an idea of how the men of the 504th PIR captured the bridge over the Amblève intact:

> *In the morning, two of my best comrades and I were selected to form a Panzervernichtungstrupp* [anti-tank squad]. *Six Panzerfauste and a machine pistol meant we were now a formidable force capable of stopping all enemy tanks. Our battle plans focused on selecting the most favourable route of withdrawal. In our old anti-aircraft post, all was quiet. The room was on the side of the road leading to Cheneux. I was about to inspect one of my platoon's quadruple guns when suddenly twelve Americans, shouting continuously, their rifles and machine pistols raised above their heads, emerged from a thicket. They shouted 'Nicht schiessen'* [Don't shoot]. [...] *I don't know how it happened, certainly nobody gave any orders to that effect, but all of a sudden everything on the Cheneux road rushed towards our bridge. There was no stopping it; the situation had become desperate. I climbed aboard the first vehicle to arrive and we raced towards La Gleize. In the meantime, the Americans had been able to occupy the heights to the right* [east] *of the road and their guns were paying particular attention to any vehicle movement. The village had changed since we passed through there on our way to the big attack. The old town was ablaze at every corner. I met up with some old acquaintances.* [...] *Fortunately for us, the American artillery also seemed to be taking a break. There was a cold drizzle and if someone had tapped me on the shoulder and said, 'Raise your hands, surrender', I don't think there would have been a happier person in the world.*[11]

## The Result of the Attack on Cheneux

The battle took a heavy toll on both sides. Before the assault, C Company had eight officers and 119 men. After Cheneux, it had just three officers and thirty-eight men. B Company paid an even heavier price, with only eighteen men fit to fight after the action. The combined losses of the two battalions amounted to 225 men, including twenty-three killed.[12] The number of SS killed in action is unknown, but thirty-one were taken prisoner. Corporal George Graves said:

*Opposite:* The paratroopers claimed to have destroyed a Panther. However, it had been immobilised in the village since the air attack on 18 December. (*Rights reserved via Lemaire*)

*At 11:30 Lieutenant Voss, Webb and I left the CP for the First Battalion to get an estimate of casualties and to find out what arrangements could be made for the dead, if any. After walking for about a mile up some heavily wooded hills we came to a junction where five German vehicles had been put out of action. The surrounding area was the worst example I had ever seen of the result of large numbers of men trying to kill each other. Broken rifles, discarded ammunition, countless helmets, bloody GI uniforms, bandages, machine gun belts, mortar shells, all sorts of odds and ends were strewn over the hill and in the ditches along both sides of the road. Dead bodies were everywhere. The surviving combatants, their eyes glassy and expressionless, were clinging to holes dug in the banks along the road. The whole scene was so disgusting that it made you want to cry out to God: 'Why was all this necessary?' Webb and I arrived at the house* [Boutet] *which served as the battalion HQ. Our worst fears were confirmed as to what was happening. The staff were in a daze. We were told abruptly and unceremoniously that the house was being fired on from three sides. They all looked so tired that they didn't seem to care whether they lived another half hour or not. The situation was bad at first battalion. The only reports we could expect would be rough estimates.*[13]

The US paratroopers claimed the destruction of four 20-mm self-propelled guns, two troop transports, six half-tracks and a 105-mm howitzer. The list of booty included the destruction of a Tiger tank, although this was, in truth, a Panther destroyed two days earlier by American tactical aircraft. In fact, photographs taken after the fighting show that the troop carriers were actually two Ford V 3000 'Maultier' semi-tracked tanks used to feed the howitzer, a 105-mm FH 18/40 belonging to I/SS-PzArt-Rgt 1. The semi-track guns were SPW Sd.Kfz. 251 Ausf D, at least one of which was a 251/9 with a short 75-mm gun, belonging to 6. and 11. Kompanien of SS-PzGr-Rgt 2. There was also an example armed with a 20-mm anti-aircraft gun and an SPW Sd.Kfz. 251/2 carrying an 80-mm mortar. The 20-mm self-propelled guns were semi-tracked Sd.Kfz. 10/5s belonging to 84. Flak Sturmabteilung.[14] The booty taken included a total of fourteen of these semi-track guns and other vehicles.[15] Four anti-aircraft guns were still intact and in working order, and were integrated directly into the regiment.[16]

Paratrooper Mike Holmstock, of B Company, was one of the few survivors of the attack. He later remembered the scene as he emerged from hell:

*The fighting had stopped and dawn was breaking. I was sitting on a low wall with Johnny Barton, and we started talking about the fighting. Then I looked at him and asked, 'Why are you shaking like that?' He looked at me wryly and replied, 'For the same reason you are!' I realised I was shaking like a leaf, I realised all the adrenaline had gone. For the first time, I looked around me. The ground was red with blood and equipment, tyres, helmets, rucksacks, rifles all strewn about. Dead bodies from both sides lay everywhere, and many wounded people wearing bandages were walking around, haggard. I was talking to my mate about where Knobby* [Sergeant Walsh] *had been wounded when the Tank-Destroyers arrived. There were several dead Germans, one in the middle of the road. The*

Another photograph of Panther 131 at Cheneux, with the coveted bridge in the background. (*Rights reserved*)

*tank fighters we had hoped for were only now arriving. I shouted at him, 'Are you coming now? It's about time! We needed you last night.' I remember the Tank-Destroyer stopped about twenty metres in front of us. In response, the tank commander said to us, 'Can one of you drag this Kraut off the road?' We just looked at him and I replied, 'If you want him out of the way, do it yourself.' He replied threateningly, 'If you don't move him, I'll run him over.' Johnny said, 'Do as you like,' so he ran him over.*

*In the first house, they had started to collect the bodies of the Germans to pile them up for the 'Graves Registration' to come and get them.*[17] *They called up the remaining men in the company, eighteen of whom said 'Present'. I said 'Oh well, they can't use us as a company any more, maybe they'll put us to rest in the rear.' The next day, some twenty replacements, fresh from England, filled in some of the ranks.*[18]

Corporal George Graves also recalled the hours immediately after the fighting: '*The captain came back to the CP telling us that we had sixteen German prisoners who made up the total of his captures out of approximately five companies of Hitler's best soldiers: the others were dead or on the run. The Germans offered to give us sixteen wounded Americans in exchange for the sixteen SS prisoners we had, but the colonel declined.'* In reality, these sixteen prisoners were Panzergrenadiere who had been captured wounded in a German first-aid post. Three from 5. Kompanie, three from 6. Kompanie, eight from 7. Kompanie and two from 11. Kompanie, plus two artillerymen and seven Luftwaffe men, were sent to prison camps. The fact that the prisoners were immobilised by wounds in a dressing station meant that no German soldier was captured alive during the fighting; clear proof that the fighting had been utterly ferocious.

The SS prisoners were not very forthcoming, with the exception of a few men who had been forcibly conscripted into the Waffen-SS and some Luftwaffe airmen. All the Soldbuchs (paybooks) were buried, either by accident or voluntarily. These were small, sturdy pocket books carried by every German soldier on duty as a means of registration and identification.[19]

George Graves continued:

> *Around noon 2/504th PIR left its entrenched positions to relieve I/504th PIR in the village of Cheneux, which was now completely occupied. The battered remnants of 1/504th PIR came shuffling energetically down the road. They contrasted terribly with the cheerful battalion that had arrived only two days earlier by the same road, with joking men full of fighting spirit. They were bearded. Their eyes were red. They were covered head to toe in mud and they stared straight ahead, their faces devoid of expression. None of them spoke. The few officers in the small column (half of those who had left for Cheneux) were recognisable from the men only by the markings on their helmets. They carried their rifles in whatever way seemed convenient, some in the manner of Daniel Boone. They had written a page of history that few people would ever hear about.*[20]

## Civilian Testimonies

For the civilians, the hours of anguish in Cheneux were just as trying. They would never forget those hallucinatory moments:

> *The SS soldiers burst into the school where we were locked in, shouting 'Nach Kathedrale, nach Kathedrale' and took us to the church, a white flag in the lead. It was a tragic moment. People were crying, lamenting: what are they going to do to us? 'Be calm, we won't do anything to you!' said an SS man. 'If you cry any more, we'll shoot you all!' said another. Then followed some really painful hours. In addition to the torments of hunger, thirst and fatigue, there was the uncertainty of our fate. The SS guards became nasty. We never quite understood their motives. First, they put the women and children on one side of the church and the men on the other. Many feared a massacre and believed their last hour had come. Madame Durieux, the priest's mother, knew a little German. She negotiated and later the people of Cheneux thought that her action had been beneficial. Outside, the*

*fighting resumed with unprecedented violence. The walls of the church shuddered with each starting shot from the mouth of the 'Royal Tiger'* [sic] *ambushed behind the cemetery walls. Shortly before evening, the last guard left, leaving the civilians alone in God's house. The din reached the ears of the civilians in the church, illuminated by the sinister glow of the fires. The SS were cornered, defending their skins in bloody, merciless hand-to-hand combat…The fury of the paratroopers from a battle-hardened unit was unleashed, and when the supply of grenades ran out, the half-tracks were stabbed. The end was near. At around 9 pm we heard frantic 'Raus, raus', the gunfire died down and the sounds of war faded. Suddenly, the airborne soldiers burst into the church. Distrustful and suspicious, they scrutinised and questioned all the civilians. In fact, some SS men had put on civilian clothes they had stolen from the wardrobes. Everyone was told not to go outside, as the order had been given to shoot on sight.*[21]

## A Critical Look at the Capture of Cheneux

The capture of Cheneux was presented as an American victory. It certainly was, but the very heavy toll could have been reduced, and there is no doubt that the assault was hastily ordered. The following points in particular are worth noting:

The position occupied by Feldwebel Karl Laun. It is easy to see why the Germans withdrew to La Gleize, as its position was so exposed from Cheneux. (*Rights reserved via Lemaire*)

a) A lack of information about the enemy force in the village despite the dispatch of a patrol.[22]
b) The initial attack was launched frontally without any action on the flanks, leading to a costly stalemate before a flanking attack was made the next day via Monceau.
c) The lack of armoured support. The Tank Destroyer was not capable of supporting an attack by infantrymen, particularly because of the open turret and the absence of a box machine gun for close defence. The only close-contact weapon was a .50-calibre machine gun for anti-aircraft defence, mounted on the back of the turret at the nape of the neck. The gunner had to expose himself to the scrap metal of the battlefield to use it.
d) Air support was not possible due to poor weather conditions.
e) The artillery did not seem to be effective. The omnipresent fog thwarted the work of the observers meaning it was unable to direct fire correctly due to poor visibility.

Who should be blamed for the price paid for this tactical victory achieved in such haste? Ridgway, the commander of XVIII Airborne Corps? Gavin, general of the airborne division? Tucker, the fiery commander of 504th PIR? No one claimed responsibility. Gavin justified it by the need to clear the entire left bank of the Amblève in order to set up a solid position that could not be bypassed. Two companies of paratroopers, totalling around 250 men, were launched in the frontal attack on the village.

Bearing in mind that the normal ratio commonly accepted for launching an assault with some chance of success is three attackers to one defender, when considering the number of German troops in Cheneux at the time, 1,200 men with significant armoured support would have been needed to take this solidly defended position. In our view, the deadly attack had been launched in haste and was very costly in terms of casualties. It succeeded only because of the valour and pugnacity of the soldiers who took part.

It should be noted that the capture of Cheneux was only the beginning of the All Americans' involvement in the Battle of the Bulge, but it marked the end of one of the most critical phases of the campaign: deployment close to the enemy. For the All Americans, a defensive phase now began, which were quickly put to the test on the heights of Trois-Ponts.

# Chapter 5

# The Battle to Reach Peiper

## 1. SS-Panzer Division Completely Torn Apart

While the SS-Panzergrenadiere held out in the pocket of La Gleize, the commander of 1. SS-Panzer Division, SS-Oberführer Wilhelm Mohnke, set up his command post in Ligneuville to try to reconstitute his position. His task was a complex one, however, given the fragmentation of his division.

The SS attempted a direct assault on Stavelot to re-establish the communication lines of the entire 1. SS-Panzer Division. (*NAC*)

Chief of Staff of I. SS-Panzer-Korps was SS-Gruppenführer und Generalleutnant der Waffen-SS Hermann Priess. (*Rights reserved*)

A dispatch rider compensated for the radio link problems. These men are riding a BMW R75 with sidecar. (*Nara*)

KG Peiper and part of KG Knittel were surrounded in the Stoumont – La Gleize – Cheneux triangle. It should be noted that not all of KG Peiper was surrounded there. 6. and 7. Kompanien of SS-Pz-Rgt 1 and most of the Tigers from s. SS-Pz-Abt 501 were still around Wanne and the Stavelot heights, where they were joined by part of the divisional artillery.

KG Knittel was roughly assembled in a bridgehead on the road leading from Stavelot to Trois-Ponts. The former was occupied by a battalion from 119th IR of the 30th ID, reinforced by elements of 743rd TB. Trois-Ponts was very lightly defended until the arrival of Vandervoort's 2/504th PIR on 20 December. Vandervoort had brought his E Company across the Salm and was a direct threat to KG Knittel's connections, which was only linked to the rest of its division by the Petit Spay footbridge, with the road to the bridge itself cut off by E Company.

Meanwhile, KG Sandig was stuck on the heights in front of Stavelot.

Reinforcements were obtained for the I SS-Panzer-Korps (Pz-Korps). Its Chief of Staff, SS-Gruppenführer und Generalleutnant der Waffen-SS Hermann Preiss, stated in his post-war report that on 20 December at midday, 12. SS-Pz-Div had been subordinated to the II SS-Pz-Korps. The latter had taken over the missions of the 277. Volks-Grenadier-Division (VGD), 12. VGD and 3. Fallschirmjäger-Division after the LXVII Armee-Korps headquarters had been bombed. In reality, it seems that this corps fell short of 6. Panzer-Armee's expectations and was replaced by II SS-Pz-Korps, which had been held in reserve until then. Dietrich's aim was to ensure that the

I SS-Pz-Korps was not immobilised. At the same time, 9. SS-Pz-Div 'Hohenstaufen', which had been ordered to leave the Stadtkyll sector via Born towards Recht, was subordinated to the I SS-Pz-Korps. However, the lack of fuel meant that only certain sections of its reconnaissance battalion, SS-Aufklärungs-Abteilung 9, could be sent forward. SS-Panzergrenadier Regiment 19 began to advance on foot, with artillery and tanks waiting for supplies to arrive. The task of 9. SS-Pz-Div was to attack from Recht through Vielsalm and then north-westwards. The aim was to clear the way for KG Peiper on the left in the vicinity of 1. SS-Pz-Div, and then to push forward with it towards the north-west.

Lieutenant Colonel Lovelady commanded 3rd AD's most powerful CCB Task Force. His mission was to completely isolate Peiper but to do so he had to annihilate the troops of KGs Knittel and Hansen. (*Rights reserved*)

SS-Aufklärungs-Abteilung 9 advanced as requested to the south-west, but came up against Task Force Rosenbaum of the 7th AD near Poteau. Blocked at this point, the Hohenstaufen took over the security tasks south of Recht in order to free up the rear of KG Hansen, which in turn was delayed by resistance from 14th Cavalry Group in Poteau on the morning of 18 December after crossing Recht. It now had to hold the Poteau crossroads against attempts by Task Force Rosenbaum to retake this strategic point and could not set off again until it had been relieved. By the evening of 20 December, it was at Aisomont on the heights of Trois-Ponts, its mission being to reach Knittel via the Petit Spay bridge.

In 1. SS-Pz-Div's sector, the Germans were well aware that the enemy had received considerable reinforcements, enabling it to advance to the point of becoming increasingly threatening. Continuous attacks throughout the morning by the armoured 30th ID from the north and west, as well as from the south-west, on KG Peiper made it clear that the subsequent effect of the breakthrough had definitively faded, even if for the moment these attacks were repulsed. Meanwhile, the presence of Task Force Lovelady in Coo prevented traffic along the Trois-Ponts – La Gleize road, completely isolating Peiper. SS-PzGr-Rgt 1, which had been reinforced, had now moved forward on the right and experienced the worst difficulties in getting to its assembly area thanks to the poor conditions on and off the roads.

On the evening of 20 December, Mohnke had little choice and was forced to exert concentric pressure on Stavelot. KG Knittel repeated its attacks from the west and Sandig from the heights south of the town. If the Germans took the town, they would be able to re-establish his lines of communication. Meanwhile, KG Hansen, with SS-PzGr-Rgt 1 and SS-Panzerjäger-Abteilung 1 accompanied by twenty-one Jagdpanzer IV/70s and

KG Hansen was delayed in the fighting in Poteau. This SS-Panzergrenadier poses after the skirmish in front of an M8 Greyhound from 14th Cavalry Group. (*Nara*)

Stug IIIs, had to make its way towards Peiper via Petit Spay. Coming from Aisomont, it found Vandervoort's E Company in its path. At the same time, 2/505th PIR was also spotted,[1] particularly its E Company on the heights of Wanne.

## Hanging at Easy Company

On the night of 21 December at around 3 am, two SPWs from KG Hansen approached the small junction of the Wanne road and the path leading to Petit Spay. The first jumped on a mine placed in front of the crossing. Vandervoort gives an excellent description of what happened next and how his men coped with the maelstrom that descended:

> *At daybreak the German infantry attempted to drive them* [Easy Company] *from their position* [on the hill] *with a vigorous attack, which was repulsed. The battalion reported to the division that E Company was engaged with elements of 1 SS Pz-Div. Lieutenant 'Creeper' Doerfler, the battalion's intelligence officer, confirmed the identification of the Germans killed during the night and early morning. In mid-morning, a large infantry attack, supported by four or five tanks, was launched against the company. The attack ended with the death of German soldiers in E Company's trenches and the capture of more Germans. The resistance probably surprised the German commander. The terrain made it necessary to temporarily hold a blocking position. The crazy American paratroopers didn't*

Bazooka teams like this one were placed on the heights overlooking Trois-Ponts by Vandervoort. (*Nara*)

*seem to know how to read a map and insisted on staying at the edge of the woods and covering the road with their fire.*

*From the mortar observation post we could see the Panzer formations manoeuvring and massing for another attack. The road was clogged with Tiger and Panther*[2] *Panzergrenadiere (in vehicles and on foot), self-propelled artillery and mobile flak. It was an exceptionally well-equipped and large armoured KG, and a disturbing sight for a unit with only a small 57-mm anti-tank gun. The young German 'Blackshirts' killed in the trenches of E Company had shown that the Germans were determined to fight their way westwards. Some of the artillery from the Panzers, mortars and 20-mm self-propelled flak guns began firing into E Company's area. With this vastly superior force pressing down on them and with their backs to the river, the position on the cliff was rapidly turning into a trap. Prudence dictated that we move the company to a more favourable defensive position on the west bank of the river. The terrain would help us separate the tanks from the infantry and put the small party on equal footing.*[3] *The deputy divisional commander disagreed. There was no better combat company commander in the 505th PIR than Bill Meddaugh. He and his company – about 140 men and officers – were proud, tough, battle-hardened soldiers. His orders were to stay and try to hold the Germans east of Trois-Ponts. If they had not been ordered to leave the position, and if they had been surrounded and captured, they would probably have been fighting under the tracks of the Tiger tanks. He kept going back and forth to the battalion command post to keep abreast of developments.*

*Determined not to lose E Company, I sent F Company across the river to the south to try and hit the next German tank attack on the flank. This would make it easier to break the engagement if we could get permission (or if I decided to go to hell with permission) to pull E Company back. F Company's sortie did little to discourage the massive Panzer attack. But the Germans must have wondered where the Americans were coming from. By mid-afternoon we could hear the sound of battle rising on the cliffs above the town.*

*In the morning, Lieutenant Cooper, leader of the 81-mm section, had joined the position of the 2nd section of E Company on the left flank. By keeping the mortars close by, he was indispensable to E Company. Captain T.G. Smith, the battalion's second-in-command, moved up to the company's CP during the latter part of the battle to maintain a symbolic battalion presence on the cliff. 'T.G.', a seasoned combat veteran, would have ordered the company back immediately, but he lacked the authority to do so. Disaster seemed imminent.*

*Faced with the bulk of a Panzer-Division, not one man from E Company left his fighting position. They were superb. The general came back to the battalion command post and ordered: 'Bring them back'. With a great sigh of relief I told my operations officer, 1st Lieutenant Charles E. 'Pinky' Sammon, to give the order to the company. I jumped into my jeep and drove off in the direction of E Company's position. As we passed the 57-mm anti-tank gun, the team was preparing to return to the town. We arrived at the company HQ just as a combined infantry and tank assault culminated in an attack on the company trenches. Four or more tanks were closing in on the open area on the right front and spraying the edge of the woods with machine gun and cannon fire. The first wave of German infantry assault was momentarily blocked on the left side of the road by a deadly fusillade across the open road. I ran to Meddaugh and told him to get his men back into town to form the battalion reserve, and to do it now! Bill passed the word to his company to withdraw. They began to retreat through the woods, accompanied by a hail of bullets that cut through the bark and wood of the trees. A company of Panzergrenadiere advanced on the road, some shouting in English: 'Halt, Americans, you are surrounded.' Meanwhile, Corporal Jerome Russell, my driver/radio operator, had turned the jeep around. Taking T.G. with me, I climbed back in and we began to descend towards Trois-Ponts, assailed by swarms of 9-mm bullets from Schmeisser machine pistols. Halfway down the road, we came across the 57-mm anti-tank gun, jack-knifed in a ditch and abandoned by its crew.*

*The left flank of E Company, hit hard by the Panzer infantry's lateral assault, kept its nerve and its weapons. But with the Germans pouring in behind them on the other side of the road, they had no choice but to hide in the thick woods and descend towards the cliff. Further to the right, the Tiger tanks and accompanying infantry were slower to close in. The soldiers of B Company made the Panzergrenadiere and their tanks pay a heavy price*

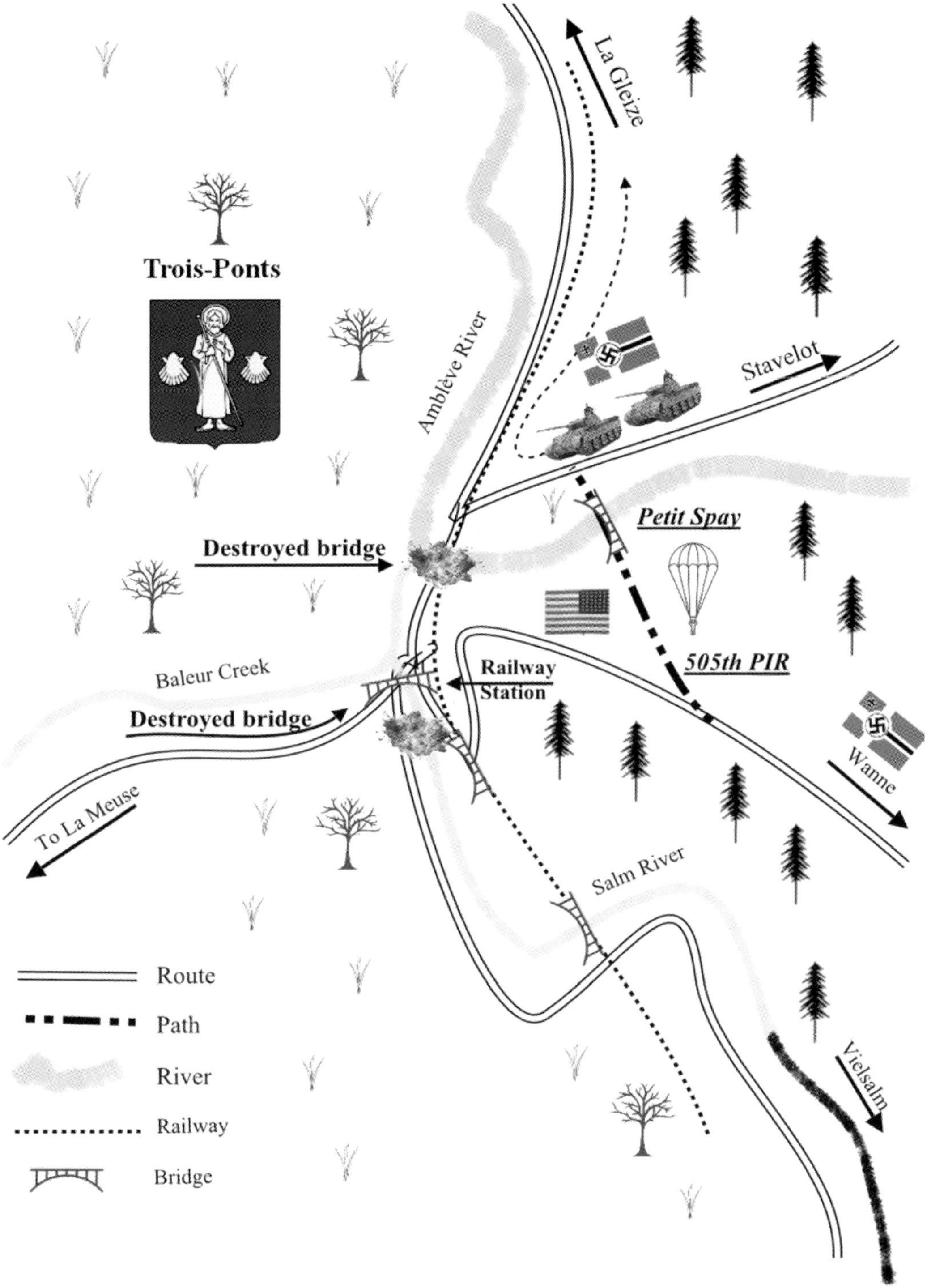


E Company, 505th PIR was in an excellent position to hinder movements and prevent access to the Petit Spay bridge: the last crossing point over the Amblève. It was ruthlessly repulsed. (*Christian Dujardin*)

*for advancing over open ground. Having been ordered to withdraw, the soldiers, armed with the lessons they had learned in close combat at Nijmegen in Holland, intuitively improvised a 'fire on foot' in the opposite direction. Moving backwards and using trees for cover, they simply fired at any pursuer who came too close.*

*When they reached the edge of the cliff, they jumped down, got up and walked the 100 metres between the two roads, the railway and the river, under the protective fire of our troops on the other side of the river. The latter had received orders to engage any German appearing on the cliff. A number of soldiers suffered back and limb injuries – sprains and fractures – as they jumped the cliffs, but no one was left behind. Other members of the company grabbed the wounded and dragged them along. This was the opportune moment for the Germans to start pushing towards the town of Trois-Ponts. B Company was momentarily disorganised. F Company was still on the other side of the Salm. D Company was downstream, blocking another German attempt to cross. The battalion headquarters, the headquarters company (and those damned engineers) were all that stood in the way of a major breakthrough. The soldiers and sappers, entrenched along the riverbank and in the houses of Trois-Ponts, returned fire with their 30 and 50 calibre machine guns. We blew up the road bridge over the Salm as soon as the last soldier from E Company had cleared the area. Other German infantrymen opened fire along the cliff. The Germans and Americans engaged in rapid exchanges of machine-gun and rifle fire at distances of 150 to 300 metres. The Germans began spraying the streets of Trois-Ponts*

Vandervoort claimed that his men fought against Tiger tanks. As with all Americans, every German tank was a Tiger. This was highly implausible, as Hansen only had Jagdpanzer IV L/70 tank fighters. (*Nara*)

*with automatic weapons. But the exposed edge of the cliff was not the ideal place for a duel with entrenched defenders. The paratroopers were content to fire the old-fashioned way and drew a lot of blood on the cliff.*

*A Tiger tank appeared on the side of the cliff road. The white skull and crossbones of the SS badge and the black and white war cross painted on its armour were clearly visible* [sic].[4] *At point-blank range, it pointed its long bulbous-mouthed cannon and began firing directly at the soldiers. A hundred feet above us, shrouded in gun smoke, it loomed off the cliff like something out of a Lindzee Prescott cartoon.*[5] *Our 2.36 bazookas barely dented its front armour plate. Fearing that wounded members of E Company were still close to the tank's position, we reluctantly brought the 81-mm mortar section into action. They chose white phosphorous shells to reduce the Germans' visibility from the cliff. With astonishing accuracy, the first shell hit the Tiger just in front of the turret. Burning globules of phosphorus shot off in all directions. The enemy soldiers around the tank scattered like quail. The Panzer driver put the menacing monster in reverse and accelerated back to the shelter of the woods. No more armoured vehicles attempted a direct approach, and the open-topped, multi-barrelled flak vehicles didn't dare expose themselves to this mortar fire with sniper-like accuracy.*[6] *The 82nd Airborne Division's artillery observer took over. Fortunately, the division's artillery was able to be aimed at the enemy position. Because of the mountains and valleys, there was a lot of dead space in our artillery range. We were doubly lucky with the town nestling under the cliff, the German artillery overran the river bottom area we were defending. As F. Company was not on the high cliff, the artillery of the 82nd Airborne Division was used to its advantage. The 1 SS-Panzer Division withdrew from the cliff until nightfall.*

*Winter days are short. As night fell, the Panzers returned, still determined to fight their way westwards. The Grenadiere made several vigorous attempts to cross the Salm that night. That day in December was not as high-profile an action as Bastogne. But in some ways, little Company E did more than the others. For twelve long hours, it held off the highest-priority and best-equipped division in the German army, convincing the commander of the 1. SS-Panz-Division to turn back and look for an easier route west than passing over the defenders of the 505th PIR at Trois-Ponts. Despite all their determination and excellent equipment, the Germans left battered and exhausted. During the night, the Germans changed their attack route to the north, towards La Gleize, along the road and railway parallel to the Amblève.*[7]

Vandervoort's account is poignant. While he describes the facts well, he is not free of exaggerations. Like many Americans, he apparently saw Tigers everywhere, believing he was single-handedly stopping an armoured division when, in fact, he found himself up against a battalion of Panzergrenadiere supported by Jagdpanzer IVs. Preiss explains: '*The enemy had crossed the Salm sector during the afternoon and by 10 am, shortly before the end of the assembly, had advanced to just before Wanne, so a battalion of the regiment had to be sent to push the enemy back beyond the Salm. By nightfall the wood west of Wanne had been cleared and the battalion had to remain there as a security battalion.*[8]' Nevertheless, the performance of Easy Company, 505th PIR, deserves to be highlighted. In any case, it had nothing to envy another company with the same designation within the 506th PIR of the 101st Airborne Division. Its fight blocked access to Petit Spay for the bulk of KG Hansen, while the threatening presence of 505th PIR in Stavelot deprived KG Hansen of a large part of its resources, meaning that many of the troops could not take part in the assault on Stavelot.

## KG Knittel Under Siege

Of course, the Americans were perfectly aware they had to keep KG Peiper isolated in order to crush it, and so began by trying to reduce the pocket formed by KG Knittel and its bridgehead on the right bank of the Amblève, between Stavelot and Trois-Ponts. Task Force Lovelady launched its first assault of the day. From 8:30 am, the Shermans moved slowly along the steep path towards Parfondruy. Arriving on the outskirts of the

This Sherman M4A3 76 (W) from Task Force Lovelady was photographed after the fighting on the heights of Parfondruy. (*Nara*)

Men from 30th ID advance up the hillside. This group of GIs has a bazooka at the rear of its squad. (*Nara*)

villa l'Épilogue,[9] the armoured column was stopped by heavy fire. The location was not suitable for an armoured assault: there was a steep embankment on the left, while the meadows, which would have allowed a tactically worthy deployment, were waterlogged and impassable. The infantrymen of E Company, 120th IR, who accompanied the tanks, did not overcome the obstacle until around 1:30 pm, when the tanks immediately rushed in and liberated the martyred hamlet of Parfondruy. On the heights north of Stavelot, L and I companies had arrived at La Borzeux wood. They were to head for Ster, which was liberated at 11:30 am, while skirmishes broke out in Renardmont.[10] The vice gradually tightened on KG Knittel, which lost the ground overlooking its bridgehead and the precious Petit Spay bridge, which enabled it to maintain a link with the bulk of the division. Renardmont was evacuated in the afternoon. At the western entrance to Stavelot, the Germans were definitively blocked in their advance. Coblenz, the officer in charge of the assault, said: '*The enemy had a perfect view of the place. At the slightest movement, the Americans responded with heavy fire: machine guns and grenade launchers. The greatest danger was posed by sniper fire.*'[11]

It was a trying time, even for hardened SS men. After the fighting, a resident of the route de Trois-Ponts found two handwritten letters from a German soldier, one addressed to his mother and the other to his father. They read as follows:

These 30th ID soldiers are seen taking advantage of forest cover to make their advance. (*Nara*)

> *21/12/1944. My dear mother. I am in a cellar. Lighting: a candle and it's freezing. Above us the artillery is thundering into the Belgian town. Here in this cellar, these barrage fires cannot shake us. We've been without food for five days. We live on what we find in the houses. There's enough. Not much bread, though. We have kilos of butter, but not a piece of bread. Today, I'm counting my 41st day of fighting,*[12] *and every day has been tough. But we'll get through it. I'll finish, because sleep is precious. Give my regards to all the parents for me. I don't have time to write to them. A cordial hello and kiss. Your Günther.*

The second letter was to his father:

> *21/12/1944, half past seven in the evening. My dear Dad, just a few lines, because the little time I have I have to sleep. Today is the 41st day of battles in the streets. They are bitter battles. As the most advanced section, it's possible that we'll still be surrounded as often as we are now. But it doesn't bother us much. To you, dear Dad, I wish a happy Christmas, a little belatedly. All the best for '45. Unfortunately, we won't have our own Christmas party again. I've also written a few lines to Mum. I apologise for the bad handwriting. I'm in a cellar where it's terribly cold. The Americans are 80 metres from us. Their artillery is pounding the town without taking their own troops into account. The*

*communiqués will certainly tell you where we are fighting. We don't know anything about the whole situation. And that's it. I've already prepared some good American cigarettes for you. All the best. Yours sincerely, Günther.*[13]

Although the soldier in question was not identified, his account sums up the atmosphere in this part of the fighting very well. The SS remained confined to the houses at the entrance to Stavelot. Tiger II 132, which was defending the perimeter on the town side, withdrew for the night. It returned in the morning and again set up a bunker in front of the Stavelot exit, where it remained for part of the day. The heavy Panzer withdrew for good, leaving the Americans free to launch the final assault. The losses on the German side were terrible, as witnessed by Coblenz's account of his return from Knittel's HQ. The constant to-ing and fro-ing between Coblenz and Knittel HQ was duc to the lack of radio and telephone communication:

*On the way there, I passed the leader of the third section. This section was part of my company. Siebert told me that after a very close fight he had driven the enemy back and that he had shot some American prisoners. He did not tell me the exact number of prisoners of war shot. I asked Siebert why he had shot the prisoners. He replied that his platoon was reduced to nine men and that he could not do without anyone to guard the prisoners.*[14]

Only the Petit Spay bridge still allowed the passage of light wagons, men, lorries and troops, who had crossed the Amblève to reinforce Knittel's units, which had been badly beaten. Ster was then occupied by L Company, 117th IR, while Renardmont was liberated by I Company. Parfondruy was in the hands of the riflemen of E Company, 120th IR, supported by Lovelady tankers. The Panzergrenadiere withdrew along the railway line, thus protecting the Trois-Ponts – Stavelot road.

## KG Hansen Joins in the Dance

Unfortunately, this American success was short-lived, as KG Hansen threw its regiment, which had already been badly beaten in the Rodt area, into the fray. I/SS-PzGr-Rgt 1 crossed the Petit Spay bridge after having repulsed Vandervoort's men, and the GIs occupying Ster, and more precisely the Masures farm, were violently attacked late in the day on 21 December by these reinforcements. The arrival of Hansen temporarily loosened the grip on Knittel.

The tank hunters of KG Hansen followed the Panzergrenadiere. One of them, a Jagdpanzer IV/ L70, arrived at Petit Spay. Only the driver remained on board; the rest of the crew had carefully crossed the bridge ahead of their tank. The Jagdpanzer set out onto the bridge, but as soon as it had crossed the halfway point, a huge crash was heard: the Panzer and the bridge disappeared in unison into the tumultuous waters of the river. It was a catastrophe for Gustav Knittel's SS-Aufklärungs-Abteilung 1. It was now trapped and surrounded, with no means of crossing the tumultuous waters of the Amblève.[15]

Overall view of KG Hansen's Jagdpanzer IV and the low-capacity bridge designed for the agricultural cart, which collapsed under the weight of the tank. (*Stavelot Library*)

The I SS-Pz-Korps Chief of Staff wrote of KG Hansen:

*The regiment's attack (minus one battalion, which had been delayed by the enemy attack on Wanne)*[16] *took place in the early afternoon. The infantry crossed the Amblève sector and attacked northwards. The Jagd-Panzer IVs*[17] *could not be brought across the stream, as the light bridge to the north-east of Trois-Ponts had collapsed when the first Jagd-Panzer was placed there. The infantry attack gained about a kilometre of ground and halted along the line north of Renardmont-Ster. KG Peiper was unable to take part in the attack as it had run out of fuel and ammunition. The attack, led by a battalion of SS-PzGr-Rgt 1 and part of SS-Aufklärungs-Abteilung 1 on Stavelot, was repulsed by the enemy. In order to make KG Peiper mobile again and therefore able to take part in the fighting, air supplies were ordered by the Korps for 21 December 1944 and granted by the Luftwaffe.*

German engineers using an inflatable boat. This photograph is claimed to have been taken at Petit Spay. Although the locations seem to correspond, we have no certainty that it was taken there. (*Nara*)

I SS-Pz-Korps did not disarm and was counting on the Luftwaffe to get Peiper out of its predicament. Indeed, the orders given to Mohnke for the following day were for the 1. SS-Pz-Div to make the bridge north-east of Trois-Ponts usable again and continue the attack with the aim of rejoining KG Peiper. The 9. SS-Pz-Div quickly reached the Recht sector and, in view of the position of the 1. SS-Pz-Div, joined the first regiment to arrive and moved with it to Vielsalm.

Preiss goes on to say: '*KG Peiper had been heavily attacked throughout the day but had been repulsed. They had reported that they had run out of fuel and only small quantities of ammunition and other supplies.*'[18] In other words, if Peiper was not rejoined very soon, his battle group would be finished.

As a result, the instructions given by I SS-Pz-Korps were completely logical. As the links between the two parts of 1. SS-Pz-Div were cut, there was only one way to re-establish them: build a bridge. The riverbanks lent themselves well to the initiative and so construction of a K-Brücke began immediately. This event also triggered a change in the German plan. It was clear that it was no longer possible to break through to the

Detailed view of Japdpanzer IV l/70 with its factory camouflage of superimposed circles. It was sent into combat without having been given a number. (*Stavelot Library*)

Meuse via the Stavelot – La Gleize sector, so the axis of attack therefore shifted south towards Vielsalm, where Preiss still hoped to break through with the support of the Hohenstaufen. This intention was an excellent card to play for two reasons. Firstly, it provided a route to the Meusc that was not yet solidly defended. Secondly, by taking Vielsalm, the road to Saint-Vith could be definitively closed and the many American troops there isolated: the entire 7th AD, the CCB of the 9th AD and the survivors of the 106th ID. General Ridgway, the American commander of the sector, now faced a major new problem.

At the end of the day, Major Robert Yates was still in command of C Company, 51st Engineer Combat Battalion. His men held the market town of Trois-Ponts, and he had the excellent idea of sending a patrol towards Petit Spay. The German pioneers were hard at work building a bridge a few metres downstream from the old one and the information was passed on to Colonel William Ekman, commanding the 505th PIR. He ordered the airborne artillery to saturate the area, Meaning it immediately became an uninhabitable hell for enemy troops.[19] The American fire was to be terribly effective as for the first time, the shells were fitted with a Pozit proximity fuze.

Charles Corbin was a section leader with Battery A, 391st Armored Field Artillery Battalion (AFAB) within the 3rd AD. On 21 December, he was ordered to report to Lieutenant Edmark of D Company, 33rd Armored Regiment (AR) at Parfondruy, to provide artillery support. He was escorted part of the way and ordered to hurry as the Germans were watching the road. He arrived at Parfondruy, where his section acted as an artillery observation post, and described the action of his division's guns in the area, also explaining why Tiger 132 fell back to Petit Spay:

> *We had nine tanks, a platoon of infantry and mortars, some engineers and medics, and we had to hold our position. Lieutenant Edmark had led D Company from Petit-Coo to take Stavelot, but he had been stopped in the afternoon on the edge of Parfondruy, on the road to Coo, by a large number of infantrymen and tanks. They had killed many Germans,*

General view of the Petit Spay site showing the collapsed bridge, the engineer footbridge that could not be completed and a Tiger II tank in the background taken by KG Knittel to attack Stavelot. (*Nara*)

> *disabled several tanks and taken a few prisoners. The fighting had stopped when we arrived.*
>
> *All afternoon we could see German troops crossing the railway line on the Stavelot road towards Trois-Ponts, but we couldn't see our artillery shells because of the mist and fog. I went up to a house on a hill behind us to get a better view. There, right under our noses, was a big German tank under the trees. After warning Lieutenant Plummer and Lieutenant Edmark, we threw the artillery on it and got it out to where one of the tanks from D Company had a good chance of hitting it. And he did, but three shells bounced off and he retreated, never moving his turret. It must have been a Tiger Mark VI. We all wondered, and I know that the tank gunner shook his head, feeling helpless as he retreated along the track on our left flank. I'd seen our 75s bounce off Mark V and VI tanks before, the last time at Roetgen where they destroyed several of our tanks.*
>
> *This tank fire caused a lot of hits on us as the Germans returned fire, and some of our own 155 attacked us. It took us some time to put a stop to it. Colonel Lovelady radioed Lieutenant Edmark as we had the only radio capable of communicating with the outside world. The road to Coo had been taken by the Germans and our infantry had been ordered out. We were isolated and feared the Germans would try to attack us for our petrol supplies. We mounted our three 30-calibre machine guns in the windows from top to bottom and sat up all night waiting. Nobody slept, but the attack never happened.*[20]

## Consequences of a Collapsing Bridge

Fortunately for the American front, KG Hansen's involvement was limited by the collapse of the Petit Spay footbridge. Reading Corbin's account, we understand that if this had not been the case, it would have been possible for the Germans to link up with KG Peiper. The American artillery also played a vital role in the battle by preventing the pioneers from establishing a bridge over the Amblève, As Preiss explains: '*The bridge positions were subjected to constant and intense fire and the new bridges that were put in place were repeatedly destroyed.*' The consequences were not long in coming, and the failure of the attempt to clear Stavelot was noted by the corps headquarters:

> *Parts of SS-PzGr-Rgt 2 had managed to penetrate Stavelot. However, they were unable to resist the enemy attacks and had to retreat. SS-PzGr-Rgt 1 gained some ground at the cost of hard fighting and considerable losses, but was unable to break through the enemy front, closed as it was, because the enemy had a number of tanks and our own assault guns could not be transported across the Amblève. In addition to the 30th ID, elements of a tank unit and a parachute division appeared on the scene.*[21]

Meanwhile, towards the rear, 9. SS-Panzer Division managed to move one of its regiments forward on foot and, by removing petrol from the tanks of the most important vehicles, move an armoured battalion into the Recht sector. An attack towards Vielsalm followed at around 10 am, which initially made good progress but failed to isolate the defenders of

Sherman M4 manufactured in 1943 and fitted with duckbills to widen its tracks, photographed near the German border. This type of equipment was used by Task Force Rosenbaum. (*Nara*)

Saint-Vith. The tanks could only manoeuvre on the road itself and in the woods to the east of Poteau, the infantry was attacked on its southern flank and had to retreat, leaving the crossroads in the hands of Task Force Rosenbaum. Thanks to the difficulties inherent in the wooded terrain and the mud, the Panzers were unable to help them. In addition, Task Force Navajo had a firm hold on the road beyond Poteau. Hopes of a successful breakthrough on Vielsalm were severely thwarted for the time being.

I SS-Pz-Korps' radio listening services were able to decode the movement of enemy forces, so Preiss revised his battle plan. He realised that 82nd Airborne Division was settling along the Salm between Trois-Ponts and Salmchâteau, heralding the formation of a firm front along the Targnon – Grandménil line. He realised he had to rely on the fact that the attacks against KG Peiper would increase in number and strength and that without supplies and petrol, it would be unable to defend itself. Preiss was also aware of the danger to the surrounded SS and therefore asked that KG Peiper be allowed to break the deadlock. This request was rejected by 6. Panzer-Armee, which instead ordered that everything possible be done to free KG Peiper with all available means, the main aim being to reduce the loss of men and equipment. Dietrich ordered nothing less than a breakthrough towards La Gleize, specifying that petrol and ammunition were to be brought to the group in armoured supply vehicles.

505th PIR deployed all along the Salm, taking advantage of the protection afforded by the railway embankment on the Liège – Luxembourg line. (*Nara*)

Of course, this was easier said than done. The state of the roads was deplorable and repairs were carried out by the engineers with limited personnel. The work detachment from the Todt Organisation that had been planned has still not appeared on the front line. For the moment, however, the weather was favourable and there was very little enemy air activity in the combat area, although only limited supplies of petrol and ammunition were available.

The missions given to the German armoured divisions for 22 December reflected the needs of the day:

> *1. SS-Pz-Div, by discovering the other sectors of the front and gathering all the forces from other sources, must re-establish contact with the Peiper group.*
>
> *9. SS-Pz-Div must leave only light security forces in front of Poteau to rush forward through Beaumont – Wanne and press east with the main body, leaving security troops west of the Salm against Vielsalm.*

A moment of rest for the paratroopers of 505th PIR after their long journey. One of them has placed a stove on the rails. (*Nara*)

Developments in the tactical situation in the Stavelot sector made one thing clear: there was no hope of success there. The Americans had concentrated too many resources and it was now virtually impossible to win. KG Peiper could not, however, be abandoned to its fate.

## Fuel: the Eternal German Struggle of the Battle of the Bulge

Reading the above, we realise that one of the determining factors in the loss of the *Wacht am Rhein* offensive was the unavailability of fuel, an issue we believe it is important to highlight. The supply of petrol was one of the biggest supply problems facing the German generals as they prepared for the offensive. In fact, it was the main reason why the offensive was postponed.[22] The defeats of the previous year and early 1944 had cut the Third Reich off from its oil wells in Europe and in the east. For several months, the Third Reich's vehicles had been running on synthetic petrol produced in insufficient quantities. In anticipation of the offensive, troops were rationed to build up a reserve

The B17s of 8th Air Forces were capable of operating over Germany even under cloud cover. On average, one bomb in ten hit its target. (*Nara*)

that could be used on the day of the attack. On the eve of the offensive, 8,000 tonnes were planned to enable the two attacking armies to reach the Meuse, and a further 8,000 tonnes to reach Antwerp, while 4,000 tonnes were held in reserve.[23]

However, this stock was only distributed sparingly to the troops. Only 50% of the total amount was entrusted to the logistics services of Heeresgruppe B, while 20% had to be kept in reserve at OB West[24] and could only be distributed with the agreement of von Rundstedt's staff.[25]

In the field, the German army distributed fuel and oil to units on the basis of Verbrauschssätzen, the theoretical quantity needed to cover a distance of 100 kilometres. The distance to Antwerp was 200 kilometres, or two Verbrauschssätzen. These are theoretical figures, because the actual distance that units could cover per Verbrauschssätz was only half of what was envisaged by the theoretical data. The amount of fuel needed to reach Antwerp was, therefore, far too low.

This was not the only problem. Indeed, SS-Brigadeführer Fritz Krämer states:

*We had enough ammunition for eight days, with a further eight days in the depots or on the way on railway wagons. I considered this to be entirely adequate. We had enough fuel for an initial advance of 200 kilometres. This fuel was not all in the divisions, it was partly in depots west of the Rhine and partly on the road (that was four Verbrauschssätzen, about 50 kilometres each). We expected to receive one new consumption unit a day from our depots. Provided there were no additional transport problems, we thought we could manage with our own fuel reserves. However, in the event of problems caused by the American air force, we would have had to fall back on captured fuel, although we had no idea how much was there.*[26]

A Panther required 720 litres of fuel. The precious liquid was available in December 1944, but it was stored too far behind the front line. (*Nara*)

The OKW's[27] plan was based on two assumptions about enemy air supremacy. On the one hand, the beginning of winter was chosen because at this time of year the weather was generally overcast over the Ardennes, thus reducing Allied air support. For the period in question, the units at the front were not much troubled by fighter bombers. On the other hand, heavy bomber missions were never interrupted because the aircraft were less sensitive to cloud cover because they flew above it. In addition, guidance beacons allowed them to be dropped with relative precision. Air strikes were therefore to continue on German communication lines. They were to have a considerable impact, amplified by the fact that the Germans kept their fuel reserves far away on the banks of the Rhine.

From the start of the offensive, Allied heavy bombers concentrated their efforts on paralysing rail traffic in the Eifel. The effectiveness of the American measures was confirmed by Krämer, who explained that the expected daily supplies never arrived from the depots because of the poor state of the roads, the American air force and other various causes that he did not specify.[28] With the bridges over the Rhine damaged, petrol was blocked on the right bank of the river. Logistical vehicles also lost a lot of time, as they had to make long empty journeys to refuel at railway filling stations in the Cologne region throughout the offensive. This was the case for the whole of 6. Panzer-Armee[29] and explains why 9. SS-Panzer Division was unable to reach its full potential at the crucial moment when it had to go into action.

Allied aircraft tracked down supply convoys, leading to a cascade of delays in the missions assigned. (*Nara*)

On the other hand, in the event of a problem, the solution envisaged at tactical level was to fall back on captured supplies. Staff theorists confirmed Krämer's account, but went further, suggesting it was a lack of information that led units to take supplies from the Americans: '*The OKW had planned 20,000 tonnes of fuel for the operation: 8,000 tonnes to reach the Meuse, another 8,000 for the objectives north of the river and 4,000 in reserve. The Armee-Kommandeure did not know this and their orders to help themselves to captured Allied depots reflected this lack of knowledge.*'[30] It is from these interrogations that the tenacious legend that the Germans were ordered to refuel in American depots originated. This usual practice at the front was, in fact, only seen as a plan B, in the event of supply interruptions, but was in no way a systematic measure provided for in the battle plan. Faced with inadequate initial supplies from the start of the offensive, Peiper tried to recover every last drop of fuel from the American depots.

## The Pozit VT Proximity Fuze

The night of 21 December was dark, foggy and cold, but that did not stop the telephone lines from heating up between XVIII Airborne Corps and 30th ID HQ. G4, in charge of logistics for the XVIII Airborne Corps, called Leland Hobbs, commander of the large infantry unit: *'I've just received an urgent request from your office, I've no idea what you want, I've got nothing like that in stock.'* An annoyed Hobbs replied: *'I've asked for 2,400 shells with POZIT detonators, the Army has agreed to supply me with 1,800 and the material is in your stores, so check!'* A few minutes later, the G4 replied: *'OK, nobody knew what it was.'*[31] Major General Hobbs was delighted and sent his instructions on the use of this revolutionary weapon: *'Tell the troops not to worry about air bursts,'* he added to those concerned.[32] This electronically triggered detonator would be used for the first time against land targets in the Stavelot pocket, although its history dated back to 1940.

There are two ways of detonating a shell: the first is by contact, the second by programmed explosion. In the case of 'soft' targets such as aircraft, vehicles and infantry, the use of shrapnel (small steel balls) is essential. Hitting a moving target with a shell is a matter of sheer luck. The shells used for this type of low-security target must explode close to the target. Any explosion too close or too far away greatly reduces the lethal effectiveness of the projectile. One of the most widely used shells at the start of the Second World War was the 'Superquick', also known as a 'selective-fire' shell. Using an internal combustion system, it could be set to detonate the charge between zero and twenty-five seconds of flight, but could also function

This schwimmwagen from one of the two KGs in the Stavelot pocket has been riddled with shrapnel. The Pozit detonator shell exploded at the optimum altitude for the most effective dispersal of the projectiles. (*Stavelot Library*)

instantaneously on impact. These settings had random results and the explosion on impact might not occur in soil that was too soft.

The development of proximity detonators began in 1940. At the start of the development programme, the army was given responsibility for finding a solution to this problem of firing at the ideal moment in a trajectory. The US Navy was chosen to develop the new proximity fuze shells, and its first challenge was to ensure that the more or less sophisticated equipment fitted to these innovations functioned correctly. The acceleration exerted when an anti-aircraft shell is fired is 20,000 G. In addition, the centrifugal force exerted by the rotation due to the rifling of the guns reaches 30,000 rpm, adding another 9,500 G exerted laterally. These astronomical figures show just how high the stresses were in a 105-mm shell weighing 17 kg.

The development of rotating projectiles continued at Johns Hopkins University Applied Physics Laboratory for three years. Numerous types of proximity detonator were studied. Several variables were taken into account to choose the ideal triggering mode: acoustics, pressure, electrostatics, optics and radio. In October 1943, after many trials, it was the radio process using the Doppler effect that generated the most hope, even though it was more complicated than the others. It had two major advantages: it worked day and night and could be used against any target that reflected radio waves. As a result, it could be used for both airborne and ground applications.

The operation of a Doppler-effect detonator was based on the difference between the frequency of the fuze's emitter and the frequency of the received signal reflected by a target as the shell moves towards or away from the target. When the shell leaves, the return wave returns to the transmitter out of phase with the distance travelled. As it approaches the target, the return pulse begins to phase with the initial pulse. When the departure wave merges with the return wave, the distance to the target is practically zero and the explosion occurs.[33]

The terms Proximity Fuze, Pozit and VT (variable time) are used to designate this weapon, which was kept secret for many years after the war. Captain Shumaker, Director of the Research and Development Division of the Bureau of Ordnance, coined the term to be descriptive without referring to this top secret technology.

The reliability of the new VT detonators was between 70% and 90%. The improvements compared with shells fired by an internal combustion system varied in a ratio of 5:20.[34] When they first came into action, Pozits could only be used in sectors where it was certain the projectiles would not land in an area in enemy hands. In 1944, Doppler detonators were allocated to the British Army's Anti-Aircraft Command, which was engaged in the defence of Britain against the V1 rocket. As most of Britain's heavy anti-aircraft guns were deployed on a long, thin coastal strip, the unexploded shells fell back into the sea, out of range of capture. The impact of the arrival of the Pozit was immediately felt during the V1 Blitz against London in 1944. Indeed, after the introduction of the Pozit rocket, the proportion of flying bombs destroyed when passing through the coastal gun belt rose from 17% to 74%, even reaching 82% in one day. A minor problem encountered by the British was that the fuze was sensitive enough to cause the shell to explode if it passed too close to a seabird and a number of seabird 'kills' were recorded.[35]

# Chapter 6

# A Fierce Battle for the Saint-Édouard Sanatorium

## Battling It Out in a Hospital Full of Children

Let us now return to Stoumont to examine the pressure on the La Gleize cauldron. While 504th PIR was struggling with the Panzergrenadiere in Cheneux, another attack was being prepared against Peiper from the north-west of Stoumont. In the late afternoon of 20 December, 1/119th IR from Targnon succeeded in taking the Saint-Édouard Sanatorium. However, although the success, achieved around 4 pm was substantial, victory was not yet assured.

Having just moved into new positions at Francorchamps, GIs from 30th ID target a German aircraft. (*Nara*)

Aerial photograph of the Saint-Édouard sector showing 30th ID's approach from Targnon. (*Nara*)

On the evening of 20 December, the GIs in the sanatorium remained alert despite the bitter cold. Supplies of cartridges for the heavy machine guns were called for and they knew next few hours were likely to be difficult and at around 11 pm, the Germans launched a very aggressive counter-attack. Between fifty and 100 infantrymen, supported by several tanks, fired from the road north of the building. The SS fought very hard, with assault waves coming screaming towards the GIs as they tried to reclaim the building from which they had been expelled a few hours earlier. Another bloody battle ensued, lasting several hours. This time, the GIs were forced to withdraw completely from the sanatorium's main building. However, a group of eleven men, led by Sergeant William Widener, continued to hold out in a small neighbouring building. The survivors of B and C companies, 119th IR, set up a first line of defence about 30 metres from the battered walls of the sanatorium, along the hedge that encircled the property.

Obersturmführer Franz Sievers was 31 years old at the time and had been in command of 3. Kompanie/Panzerpioniere Battalion 1 since 15 October 1944. He took part in the attack and described what happened:

> *On 20 December we were expelled from the Festung by the furious 'Amis'.*[1] *Sturmbannführer Werner Poetschke ordered me to launch a counter-attack to retake the positions we had lost. The counter-attack began at 11 pm and we succeeded in driving the GIs out of the 'Festung', but it was impossible to retake the old main front line because the Americans*

> *had established strong defences there. Shortly after midnight, the 'Amis' attacked the sanatorium again with tanks and bazookas. There was fierce fighting.*[2]

The terrain favoured the German counter-attack as the starting point was higher than the American positions below on the road. During the fighting on that cold winter's night, three Shermans of from 740th TB were destroyed. The driver of the only Sherman to survive the attack recalled:

> *I was dozing when all hell suddenly broke loose. I heard a big explosion, followed by another and another. Looking through the periscope, I saw that the three tanks in front of me were on fire. The thought of my trapped buddies crossed my mind and you can imagine how I felt. From that moment on, everything seemed like a madhouse. I could see a bunch of people running backwards, silhouetted by the flames of the tank fire. I could swear the Boche were swarming our tank. A mortar round hit the tank just about*

Three Shermans from 740th TB were lost during the German counter-attack on the night of 20–21 December. The Saint-Édouard Sanatorium is visible in the background. The upturned turret shows that the ammunition in one of the tanks exploded, while the other was set on fire. (*Rights reserved*)

> *where the transmission meets the hull of the tank. The explosion blew the helmet off our gunner. He looked up from the turret to see where the shots were coming from. Someone jumped on our tank and shouted to Willie Morris, our tank commander, that the fire was coming from the castle on our left flank. I remember the loader, Corporal William Waddel, struggling like hell to feed the on-board weapons. The coaxial machine gun was red-hot and he didn't hesitate to take it apart with his bare hands to change the barrel. I noticed that his hands were bleeding, but he carried on as if nothing had happened. When I then looked out of the periscope, I saw flares flying over our Sherman. The coordination of the crew, tank commander, loader and gunner worked remarkably well. It's certainly thanks to our training. When we ran out of ammunition, the tank commander, Willie Morris, ordered me to start us up again in the shelter of a house.*[3]

The three burning tanks of 740th TB clogged the road, forming an obstacle that prevented Peiper's Panzers from extending their counter-attack by pursuing the fleeing defenders. In addition to the loss of the three tanks, the report indicated that B and C companies were in a sorry state. It is therefore quite possible that they would have been on the verge of collapse had the German advance been more determined. Eventually, the sanatorium was taken over entirely by German troops. Lieutenants Anderson, Hendley and Heginbotham and the Doughboys were captured and taken to Froidcour Castle,

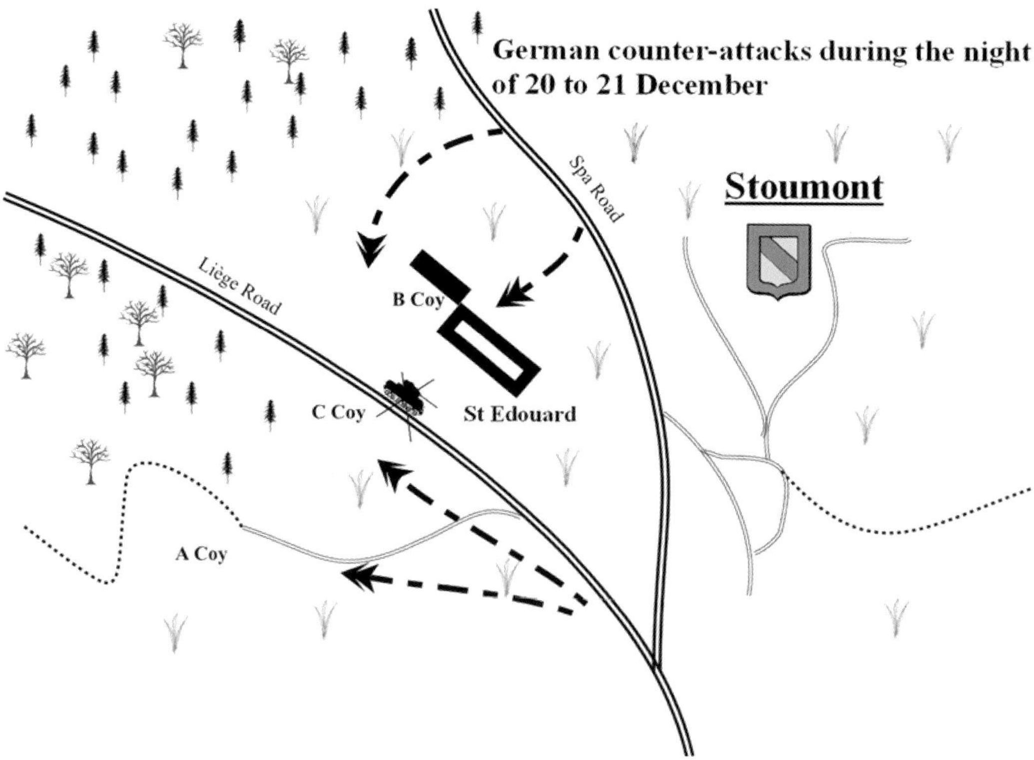


The Germans counter-attacked from two directions to retake the Saint-Édouard Sanatorium. (*Christian Dujardin*)

which was used as a field hospital for the wounded on both sides, as well as functioning as a prison.

There was consternation in the sanatorium, as we return to Abbé Hanlet's invaluable testimony:

> *Suddenly, around midnight, gunshots rang out around the house: a shell fell in the 'expense', 2 metres from the people, filling the corridor with gunpowder and smoke; and no more water to take the recommended precautions. One sister soaked how many handkerchiefs in a bucket of water that had been used to wash the cobbles! The Germans were here again! What a surprise! Soon German soldiers came down into our cellar, machine guns under their arms. What a thrill for these brave Americans. They were still rejoicing over the victory. We were stunned! The joyful Germans searched their prisoners, disarmed them with a sneer, smashed their rifles by throwing them on the ground with violence, howled in anger, belching out the worst insults. 'Ah! Ah!' cried the leader of the gang, a tall black devil, mockingly, brandishing the papers of an American officer, 'Here's a lieutenant!' And soon the sad procession of prisoners passed in front of us, silent, their hands clasped on their heads. Thirty-three of them entered the bread cellar, where they stayed for a few hours before being taken to Froidcour Castle, where they were freed by their compatriots two days later.*

The GIs defended their hard-won positions at the sanatorium tooth and nail. (*Nara*)

The Task Force from 3rd AD joined the surviving infantrymen of 119th IR, who were driven out of Stoumont to retake Saint-Édouard and Le Rouat. (*Nara*)

*There were also wounded. One of them, an American, had a serious injury to his right arm and was bleeding profusely. The sister nurse tried to stop the haemorrhage with a tourniquet, but soon the unfortunate man's condition worsened and the tourniquet had to be administered in a hurry. After a while, the dying man came to. 'Thank you,' he said to the priest, 'I've understood everything you have said and done. My wife is very Catholic: she'll be happy if I die. Thank you very much!'*

*In the meantime, a late prisoner, a telephone operator, was discovered under some mattresses at the other end of the cellar. The leader of the enemy gang was furious: 'We should burn everything here', he said, giving the priest a nasty look.*

*'And why is that? What harm have we done?'*

*'You're hiding prisoners.'*

*'There are only women and children praying here. You are in a children's asylum that the combatants should have respected instead of turning it into a battlefield.'*

*The commander relented: 'Is this your wounded American? I don't think he'll get any further.'*

*'It's possible, but he's lost too much blood.'*[4]

## New Unit Puts Pressure on Peiper

At 3:30 am on 21 December, Task Force Jordan was placed under the orders of 3/119th IR, with Colonel Bision leading the powerful detachment in a joint attack at dawn.[5] The battle group made slow progress towards Stoumont but was stopped at around 2 pm 200 metres from its first objective, the Saint-Édouard Sanatorium. The advance was halted before the last hairpin bend in sight of the building, preventing it from relieving its defenders: the GIs of 1/119th IR. The 33rd AR's After Action Report did not specify the reasons for the failure, except that six German tanks were spotted on the edge of the forest just north of Targnon.[6] A similar event blocked the attack by Task Force McGeorge on the outskirts of Borgoumont to the north of La Gleize,[7] the presence of the Panthers and Tigers seemingly enough to calm the ardour of the US soldiers.

Having been practically wiped out on 19 December, Lieutenant Knox had been integrated into L Company, which had otherwise been saved only by a hasty retreat. The survivors of the fierce fighting set up a roadblock on the heights near the hamlet of Chefna, and Knox was ordered to take part in the assault north of Stoumont, which failed so close to its goal:

> *This 20th December is my birthday, I'm 25. An armoured column met us at the roadblock. I'm feeling much better. I dozed off for a few minutes. The day passed without incident until about 6 pm. We received orders to return to Stoumont, assembled and marched back to our starting point. I had never seen my men so sad. Morale was close to zero and they knew who they were up against: the terrible 1. SS-Panzer Division, the cream of Nazi armoured troops. The commander of L Company, Captain Stewart, was not in favour of this decision. He pressed Colonel Sutherland for reinforcements and artillery support. I went to the battalion HQ to get the attack plan. It was amended four times. Lieutenant Colonel Brown, the battalion commander, was with us. Although he wasn't directly involved in the attack, his presence comforted us. Captain Stewart took instructions from the battalion commander. The latter gave him the time of the assault: 5:30 the next morning. We set off at 6:30 am. The fog was very thick. Our company, although very hard hit by the fighting on 19 December, was the one that had suffered the fewest casualties. At around 8 am, we arrived above the town, where the fog was so thick that we could only see 25 metres. We were at the edge of the woods, about 500 metres from the sanatorium. The time of the artillery barrage was changed and finally set for 12:45 pm.*
>
> *The artillery barrage started and we went straight into the attack. No one was enthusiastic, but they knew they had to 'Go for it'. It was so foggy that one of my men called Collin found himself 10 metres from a German machine gun. Unaware, he rushed at the machine gun and his BAR jammed at exactly the wrong moment. He fired into the barrel of the MG 42 to divert it and put the gunners out of action with the butt of his BAR. He was the hero of the day. Despite this dazzling feat, there was still a lot of shooting and the fog stopped our attack. We lost contact on our right and all we could do was retreat.*

When the attack was stopped, Lieutenant Knox emphasised the extreme nervous fatigue of his men. (*Nara*)

> *Captain Stewart rejected any idea of retreating and persevering with the attack. We had exhausted all our moral and physical resources. Our energy was completely shattered. I never thought my boys would weaken like that. Finally, we received a message to hold our position for the night. We dug our foxholes under the shelter of the M5 light tanks. I was particularly exhausted that night.*

Knox's testimony helps us to understand why the attack failed so close to its goal: the GIs were simply exhausted. At the end of the day, General Boudinot from 3rd Armored Division arrived and took command of the CCB.

## 1/119th Attack Saint-Édouard

The attack on the Stoumont sanatorium, the keystone of the German defence in the sector, resumed on the morning of the 21st, preceded by Tank-Destroyer fire. From a well-hidden position behind a house, 150 metres west of the building, a Tank Destroyer fired 240 shells at the thick stone walls. Sergeant Widener, who still manned an annex to the imposing building, briefed the crews to direct their fire. Later, several Tank Destroyers arrived and fired a few hundred more rounds into the building. A Panther

An M36 Jackson fired no fewer than 240 shells at Saint-Édouard. (*Nara*)

tank, lurking on the east side of the sanatorium, prevented the infantry from retaking it. Meanwhile, a bazooka team tried everything and approached the Panzer manoeuvring behind the building, but machine-gun fire put an end to their courageous attempt. The tanks of 740th TB, under the command of Captain Berry, were unable to engage the German beast because of the steep, muddy slope that provided access to the stronghold's ground level. The sappers finished their work, despite the scrap metal of the battlefield, creating a path of logs and stones. The 75-metre-long path was built on the west side of the village, providing access to the plain to flush out the enemy. Three Shermans and a Tank Destroyer moved towards the top of the sanatorium. Lieutenant Powers was in the lead and managed to sneak up on the right side, from where he was able to neutralise the Panther tank that was threatening to prevent any manoeuvre around Saint-Édouard. The Tank Destroyer and Shermans covered the withdrawal of Sergeant Widener's men and eleven other survivors of the fierce fighting who had taken refuge in an annex to the main building. As soon as the infantrymen were safe and sound, the US tanks withdrew under fire from anti-tank guns from the heights of Saint-Édouard.[8]

Abbé Hanlet recounted the tragic events, which, it should be remembered, involved a large number of terrified children in the cellar corridor:

*From the afternoon until the evening, the fighting continued with increasing fury. The American tanks were firing non-stop at point-blank range at our walls, which were*

The American engineers were able to install a log track to enable the tanks of 740th TB to approach Saint-Édouard. (*Nara*)

*collapsing over our heads. Grenades fell with a clatter on the pavement of the great hall and we were shaken with every blow. In the kitchen, a grenade pierced the granite and toppled the cellar ceiling. Around the window sills of our underground passageway, bullets rained down like hailstones in a thunderstorm. At any moment, the house was shaken by a burst of shells. Since the previous day, the population of our shelter had increased by around twenty people from Stoumont and forty evacuees from Elsenborn (who had already taken refuge for a few weeks in the hostel, which had become uninhabitable). During the battle, this crowd of 250 people, moving away from the windows at either end, gathered towards the centre around the sisters. People crammed together. We lay on the ground, making ourselves small. We wanted to go underground so we wouldn't be crushed by the house that threatened to fall on our heads. We prayed, we begged! Rosary after rosary. Invocations were shouted, answered by the pleas of the crowd that was stretched to the limit.*

*Another American, wounded in the knee, was brought in on a stretcher, followed by two wounded Germans. One of them, seriously wounded in the head, was lying on a bench next to the large, wounded American who had just been administered treatment. The German ambulance driver complained about being deprived of the necessary medicines.*

The left wing of the building is about to collapse. In the cellars, the children's worst fear was that the building would collapse on them. (*Nara*)

*'But,' said the priest, 'there's an ambulance driver wearing a Red Cross armband who must have everything he needs in his bag of bandages. Can I call him?'*

*'Certainly. Do it quickly!'*

*And there was the American medic helping the German ambulance driver, devotedly treating the enemy soldier, applying stitches, giving injections, bandaging wounds and giving the poor wounded man a drink: the parable of the modern Good Samaritan on the battlefield of the Ardennes in the twentieth century! Then there was the dying man from earlier, back on his feet. The German leader took pity on him, offered him a cigarette, put it to his lips and lit it. The wounded Samy smoked: he was happy, he seemed to have come back to life. But what was he looking for in his tunic pocket? A small chocolate packet, which he passed to the priest, saying, 'For the German comrade'. The priest accepted in recognition of his enemy's generous gesture, but said quietly, 'I'll never be able to eat this, it's covered in blood.' Indeed, the chocolate wrapper was stained with blood. A moving picture of Christian charity in the midst of so much carnage and horror.*

*In the evening, to our great surprise and against all expectations, it was the Germans who came to find us in the cellar. They looked tired and discouraged. The expected reinforcements had not arrived, they said. For three days they had been occupying the hill of Stoumont, which overlooked the Amblève valley and the road to Liège. There were only about twenty of them left at Saint-Édouard, in Festung Saint-Édouard, as they called it.*

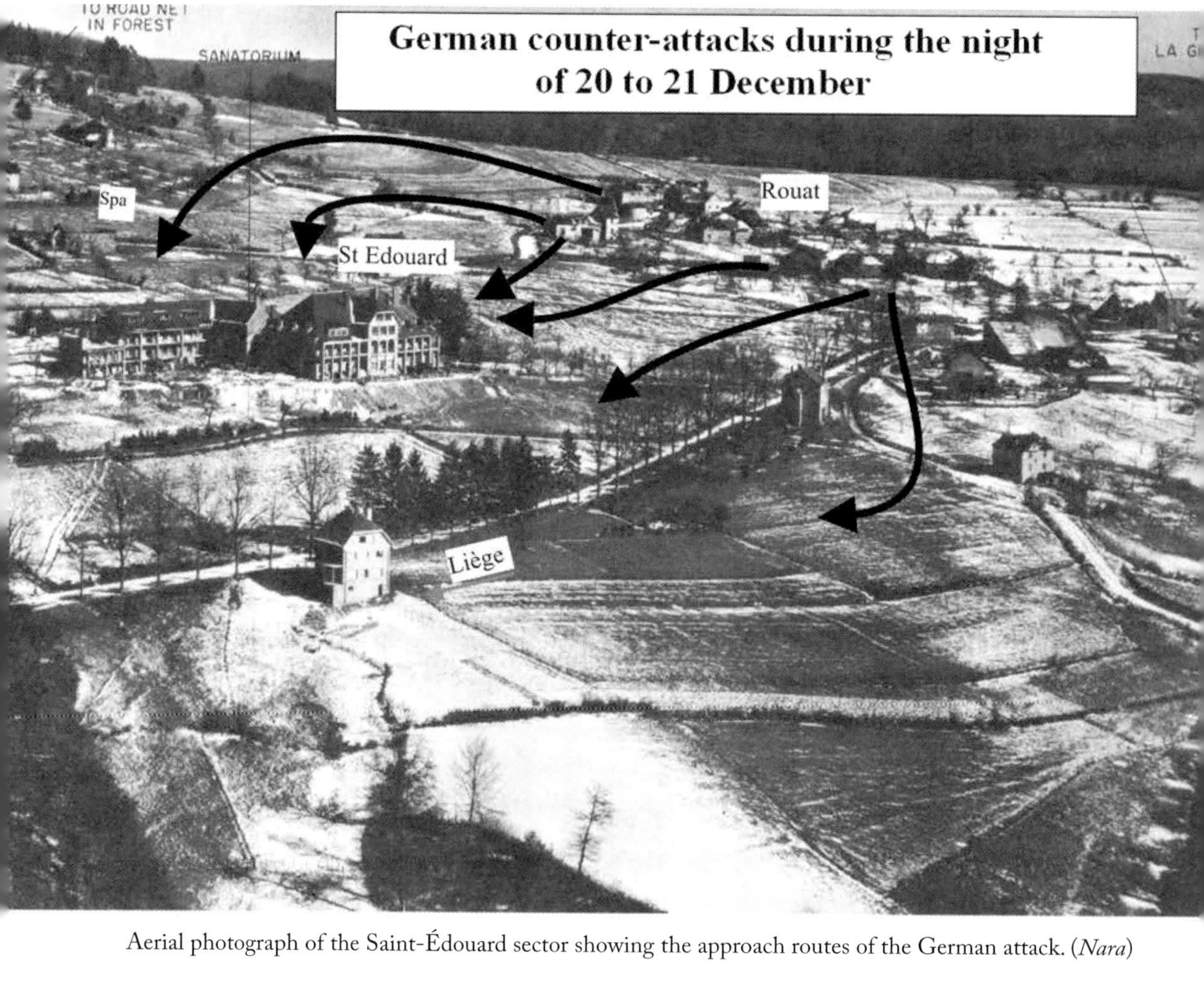


Aerial photograph of the Saint-Édouard sector showing the approach routes of the German attack. (*Nara*)

*We asked them to evacuate as soon as possible, as our shelter was not safe: the vault was cracked in several places and had even been pierced by a shell; it would give way if any more shells hit it.*

*'Impossible,' replied our "protectors", 'the house and village are still in enemy hands: the first person to venture onto the road would be shot.'*

*'You won't be able to leave until we've gone.'*

*'At least,' we insisted, 'don't shoot tonight, so as not to provoke a counter-attack on our house, which won't be able to withstand any more shots.'*

*'We're going to fire a few rounds to see if the enemy responds. If he leaves us alone, we'll stop firing too, and you can sleep in peace, and so can we, because we haven't done it for eight days.'*

*They did not keep their word. Throughout the night, the Germans regularly fired the big gun they had placed in front of the house, opposite the cellar under the great hall, every ten minutes or so. Fortunately, the Americans only responded at first with a few shots aimed at the village. They had other things to do: they were taking advantage of the night to prepare the next day's liberation offensive.*

## The Final Assault on Saint-Édouard

On the morning of 22 December, all the GIs were forced to attack without waiting for tank support. The three tanks destroyed during the night were still blocking the road, preventing any vehicles from passing, so the infantrymen were asked to use smoke grenades for protection instead.

The assault was scheduled for 12:45 pm, with A Company going into action at the appointed time, and the enemy returning fire from mortars and 20-mm anti-aircraft guns. A Company was pinned down by MG 42 fire, but B and C companies continued the assault, requesting more protective fire from tanks and mortars. Uncle Sam's sappers proved their self-sacrifice and courage, and under the scrap metal of the battlefield were busy clearing away the wreckage of tanks blocking the road to the centre of the village. A Panzer was spotted behind the sanatorium and the GIs called for reinforcements, which were quickly provided: 1/119th IR, which had remained behind in Targnon, was ordered to support 2/119th IR, which was struggling to seize the keystone of the German defensive system. Despite a fierce firefight, at 1:40 pm the Doughboys once again reoccupied the sanatorium and the tanks were ordered to stop firing on the building. American losses were dramatic, with C Company paying a particularly heavy price.

*The next day, 22 December, we received orders just after midday to attack again at 2:15 pm. This time, we would certainly have tanks with us. The usual artillery preparation would be given. The men's faces reflected terror. I wondered if the men were going to start, they looked so overwhelmed. At the appointed time, the captain shouted to the men: 'Forward, the tankers are doing a good job, let's go.' It was an almost miraculous intervention; the lads went for it with the tanks. K Company went off to our right. We moved into an open*

Civilians evacuated after the fighting. The Ardennes was completely devastated. (*Nara*)

*area. Nobody was firing, not a single shot. The Germans had withdrawn! We arrived in the village and found our old jeep. The men were completely different now. And so ended the story of Stoumont. It had been difficult. I found two of my men who had been hiding in a cellar. The Germans had never found them.*[9]

SS-Obersturmführer Franz Sievers would be tried at the so-called 'Malmedy' trial in Dachau. (*Nara*)

Obersturmführer Franz Sievers described the relentless battle from the other side:

*Using bullets and knives, the Americans dislodged us room by room. The last place we resisted was the kitchen. We held out all afternoon in that room. Although the GIs occupied a large part of the building, the tanks and tank destroyers continued to fire on the 'Festung'. We evacuated our last point of resistance after a bazooka was fired into the kitchen.*[10]

Marie Gabriel was caught up in the hell of Saint-Édouard. She was 6 years old in 1944 and had been an orphan since the age of 3. Brought up by an aunt, she had to be placed in a sanatorium because of health problems and so she and her older sister were sent to Saint-Édouard, where they could have better nutrition and peace of mind. However, the arrival of Peiper's troops meant this was not to be and her account of a wartime childhood brings back vivid memories:

> *On Thursday, 21 December, we had a particularly bad night, during which the preventorium was bombed non-stop. We didn't sleep a wink. Screaming, crying…It was dark, there was no light, everything was cut off. We had no water. We were forbidden to take the blanket off our face. I think that day most of us thought we were living out our last hours. That was the last night we spent in the cellars. In the laundry room, which was an annex of the large cellar, we fetched water for drinking, when there was any. A corner of this room was also used as a public toilet for the 200 people taking refuge in the cellars. I was starting to get hungry, and it was high time this ended. One day I went into this famous laundry room and as I was getting into position I spotted a pair of black boots. I immediately looked up. It was a German officer…I say officer because he was wearing a kepi. He was looking at me, but kindly. He was eating a huge slice of cottage cheese. I loved cottage cheese. I was starting to get hungry and my stomach was rumbling. He probably realised that and handed me his sandwich. I pounced on the sandwich and prepared to eat it in secret so that I wouldn't have to share it with anyone. But my sister was looking for me. She found me, stood in front of me and said, 'Who gave you that?' She looked at the German and said, 'He's a dirty Kraut! You don't have to eat that sandwich.' She took it and threw it in the excrement. I blamed her, and I still blame her today. For God's sake, my cottage cheese sandwich. The guy did nothing, just ran his hand through my hair and left. It was clear to them that the war was over. Looking back, I can see that the look on that guy's face was one of affection. My sister, who was 10 years old, certainly understood things in a different way to me.*[11]

## 2/119th IR Attack

While Task Force Jordan, flanked by 3/119th IR, moved towards Saint-Édouard, another attack was led by 2/119th IR, commanded by Major McCown. Its mission was to take the defenders of Stoumont by the rear by cutting the road between the besieged village and La Gleize. To get there from Targnon, they had to climb a steep path through the woods, cross the muddy fens at the top and then descend into a wooded valley. All along the route were muddy paths dotted with peat bogs. The group set off at 11:40 am on 21 December and at 12:40, McCown informed his regimental CP that he had reached the halfway point.[12]

At 3 pm, the first elements arrived at the objective and began cutting down a few trees and laying mines. At 3:12 pm, the bulk of the unit moved back into the woods, while a squad of bazookas remained to defend the roadblock that had just been set up. The

An officer gives instructions to his men before taking action. (*Nara*)

Germans noticed enemy troops in their rear and immediately launched a strong armoured patrol. Believing they were no match for the armoured vehicles, the bazooka squad went into the woods at 3:50 pm and were pursued by SS-Panzergrenadiere through the forest. Nevertheless, the GIs managed to lose them at around 4:20 pm.

However, the unit's commander, Major Hal D. McCown, was captured during the fighting. He wrote in his report:

> On the *afternoon of 21 December, at about 4 pm, I, my radio operator and my orderly were captured by a German patrol who had us*

Lieutenant Colonel McCown in the Korean War, when he commanded 17th IR, 7th ID. (*Nara*)

*in their sights from all sides. We had fallen into a trap. A machine gun fired over our heads and individuals from another patrol approached us from three directions. By this time, I had moved away from the front line to inspect my battalion's outposts flanking Stoumont behind the Germans. I was taken back to the enemy HQ at Stoumont and, as I passed through the town, I saw the Germans everywhere preparing to leave. The opposing commander told me later that it was the appearance of my troops in his rear at Stoumont that had prompted him to evacuate the town that night. I was led back to the main headquarters at La Gleize through several areas where fire was being exchanged between my men and the encircled Germans. Knowing my own plans for the capture of Stoumont and seeing that they had been put into effect by this time, I expected to be recaptured before I reached La Gleize, but this was not the case.*[13]

The American attack was repulsed in this sector on the evening of 21 December, as Peiper committed his 1. and 2. Kompanien of Panthers and Grenadiers from III (Gep)/ PzGr-Rgt 2.

## Peiper Retreats to La Gleize

McCown's mission may seem like a failure, but it had a considerable impact on Peiper's decisions that evening, as he later explained to his American interrogators:

*Around noon on 21 December, the situation in the pocket was discussed with all the KG unit commanders at a conference in the command post. This conference was the result of the following radio message from Mohnke: 'The Division intends to advance through Trois-Ponts and relieve KG Peiper.'*

*However, neither Stoumont nor Cheneux could be maintained for much longer under current conditions. To remain in line with the division's intentions, it was decided to concentrate all available KG elements around La Gleize, a village of around thirty houses, and to keep the Cheneux bridge open.*

*The need to concentrate forces became particularly apparent when the American engineer assault detachment managed to reach the Stoumont – La Gleize road without incident, effectively blocking the road by blowing up trees and subsequently undermining it.*

*During a counter-attack against this assault detachment, which had dug in on the road, a number of American soldiers were captured, including a major and his radio operators. On the evening of 21 December, the German lines fell back to La Gleize. The withdrawal from the Stoumont area and the retreat of the Cheneux defence line to the area just behind the bridge proceeded without incident or enemy interference.*[14]

These decisions show that things were going from bad to worse for the Germans. Their defence was severely affected by the lack of petrol and ammunition and they could afford virtually no tank movement because they had to be economical with their ammunition.

McCown's attack convinced Peiper he had to tighten his positions around La Gleize, leading to a gradual withdrawal of the SS. (*Nara*)

McCown's attack made it clear to Peiper that he had no choice but to tighten his defences further and abandon his command post at Froidcour Castle. Given the news he had received, Peiper's decisions were logical. La Gleize became the last redoubt where he would wait for help. The report written by the American major after the event would prove to be an invaluable source for imagining the atmosphere in the cauldron of La Gleize, which we will return to later.

## The SS Evacuate Saint-Édouard

Oskar Siegmund was a member of the vehicle maintenance staff in the Diefenthal Battalion. He confirms the order to withdraw to La Gleize, writing:

> *On 22 December we withdrew with the SPW to the orchards of La Gleize. There was still only infantry fighting, the grenadiers were in the front line. Comrades told me that Peiper was linked by radio with the division in front of Stavelot. He was quoted as saying,*

An abandoned Sd.Kfz. 234/1 near Saint-Édouard, photographed by the American technological intelligence services. This reconnaissance vehicle was armed with an MG 42 machine gun and a 20-mm cannon. (*Nara*)

> *'We are cut off from everything and continually attacked by the Americans. We needed petrol, code name "Otto". The reply we got was, 'We're doing what we can'. Certainly, our comrades tried to cross the Amblève, but none of them made it to the other bank alive. Of course, we did throw jerry cans of petrol into the river so that it would reach us, but none arrived. There were also 'releases' into the air, but nothing essential arrived.*[15]

On Friday, 22 December, at around 10 am, General Boudinot went to the front line as usual to analyse the situation, which seemed to be inextricable because access to the village of Stoumont was blocked at Saint-Édouard. He noticed that there was no fire coming from the building, while two civilians reported that the Germans had left during the night.

Lieutenant Colonel Harrison ordered a reconnaissance party to verify this, and the patrol found the place empty of the enemy. Consequently, First Battalion occupied it without firing a shot. Two or three seriously wounded GIs who had been left behind by the Germans in the sanatorium reported that the enemy had left the building at 4 am.

View of Stoumont after the battle. On the right is Panther 225 belonging to Rottf Franz Brahms, which was destroyed at dawn on 19 December during the attack by KG Peiper on Stoumont. (*Nara*)

SS-Unterscharführer Herzog's Panther 234 destroyed during the American attack on Saint-Édouard. (*Nara*)

There were still signs of enemy movement in the village, but when First and Second battalions attacked from the west, only German rearguards were encountered. Luckily, their resistance proved light and Stoumont was finally in American hands by mid-morning.

The civilians trapped in Saint-Édouard finally saw their martyrdom come to an end. Abbé Hanlet concluded his diary by writing:

> *On Friday, you wake up – if you can call it that, because who has slept? You wake up with the idea that you have to leave at all costs. Sister Superior and all the sisters were of the same opinion; the situation was becoming untenable: we had to leave. But when? Where to go? So many questions put off until later. For the moment, it was a question of organising the departure, so as to be ready when the time came. Orders were given to pack by candlelight. The house seemed to be completely calm: the Germans have gone! We waited for the Americans to evacuate. Sister Superior, another sister and the gardener, carrying a white flag, took advantage of the lull and went to Froidcour Castle to ask our devoted burgomaster for advice and to find a doctor for two sick old men. But as soon as they left*

Brahms' tank was moved back 100 metres. It is easily identifiable by its gun, which was mutilated by the ricochet of an American shell. (*Nara*)

*the village, the valiant little troop was surprised by a fresh burst of cannon fire and had to take refuge in the cellar of the doctor's house. The sisters would not be able to join the evacuees from Saint-Édouard in Lorcé until the following morning. In the meantime, it was a worrying period for the inhabitants of our underground passage, who were still awaiting their liberation!*

*Soon a fantastic cannonade broke out. The Germans, who had withdrawn to higher ground, fired on the Americans as they stormed up the road towards the village. A formidable artillery duel broke out over Stoumont: the Americans fired to clear the ground and drive out the Germans, while the Germans protected their retreat and delayed the American advance. Using a thin iron bar and a towel, we made a white flag, which one of the two wounded Americans, abandoned by the Germans, waved in front of the house. As the fire became furious, our soldier displayed his white flag prominently on the balustrade and returned to the cellar. The owner of the B&B then came to tell us that some soldiers (whose nationality he didn't know) were asking for two sisters or two civilians to talk to. So we immediately sent a sister and two civilians with a white flag. But we heard footsteps above us. We went to have a look. It was Americans inspecting the buildings. Soon, after talks, an American officer came to tell us that in ten minutes we would be able to leave. The two wounded were released: the man with the knee wound could walk (he was our flag bearer earlier); the man who had been administered on Wednesday evening was carried off on a stretcher. They happy! Saved!*

*We went up to the ground floor, then upstairs: everywhere, on the steps and in the rooms, we came across the corpses of soldiers, lying on their backs, arms outstretched, mouths open, bathed in a pool of blood, which we had to step over.*

*Everywhere, the path was blocked by piles of rubble, beams, bricks and plaster. Large holes pierced the thick walls. Familiar rooms had become unrecognisable and the inhabitants of the house wondered which room they were in. The classrooms, bedrooms and halls in particular were the scene of the fiercest fighting. The chapel had been shelled and the statues broken, but the altar was intact. We said a prayer for the victims of this battle and asked God, who had saved us, to welcome in his mercy the combatants who had fallen during those tragic days.*

Photograph taken on 25 December in the village of Bras-sur-Lienne, a few kilometres from the battlefield, as villagers evacuated their destroyed homes. (*Nara*)

*After a few minutes, the Americans came back to get us and, by the staircase that went up from the cellar to the pavilion, the long procession of 250 evacuees from Saint-Édouard left the ruined buildings. The evacuation was difficult and painful, through thick mud where the girls lost their shoes and socks, got stuck and fell. The soldiers, taken with pity, carried the children in their arms through the marshes; one of them put a pair of his socks on the feet of a little girl, which the little girl soon lost in the mire. At the end of the day, after wading through the mud for a long time and stepping over piles of scrap metal and corpses, the long caravan, marching through the neighbouring meadows and along the roadside lodge, arrived on the main road, crowded with cannons, lorries, tanks, jeeps and, above all, soldiers, who were going to chase the invaders out of the country for good. That Friday afternoon, the village of Stoumont was taken back by the Americans.*[16]

As the Americans had regained control of the sanatorium, they evacuated the refugees. The testimony of our little orphan, Marie Gabriel, ties in perfectly with that of the abbot:

*We got out as quickly as possible in tight ranks. We didn't even get the bodies out. When we came out of the cellar, the corpse of a German soldier was lying with his eyes open. The American who was helping us out of the cellar took us on the penultimate step and lifted*

Peiper's retreat gave the GIs a brief respite after several trying days. (*Nara*)

*us over the corpse. It would have been easier to remove the body …when we came out of the cellar, we were dressed very roughly. I had a pair of shoes that probably weren't worth much anymore. Don't forget that it was wartime …In the rush, I must have lost my shoes. I ended up barefoot in the mud. It was cold. I was crying. An American took me in his arms and put a pair of socks on my feet. I stayed with my GI. In the meantime, the others had got into the trucks and then left, which had the effect of clearing the view to the toilets at the back of the yard. This enabled me to see the corpses of German soldiers lined up in this courtyard. The others didn't see them. The American took me in his arms. I don't think I would have let go of him again, it's so good to feel sheltered. He then carried me down the meadow, which was nothing but a muddy field. We headed for the lorries below.*[17]

In the early afternoon, Task Force Jordan attacked the hamlet of Rouat, north of Stoumont. The assault was preceded by thirty minutes of artillery shelling. C and B companies had retaken possession of the entire sanatorium, and the village was easily recaptured with the help of Task Force Jordan, which had retaken the hamlet of Rouat with some difficulty. After some heavy fighting, at 5:15 pm the unit declared Stoumont liberated, along with the destruction of the 75-mm Pak anti-tank gun and the disabling of twenty enemy positions. The 1/119th IR paid the heaviest price for the recapture of Saint-Édouard Sanatorium. Total casualties during the battle were 106, including 18 killed, 60 wounded and 28 missing. Of those missing, 24 were released during the recapture of La Gleize.[18]

Chapter 7

# In the Cauldron of La Gleize

## Concern for the Injured

At the end of the 21 December, Peiper moved to La Gleize. He set up his HQ in the centre of the village along the main road, protected by the imposing Tiger 204. Before leaving Froidcour, the battlegroup commander had gone down into the cellars of the château, where wounded from both sides were housed. Peiper explained in the immediate post-war period:

> *During the fighting for Stoumont and Cheneux, over 100 Americans were taken prisoner on the evening of 21 December. A number of rooms were reserved for this purpose in the Château de Froidcour, the same building that contained the KG evacuation post, where around 120 wounded Germans and a number of wounded Americans were treated.*

After regrouping at La Gleize to wait for help from outside, KG Peiper came under heavy shelling. Panther 221, fitted with Stahlrollen, was abandoned to the scrap merchants. (*Rights reserved*)

A GI from 30th ID advances along a country road. The US division gradually tightened its grip around the cauldron. (*Nara*)

*After the evacuation of the Stoumont positions, Froidcour was left outside the German lines at La Gleize. Consequently, all the German wounded who were able to walk and all the POWs, with the exception of the wounded, were taken to La Gleize in the late afternoon of 21 December 1944, before the German front was withdrawn. Around eighty wounded Germans and all the wounded Americans were left in the château under the care of a German medical sergeant and two American medical soldiers, who had been working at the clearing station since their capture at Stoumont. The wounded were treated by a German doctor for the last time on the morning of 22 December and, in the afternoon, they were evacuated by American ambulances.*[1]

In this post-war report, written at the request of the American authorities, Peiper describes in great detail the care he gave to the wounded. There is no doubt that he was telling the truth as his claims are confirmed by the American medic Everett Schmid, who was taken prisoner during the capture of Stoumont and requisitioned to serve as nursing staff at the Château de Froidcour. He states that: '*On 22 December,*[2] *when Colonel Peiper left the château*[3] *and came into the cellars, he spoke to me and told me that he would have to abandon the wounded who were unable to walk. He wanted me to stay there with the few other American nurses to take care of the wounded. He also wanted to exchange American prisoners for German wounded if possible.*'[4] However, it is important to remember that at the time of writing his statement, Peiper was under investigation for war crimes committed by his unit during the operation, and it was therefore in his own interest to show himself in a good light.

## In the Cauldron of La Gleize

The report by Major McCown, who was quite surprised by what he discovered about his opponents, gives an idea of the atmosphere in La Gleize at the time:

> *One astonishing fact to me was the youth of the members of this organisation – the majority of the men enlisted were 18 or 19 years old, recently recruited, but, from my observations, perfectly trained. There were a good number of soldiers and non-commissioned officers from the years of fighting in Russia. The officers were mostly veterans, but also very young. Colonel Peiper was 29, the commander of his tank battalion was 30, and the captains and lieutenants were between 19 and 27. Morale was high throughout the time I was with them, despite the extremely trying conditions. Discipline was very good.* [...] *The physical condition of all the personnel was good, except for a lack of adequate food, which became more pronounced just before I escaped from the unit. Equipment was good and complete, with the exception of a few reconditioned half-tracks among the motorised equipment. All the men wore practically new boots and had adequate clothing. Some of them wore parts of American uniforms, mainly the knitted cap, gloves, jumpers, shoe covers and one or two coats. However, I did not see anyone in American uniform or civilian clothes. The relationship between the officers and men, especially the commanding officer, Colonel Peiper, was closer and friendlier than I expected. On several occasions Colonel Peiper visited his wounded and on several occasions I saw him pat heavily laden men on the back and say a few words of encouragement as we climbed the steep hills.*
>
> *Later, on the night of 21 December, at around 11 pm, I was again taken to the cellar of Colonel Peiper's headquarters. I found him in a very different mood from his previous cold and impersonal attitude. We talked together from 11 pm until 5 am the next morning, our subject being mainly his defence of Nazism and what Germany was fighting for. I have met few men who have impressed me in such a short space of time as this German officer.* [...] *A holder of the Iron Cross with oak leaves, he had fought in Russia for a long time and briefly at Mortain and Caen. He was totally confident in Germany's ability to defeat the Allies.* [...] *As far as the treatment of prisoners by the SS is concerned, I can say that at no time were the prisoners mistreated. Food was scarce, but it was almost as good as that*

The children locked in the school were evacuated to the village church, and were traumatised by the sudden change in tone of the SS. (*Nara*)

> *of the Germans themselves. US prisoners were always put in cellars to protect them from the extremely heavy American artillery barrage. I was taken for a short time to the main prisoner compound, which was a large, well-built, two-room cellar, far superior to any I had seen at La Gleize. The place was considerably overcrowded and allowed the guards to rough up the men a bit. I organised the whole group of some 130 people into sections, appointed a first sergeant, laid down a few rules and got the German adjutant in charge of the prisoners to adopt a fairer method of distribution.*[5]

## Pressure Builds on La Gleize

On 22 December, Task Force McGeorge set off again from Borgoumont to attack La Gleize at 3:15 pm. The unit made slow progress towards the village, but was once again thwarted on the banks of the Nabonru stream. I Company came across an infantry entrenchment that was well equipped with anti-tank weapons, as two Shermans were lost under fire.[6] Once again, the Americans withdrew to more defensible positions on the edge of Borgoumont, where they spent the night. Doctor Bastin provides details of the operation:

This GI from 30th ID, photographed after the battle, shows a face severely scarred by the fighting. (*Nara*)

> *Only the next day did we learn the result of the reconnaissance carried out on the outskirts of the village after this pitiful expedition: one prisoner. It was easy, the man surrendered; he was discovered 100 metres from Borgoumont, digging a hole at the foot of a haystack. Then came the drama at Le Chenay. American soldiers entered the isolated farmhouse and found the bodies of two men still warm. We would later learn that they were the owner, Mr Istasse, and Mr Arthur Delvenne (82), who had taken refuge there the day before. Mrs Istasse, hit in the stomach by the bullets, was lying on the first floor, but was not discovered until 24 December. Nothing could be guessed of the twists and turns of this tragedy.*
>
> *It was almost evening, and the cannon had stopped firing during the afternoon. Now it was ringing again. You get used to all the misery and I fall asleep reassured by the presence of friendly troops in position in the bocage around my house. Wednesday seemed a very sad day. This was not the opinion of the soldiers, who were already satisfied to have taken the initiative again, without encountering much reaction.*
>
> *At other points in the sector, the results were more satisfactory. From Trois-Ponts, the Amblève road was retaken as far as Roanne – Coo. The Maréchal mill, at the foot of La Gleize, which had been occupied from midday on Monday, was liberated forty hours later. At the two advanced points, Targnon and Les Forges (Chevron), the Germans were also on the defensive. They never stopped at Rahier, which they rushed through. They only occupied La Gleize, Stoumont and Cheneux.*[7]

At the end of the afternoon, the soldiers returning from Stoumont and the local civilians had no choice but to take shelter in the cellars as the American artillery was unleashed.

The Ardennes village was literally bludgeoned. Poetschke, the leader of the Panther battalion, was in the cellar of the school, opposite the church. The officers commanding the various units that had survived were gathered there to take stock of the situation. Obersturmführer Rumpf, commander of 9. (Pi) SS-Panzer Regiment 1, went down into the cellar to give his report. He stated that one of his Pioniere was suspected of having tried to desert as he had stayed behind during an assault and had taken off his SS badges. Peiper replied curtly: '*Shoot him immediately and inform your men of the execution.*' Peiper had to be ruthless to avoid panic or desertion in his troop.[8] Feldwebel Karl Laun's diary explains:

> *On* the *morning of 22 December, we received new orders to set up a defensive perimeter around La Gleize. With this order, the Landsers began to realise that we were isolated and surrounded. I had a premonition. Like a bolt of lightning, I realised the seriousness of the situation. The Yanks must have caught us here with the SS – caught together, hanging together. And those crazy SS men might want to fight to the last man, including us…*
>
> *The boys in my section had become taciturn; passively, they'd accepted their food. Like robots, they carried out the orders I gave them from the battery commander. I knew very well that only extreme vigilance and interest could enable the men to get through this critical moment, but these qualities were as lacking as the motor fuel in the petrol tanks.*

The cohesion of KG Peiper disintegrated in defeat. Troops from the Luftwaffe looked askance at the SS, who were reputed to be fanatical. The latter's face showed both fatigue and determination. (*Nara*)

This Sturmpanzer 38(t) Grille Ausf M was found abandoned in the village of La Gleize. With no ammunition, it was of little use to Peiper. (*Rights reserved via La Gleize Museum*)

> *We occupied the south-east side of La Gleize, opposite the railway bridge. Everyone was digging to get as much cover as Mother Earth will allow. Using a wood saw, we felled a few trees and rolled them onto our foxholes to protect ourselves from shrapnel. We added a few shovelfuls of earth, but this improved bunker was an inadequate shelter against Yankee mortars. On the other side of the river* [L'Amblève towards Cheneux], *we could see the American infantry. In the evening, the American artillery was unleashed. We crawled into our trenches like moles. I was overcome by hunger, but despite that, I didn't dare go and get one of my American rations just 30 metres away. Artillery shells were falling as fast as hail on our positions.*[9]

The NCO's tone is disillusioned, to say the least. His account shows him distancing himself from the SS men trapped in the cauldron with him. It's a rejection mingled with a form of fear generated by the SS' apparent determination not to give up and to drag him and his comrades into a battle that he knew was already lost. Contrary to what he believed, the SS were not going to fight to the bitter end. Peiper also knew that his troops were not going to hold out much longer, explaining:

> *On the morning of 22 December, the situation in the pocket was very serious. Fighting had developed over each of the thirty houses in La Gleize. Artillery fire did not cease during the night and became more intense, concentrating on the German positions on the*

*outskirts of the village during the afternoon. At around 2 pm, the American forces launched a concentric attack along both sides of all the roads leading to La Gleize. In a close battle lasting two hours, during which fierce fighting took place for individual houses on the outskirts of the village, the defenders of La Gleize succeeded in pushing back the attackers and re-establishing the old line of resistance on the outskirts of the village, although several serious penetrations did occur. The houses set alight by the American incendiary shells and the smoke screen masking the area added considerably to the confusion. At dusk, around 5 pm, the light faded and the ensuing calm allowed the defenders to concentrate on the necessary rescue missions and on clearing the combat zones. It was at this point that the last hope of a rescue through the division's units had to be abandoned. In the last radio order received, the division ordered the encircled forces to fight their way out of the pocket.*[10]

At this point, there was no question of abandoning the vehicles, as refuelling by parachute was planned for later that night, and so Mohnke therefore ordered a mechanised breakthrough to reach the German lines.

## The Failure of Aerial Refuelling

At around 8 pm, a general alert was issued to all American units in the area after the intelligence services had deciphered a worrying message: around twenty aircraft were due to drop around 300 Fallschirmjäger (parachutists).[11] The alert further increased the crushing stress on US fighters in the sector. Luftwaffe planes were seen flying overhead at around 8:30 pm and while parachutes were indeed dropped, instead of men they carried the containers that were supposed to supply Peiper. The airborne supply operation was

Junkers were tasked with refuelling KG Peiper. (Rights reserved)

a failure, with very few containers reaching their destination.[12] However, it should be noted that 33rd AR stated in its report: '*At 9 pm, enemy paratroopers were dropped in the Stoumont area. At 9:25 pm, five of them had been captured.*'[13] Yet, according to German reports and eyewitness accounts, all of which agree on this point, no troops were dropped. The parachute drops were only for supplies. Feldwebel Laun added:

> *During the night, a big JU 52 buzzed overhead and threw out barrels of petrol. Many of them landed on the American side – where there was a glut of the stuff – without our unwitting contribution. In the distance, behind our lines, we heard the grunt of the Werfers* [mortars]*; yet another opportunity to delude ourselves. 'Hurrah, they're coming!' But nothing came. Another blow to morale was not long in coming. We were told that the SS Hitlerjugend and Hohenstaufen divisions would make their way to us. But nothing arrived. Only the monotonous whine of the enemy artillery became more intense. Early in the morning, I found my blanket. It was frozen and stiff. But our American comrades sympathised with us and obligingly sent a few phosphorous grenades to warm us up.*[14]

Reading Laun's diary we understand that the Luftwaffe parachute drop was a complete failure. Meanwhile, I SS-Pz-Korps was immediately informed by a message from Peiper. Preiss noted: '*The air supply had arrived in the early hours of the morning and provided the group with 1.5 cubic metres of petrol. This amount of fuel was just enough to operate the radio and get a few tanks into firing position. The corps was then informed by the Army that no further supplies could be expected from the air.*' The tank capacity of a Panther was 720 litres, meaning the 1,500 litres that Peiper received would not allow him to do anything more than make short trips to adjust his equipment. At I SS-Pz-Korps headquarters, there were no illusions about the fate of the precious armoured Kampfgruppe.

These containers were parachuted early in the evening, but only 10% of the cargo reached Peiper. (*Nara*)

View of the refuelling container photographed in the ruins of La Gleize. Peiper only received 1,500 litres, barely enough to move a few tanks and run his generator to power the radio. (*Rights reserved via La Gleize Museum*)

## The Americans Keep Up the Pressure

During the night of 22–23 December, in the direction of Cour, the Germans took advantage of the American retreat to regain ground and set up a new roadblock 400 metres higher up in the direction of Borgoumont, at 'Les Tchéoux', north of La Gleize.

McGeorge's battle group launched a new assault at dawn, only to come up against the new roadblock at Tchéoux and find itself immobilised. The roadblock set up by troops of 1. SS-Panzer Division was solidly defended, with a Sherman and Tiger 334 forming an impenetrable bunker.

The origin of this Sherman capture should be noted, however. It was not in the Peiper column at the start of the offensive and only appeared at this point in the battle. It could therefore have belonged to three different units: the 740th TB, 743rd TB or 3rd AD. The most likely scenario is that it came from 740th TB and was one of the three Shermans lost during the counter-attack against Saint-Édouard on the night of 20–21 December. With Peiper firing on all cylinders, this reinforcement taken from the enemy

The Sherman destroyed the Tchéoux site photographed on the heights overlooking La Gleize to the north. The photograph shows Serge Fontaine. However, the M4A1 was later definitively neutralised by a shot fired into its transmission block. (*Nara*)

would obviously have been welcomed, as placing it at the head of a column could have a surprise effect. There were no German accounts of its presence, and although the tank is listed among the vehicles lost at La Gleize by the Germans, it is possible that Peiper was unaware of its use in his ranks.

Our hypothesis is based on two factors. Firstly, 740th TB lost three tanks at Saint-Édouard, but only two were photographed at the scene of this confrontation so it may therefore have been this third vehicle. In addition, 740th TB equipped itself urgently in the depots and the equipment it lost did not have its markings, which is why it would have been counted as a capture vehicle.

The German tanks counter-attacked at 10 am on 22 December. The column of Panzers, preceded by the Sherman M4A1 76 (W), could be seen from the Roanne heights before entering Les Tchéoux. The tanks came under heavy American artillery fire and the Sherman was destroyed during this attack. It became blocked in the middle of the road and while the crews of the other Panzers tried to free it using cables, it was to no avail. As the artillery continued to rain down, the track of one Panzer broke in front of the hotel and the tank, reversing, slid down the side of the road, unwinding its thick ribbon of steel. The Germans gradually retreated, losing a third tank in the process. They returned to their lines at around 3 pm, held in check by a torrential rain of shells of all calibres.[15]

During the counter-attack on Tchéoux, one of the Shermans from 33rd AR was destroyed during the assault. The presence of duckbills suggests that it did not come from 743rd TB. (*Rights reserved*)

At around 3:30 pm, a section of five Shermans was called in to support the infantrymen. The uneven, wooded terrain prevented the American tanks from helping their brothers in arms, who were forced to dig in on the spot. During the night, patrols from Task Forces Jordan and McGeorge made contact. When the combined action of infantrymen and tanks proved useless, the unit withdrew to Borgoumont before heading for Roanne. A section of Shermans from A Company 743rd TB, accompanied by infantry, remained on the solid positions at Borgoumont to prevent a hypothetical German attack.

On 23 December, there was a marked change in the weather as a high-pressure system accompanied by a cold front settled over the Ardennes. The gloomy, very foggy weather in was replaced by immaculate blue skies and with the fog gone, the newfound brightness revealed the position of all the KG Peiper tanks on the hill overlooking the village. The Shermans of 743rd TB and 33rd AR and the Tank Destroyers of 823rd TDB opened fire. So many shells fell on the Panzers that they were unable to retaliate. In the cauldron of La Gleize, ammunition continued to run out, as Oskar Siegmund explains: '*23 December. No petrol, no ammunition and no action from the division. Today the Americans attacked from the north. They got as far as the edge of the village and we couldn't fight back. The Luftwaffe men lent Peiper their radio transmitter and he got in touch with the division*'[16] Peiper was still counting on the parachute supplies promised by the division.

# Chapter 8

# The End of the Stavelot Pocket

## West of Stavelot, Nothing New!

Another gloomy, foggy and cold day dawned over Stavelot on 22 December. Third Platoon of A Company, 1/117th IR, supported by a section of the heavy company and by Shermans B15, B18 and B19, prepared for the assault, while the other two armoured vehicles in the platoon, B16 and B17, provided support.[1] In a

Infantry battalions had a company of heavy weapons, which were distributed among the rifle companies as required. (*Nara*)

single burst, the three tanks attacked the last houses on the road to Trois-Ponts, firing explosive shells into the walls of the buildings occupied by German soldiers, while the infantrymen threw grenades into the cellars. As a diversion, I Company, 117th IR, which had taken the hamlet of Parfondruy, launched an assault on the villa Lambert. The building was located on the western edge of Stavelot, more precisely on the outskirts of the town along the road towards Trois-Ponts. The aim was to surround the SS but to reach the imposing building, first a vast open area had to be crossed. The price was too high and the American attack was halted. However, this relative failure did not prevent Captain Kent's force from taking over all the houses along the street. A dozen SS men were taken prisoner, including one with an impressive wound: bleeding profusely, his arm was practically severed and was only held together by a flap of skin. One of the German prisoners asked for a knife and surprisingly, a bilingual GI handed him his bayonet. The SS man made the wounded man, who appeared to be his superior, lie down and, with one clean stroke, cut off the piece of flesh holding his arm, which had been severed halfway through the humerus.[2] The wounded man was none other than the bloodthirsty SS-Untersturmführer Dröge ,who had killed the civilians at Parfondruy. Despite treatment by the US medical service, he died of his wound a few hours later.[3] At the same time, the Americans discovered a horrifying sight: the twenty-three victims of the Legaye house who had been shot dead by Siebert's SS. The sight of the body of 4-year-old Pol Prince was particularly poignant. A feeling of hatred towards the enemy quickly spread among the American fighters. Captain Kent shared his subordinates' aversion to the enemy's misdeeds but despite his feelings, he had to use all his authority to prevent his men from carrying out a full-scale lynching. The prisoners had to be interrogated and taken to the rear: regimental orders.

The commander of the Schnelle Gruppe, Knittel, learned that Coblenz, the leader of 2. Kompanie, and other soldiers had been taken prisoner. He sent a group of infantrymen supported by Tiger II 133 to come to their aid. This time, the Shermans of 743rd TB did not waiver and as soon as the Panzer appeared in their sights, a barrage of anti-tank shells rained down on it. The Tiger's thick armour resisted until a lucky shot put the big beast out of action. A projectile ricocheted off the gun mantlet, piercing the roof of the front compartment and killing the radio gunner. The turret ring was also damaged, preventing it from rotating. The driver put the tank in reverse and drove off, presenting the front of the Panzer, the most heavily armoured part of the tank.[4]

The noose was beginning to tighten around KG Knittel.

## The Light Tanks Fall Back at Coo

Hansen was ordered to reach the cauldron at La Gleize, where he knew Peiper was surrounded and out of fuel. Delayed by the collapse of the bridge and prevented from crossing the Petit Spay, III/SS-Panzergrenadier Regiment 1 of KG Hansen crossed the Ardennes river on a monkey bridge that had been hastily built at a place called Les Sept Montagnes.[5] Once on the right bank, the Panzergrenadiere climbed the steep, slippery

Lovelady's Shermans were M4A3 75s (W), like this one. Mounted on Shermans that were less vulnerable than the pre-January 1944 versions, the tankers dared to venture into urban combat. (*Nara*)

slopes of the northern side of the valley and bypassed Major Stalling's powerful roadblock at the Trois-Ponts viaducts. Around 4 pm, Lovelady's combined forces were cut off from their base and the SS cut the Coo – Parfondruy road at the edge of the Baillettes wood. While some of the SS remained in the woods, others descended towards the main road leading to La Gleize. Oberscharführer Nebel, head of 12. Kompanie, remembered:

> *On the morning of 22 December, I received the battalion's order to explore the hillside along the road to Petit-Coo with a few men. After about 2 kilometres, we reached a clearing and spotted a gun in a farmhouse firing towards the road.*[6] *Despite good camouflage, we were discovered and received mortar fire. We withdrew to our starting position. After the battalion commander returned, we received the final order to attack. The aim was to relieve KG Peiper, trapped at La Gleize. We marched to the left of 11. SS-Kompanie, over the wooded hill and attacked Petit-Coo. The outskirts of the village were reached. The battalion penetrated further into the village, while I was ordered to find a command post in the village itself.*[7]

The Panzergrenadiere attacked the block of houses where a HQ and a first-aid centre for the wounded had been set up. The area was defended only by a section of M5 Stuart light tanks. Sergeant Aurio Pierro was one of the tank commanders and recounted the event with great emotion:

The SS fought to the death in the Petit-Coo battles. (*Nac*)

*I've seen more than my fair share of front-line fighting in France, Belgium and Germany. I witnessed death (including that of my own tank mates). My most harrowing experience was during the Battle of the Bulge at Petit-Coo, Belgium. I was a member of TF Lovelady. I was a tank commander in the 1st platoon of B Company. I was responsible for protecting a building used as a first-aid post. The 1st platoon was made up of five M-5 Stuart light tanks and we had to withdraw or risk being surrounded and wiped out. I had no choice but to leave the half-dozen wounded GIs in the first-aid post with several medical staff. However, one of the tanks somehow disappeared and was no longer with the unit. I don't know where the platoon commander was. Naturally, I took command of the four tanks. I had the men form a defensive position at a bridge within sight of the station and surrounding buildings. The bridge crossed a railway line. The German infantry had to take this bridge to allow their reinforcements to reach a German task force led by the famous Colonel Peiper. But by this time, the infantry advance was now blocked at Petit-Coo. Our Stuart tanks, which were faster and lighter, with three .30-calibre machine guns and a 37-mm gun with an anti-personnel charge, were more feared by the infantry than the Shermans.*

*Our two Stuarts set off at full speed towards the station. The infantrymen clung to the top of the tank. The machine guns aimed at the buildings closest to the road set fire to several of them. As the platoon approached the first-aid post, I moved my tank forward. I stopped in front of the building. Armed with a .45 pistol, I got out of the tank and entered the station. As I did so, a German bazooka exploded nearby. Shrapnel from the explosion hit me in the back and knocked me to the ground. Slightly wounded, I climbed back into my tank, while a German bazooka and small arms fire came from three sides. The tanks returned fire with their machine guns and 37-mm cannon, while the riflemen fired from every protected position they could find. The tank behind me was destroyed by a bazooka, and one of the crew was killed. One of the other tanks manoeuvred behind the station. Some of the Doughboys entered the building, while the tanks continued to fire. Just then, a bazooka rocket penetrated my M5 and started an internal fire; my crewmates and I escaped to join our soldiers. The building was partly on fire. Now we were surrounded by Germans. A full-scale siege began. There were around thirty of us. The wounded took*

A light tank M5A1 with a 37-mm cannon capable of firing highly effective bullet boxes against infantry. (*Nara*)

*refuge on the ground floor, while the others fired through the windows. Incredibly, the Boys also had three German prisoners of war to look after. They had been captured in the building when the riflemen first burst in. Bullets come through the windows and small cannon shells pierced the brick walls.*

*A number of smoke bombs forced us, including the prisoners, to take refuge in the cellar. Miraculously, none of the group was killed. The Germans probably assumed that there were many victims inside. In this large, dark cellar, with no view of the outside except through a back door, they knew that this was where we would have to fight our last battle. The fire above the building was still smouldering. I suppose the Germans didn't know that there were still fighters in the building, so we remained relatively calm.*

*Suddenly, a shout came from outside through the back door of the cellar. It was in English: 'This is your last chance!' with a strong Germanic accent. Nobody answered, which confused the Germans. The firing outside continued sporadically. With no radio available, we had no idea if help was on the way. Finally, I rushed out the back door to see if the radio was working in the Stuart still parked there. A dead German soldier lay beside the door. Incredulous that no one was shooting at me, I climbed into the turret. It was incredible that the Germans hadn't destroyed the inside of the tank. I managed to reach battalion HQ by radio. They authorised us to evacuate the station as far as possible. This meant escaping via the railway tracks that led behind the building and towards the American lines. I then returned to the cellar, still apparently unnoticed by the Germans.*

*Within the hour, the firing outside ceased. Although the town was still under enemy control, the fighting seemed to be over. The group prepared to exit cautiously through the back door. With the exception of several seriously wounded men and prisoners of war, we began our escape – about twenty-five men in all. Tragically, a distant machine gun from an unknown position fired at us. At least three GIs were killed and several others wounded by what turned out to be friendly fire from an American unit that had just arrived on the bridge. Despite all this, most of my group managed to reach our lines.*[8]

For his actions at Petit-Coo, including bravery under fire, the survival of most of his men and the immobilisation of a large enemy force, Sergeant Pierro was awarded the Silver Star and Purple Heart.

Overwhelmed by enemy infantry, two of the M5s withdrew about 300 metres away and while Hansen's soldiers reorganised, they quickly set up a roadblock. This was ideally placed at the bridge over the railway line between Liège and Luxembourg. At this point, the road was at a right angle and was therefore easy to defend because the enemy had no tanks. On learning of the attack, the S-3 of 117th IR,[9] Major Singleton, could only find a section of sappers from 105th Engineers to send to reinforce the Stuart light tanks, which were in a bad way. Singleton was reprimanded by Colonel Frankland, the regimental commander, who forbade the sappers to be used in an attack.[10]

A squad assembling for the assault. The riflemen were supported by a bar and a bazooka team. (*Nara*)

After the fighting, the few prisoners were brought back for interrogation by the S-2 team. (*Nara*)

The situation was now very confused. KG Peiper was trapped in La Gleize, while a fraction of Lovelady's troops, commanded by Stalling and based at the Trois-Ponts viaducts, were also surrounded. Stalling's roadblock was attacked from three sides, although he put up a fierce fight. In addition, the combined tank and infantry force (E Coy, 120th IR) at Parfondruy was cut off from its base, so Lovelady ordered the company to return to Coo. To do this, it had to regain access to the main road and make contact with those surrounded at the viaducts. Four Shermans were also sent to assist L Company, 117th IR, which was practically surrounded at Ster. Delayed by skirmishes, they arrived at 10:15 pm. The riflemen of E Company, 120th IR, tried to reach Coo by the most direct route, via the Parfondruy – Coo road, but their progress was quickly halted at the Baillettes wood, which was occupied by the SS of I/SS-PzGr-Rgt 1. The Americans broke off contact and headed for Roanne via Renardmont. They made their way back down the valley and finally made contact with the Coo roadblock at 10:20 pm after an 8-kilometre journey. With the arrival of the infantrymen, the sappers from 105th Engineers were thus relieved.[11]

## Counter-Attack at Petit-Coo

Weather conditions had been relatively stable since the start of the offensive. There had been no wind, while an omnipresent fog restricted visibility. Light rain soaked the ground and temperatures were around 5°C. Yet as we have seen, on 23 December, a high-pressure system moved in over the Ardennes, with temperatures dropping below 0°C. In Stavelot, the daytime temperature failed to rise above -0.5°C, before dropping to -6.3°C at night.[12] This change in the weather conditions marked a turning point in the battle, as thick cloud cover gave way to a magnificent cloudless blue sky. The Allied air force, which had been virtually grounded until then, now took control of the third dimension and paralysed the German logistics system, which was already in a bad way. At the roadblock of the railway bridge in Coo, the GIs from E Company, 120th IR, and Lovelady's tankers were ready for action. Their assault was launched in the early hours of the morning and according to the testimony of SS-Oberscharführer Nebel, the attack took the SS by surprise:

> *I left with Sergeant Stork and medic Erdelen. On the roads, the men from 11. and 12. Kompanien were under the protection of the houses. Some of them were on fire. At the corner of a street, I entered a shop. Suddenly, a burst of MGs went over my head into the shop. Stork and Erdelen climbed out of the side window of the house and we hurried up the stairs to discover a tank next to the house opposite. 'Let's get out of here!' I said. Through a window in the cellar at the back of the house, we reached the garden. Behind a hedge, we joined the first men of our battalion unharmed.*

1/120th IR, 30th ID was decisive in taking Petit-Coo. (*Nara*)

The sprocket of this M5A1 light tank is being dismantled after the machine suffered damage to its left track. The photograph was taken after the action, when the maintenance units were able to intervene. (*Nara*)

On the American side, the attack was carried out with great alacrity. Staff Sergeant Paul Bolden took part in the assault on the village and his attitude was exemplary of the fighting spirit shown by 1/120th IR, 30th ID. That morning, his action would prove decisive in the capture of the small town. His citation would later read:

*He deliberately attacked a formidable enemy strong point at Petit-Coo, Belgium, on 23 December 1944, when his company was pinned down by automatic and small arms fire from a house 200 metres from the front. Mortar and armoured artillery shells pounded the unit as Sergeant Bolden and a comrade, on their own initiative, moved forward under a hail of bullets to clear the ever-increasing fire from the German position. Crawling towards a powerful and vastly superior force, the two men reached the house and took up assault positions. Sergeant Bolden under a window, his comrade opposite where he could deliver covering fire. Sergeant Bolden quickly threw a fragmentation grenade and a white phosphorous grenade into the building. Then, realising that he was up against enormous opposition, he rushed to the door, opened it and shot thirty-five SS soldiers who were trying to reorganise after the damage caused by the grenades. Twenty Germans died under his machine-gun fire before he was hit in the shoulder, chest and stomach by shrapnel that killed his comrade across the street. He withdrew from the house, waiting for the surviving Germans to come out and surrender. When there were no more in the doorway, he gathered his strength, overcame the extreme pain and boldly went back into the house, firing as he went along at anything that moved. He had killed the remaining fifteen enemy soldiers when his ammunition ran out. Sergeant Bolden's heroic advance against all odds, his fearless attack, and his magnificent display of courage in returning to the building where he had been severely wounded, paved the way for his company and ensured the success of their mission.*

## The Fighting on Stavelot Ridge

At 11:15 am, the American attack was successful and Petit-Coo was finally free of German soldiers. The men of E Company barely had time to recover from the bitter hand-to-hand combat before they had to go back into action. It was important to keep up the pressure on the SS and re-establish contact between the distant companies: the tankers in Parfondruy and the L Company boys of the 117th, who had been badly beaten

The 81-mm mortars of the heavy company sprayed the last pockets between Stavelot and Trois-Ponts. (*Nara*)

General Hobbs (right) is pictured here being congratulated by General Simpson, commander of 9th Army. (*Nara*)

by III/SS-PzGr-Rgt 1 in Ster. By mid-afternoon, the E Company riflemen were almost able to join the tankers at Parfondruy. However, they were again blocked about 500 metres from the objective. It was impossible to join up with the men of L Company, at Ster because the SS were in firm command of the roads and woods leading to the objective.[13] Following this failure, it was decided to send F Company, 120th IR, as reinforcements. Its mission was to insert itself between E Company, which had to reach Parfondruy, and L Company (117th), which found itself surrounded at Ster.

At 3:20 pm, the reinforcements were dropped off as close as possible to the front line. General Hobbs, commander of 30th ID, wanted to finish the job and so he released G Company, 120th IR, hitherto held in reserve for the division at Francorchamps. The company moved north-north-west of Stavelot to link up with A Company, 117th IR, which was holding the western part of the town and then with the tankers at Parfondruy. Total confusion reigned. Two battalions of SS-PzGr-Rgt 1 and the Schnelle Gruppe Knittel on the German side were pitted against eight US infantry companies and two Sherman companies, as well as a few elements of Tank Destroyers, M5s, sappers, etc. All were fighting in an area 3 kilometres$^2$.[14] The chaos was such that it was largely responsible for the death of I/SS-PzGr-Rgt 1's commander. Günther Junker witnessed the officer's death at close quarters:

> *At dawn, I noticed that troop movements were taking place on the other side of the forest. Following my report to the battalion, the order was given: 1. Kompanie was preparing to attack! When I saw that a machine gun was positioned in front of us, I sent another dispatch rider to the command post. Unfortunately, in the semi-darkness, it was impossible to distinguish between friend and foe. The van took SS-Sturmbannführer Emil Karst and other commanders with him to observe for himself. The overconfident commander was immediately shot in the woods. A comrade, who wanted to retrieve him, also fell. My section then had to clear the edge of the forest and I was wounded. At the command post, the commander's grave was already dug.*[15]

Deprived of support from the tanks blocked on the other side of the Amblève and of heavy weapons, the two battalions of SS-PzGr-Rgt 1 failed against the stubborn defence of the GIs.

At 4:24 pm, an order came down the American ranks, which seemed bizarre, to say the least: all units in contact with the enemy were to wear gas masks.[16] However, fighting with a gas mask was complicated as it reduced peripheral vision and impeded breathing. In which case, the order may seem counter-productive considering the situation the GIs found themselves in. But it made sense as it allowed them to adapt to the particular circumstances of the battle. Indeed, Germans were regularly spotted wearing the clothing

SS-Sturmbannführer Gustav Knittel receives the order to evacuate the Stavelot – Trois-Ponts pocket. (*Nara*)

Germans captured wearing US gear were taken to the Stavelot ponds behind the town's tanneries and tied to trees to be shot. This photograph of the same location was taken in early January 1945. (*Stavelot Library*)

of American soldiers, and an SS man in American uniform even stabbed a soldier from 117th IR in the Rue des Tanneries in Stavelot. To avoid any further misunderstandings such as this, it became compulsory to wear a gas mask in full view of the enemy, making it possible to distinguish between friend and foe at a glance.[17]

Night falls early in December in this part of the world, and it was around 7 pm when F Company, 120th IR, took advantage of the darkness to break Ster's encirclement and make contact with L Company, 117th IR. However, confusion still reigned in the 3 $km^2$ battle area.

## CCB Withdrawn From the Stavelot Sector

At 7:45 pm, an injunction from 1st US Army command reached XVIII Airborne Corps and 30th ID simultaneously: *'Disengage the CCB from the 3rd AD with immediate effect.'*

General Ridgway was forced to redeploy his forces in the face of threats to Vielsalm. He is pictured here in February 1945 after the Alsace campaign. The XVIII Airborne Corps insignia is clearly visible on his left shoulder. (*Nara*)

These paratroopers from 505th PIR mined the railway bridge over the Salm, the blasters being protected by a sniper equipped with an M1, adding a touch of cheap drama to the scene set for the Signal Corps. (*Nara*)

The news hit like a bomb; the CCB's three Task Forces were still in action and the resulting melee was such that it was virtually impossible to break them off. Operations were planned for the following day: Task Forces Jordan and McGeorge were to attack the last encircled Peiper stronghold at La Gleize, while Task Force Lovelady was at the centre of violent clashes. Lieutenant Colonel Lovelady replied that it was impossible for him to withdraw his forces, as his roadblock at Trois-Ponts was still surrounded and the other units in contact with the enemy were unable to withdraw. Once again, the telephone lines were hot between the HQ of 1st US Army, XVIII Airborne Corps and 30th ID, and General Ridgway, commander of XVIII Airborne Corps, could not immediately obey the order.

The reasons for this decision by the Allied High Command are open to question. It could be explained by the arrival of 2. SS-Panzer Division on the banks of the Salm at a time when Saint-Vith was in the process of being evacuated. It was absolutely necessary to reinforce the sector on the ridges overlooking the Salm. The 82nd Airborne Division's position south of Trois-Ponts was stretched too thin; 505th PIR extended from Trois-Ponts to about 2 kilometres north of Vielsalm; 508th PIR extended from Vielsalm to bend westwards from the Thier du Mont ridge; and 325th Glider Infantry Regiment

General Maurice Rose was forced to muster his forces to deal with a crisis developing south of Stavelot. (*Nara*)

Task Force Kane from 3rd AD took up position at Manhay. The Shermans were held in a waiting position. The crews had taken great care with their camouflage in order to be spotted as late as possible by the Panthers. (*Nara*)

moved to its right. As we have seen, these movements were discovered by I SS-Pz-Korps through eavesdropping on their radio communications. 504th PIR, which had just suffered heavy losses at Cheneux, was still blocked in the La Gleize sector and would remain there until KG Peiper was made ineffective. Further south, General Maurice Rose's 3rd AD attached to XVIII Airborne Corps was in difficulty near Samrée-Hotton and urgently needed to recover its CCB engaged in the Stavelot – La Gleize sector.

This decision was all the more crucial as 6. Panzer-Armee was determined to kill two birds with one stone: recover KG Peiper and push westwards into a sector where the breakthrough seemed to have been successful. On 22 December, the Chief of Staff of 6. Panzer-Armee, SS-Brigadef ührer Fritz Krämer, also prepared his plans for the following day. On the strength of the information he had received from I SS-Pz-Korps, he was determined to take advantage of the gaping hole behind Vielsalm, opening the way to the Meuse via Baraque de Fraiture and Manhay. In his account of events, he says:

*In I SS-Pz-Korps, enemy pressure became stronger, which weakened the attacks to rescue KG Peiper. They were unable to make contact that day either. The army again ordered I SS-Pz-Korps to free KG Peiper by all means and to prevent valuable troops and equipment from falling into enemy hands. As air supplies were not sufficient, attempts were made to supply desperately needed fuel using armoured vehicles. These attempts also failed. The Peiper group suffered heavy losses under enemy artillery fire. Serious difficulties were encountered in treating the wounded. As was later reported, the battle group commander, Obersturmbannführer Peiper, organised a truce for a few hours on 22 or 23 December in order to exchange the wounded.*

*During their advance on Vielsalm, II SS-Pz-Korps and 9. SS-Pz-Div had to walk on foot because of the poor state of the roads, whereas the advanced units of 2. SS-Pz-Div had made contact with the enemy at Oxerreux.*

*Here, the army perhaps had the opportunity to 'kill two birds with one stone':*

*a) Open the enemy defensive front in the La Gleize – Bra – Brezee – Marche line.*

*b) help the Peiper group by a push on Manhay – Werbomont (while exploiting the good roads in the north-west direction in the Meuse Liège – Huy sector).*

*The army therefore ordered II SS-Pz-Korps to dislodge the enemy with a rapid thrust and gain the Aisne sector between Mormont and Érezée. With 2. SS-Pz-Div it was planned to gain further ground in the aforementioned sector. The army was considering adding 116. Pz-Div or the Führer Escort Brigade.*[18]

An armoured infantry unit accompanied the Shermans to defend Manhay. The Americans played the interoperability card between their different weapons to resist the German assault. (*Nara*)

Meanwhile, 30th ID was stepping up its push against Peiper, which was surrounded at La Gleize. (*Nara*)

So the option envisaged by Preiss on the evening of 21 December gained ground in the German general staffs. The 6. Panzer-Armee's northern axis of attack was abandoned and everything would be focused in the direction of the Fraiture barracks and Manhay. Things became more complicated for Ridgway, however when he had to quickly withdraw his troops from Saint-Vith and reconstitute a solid front on the western heights of the Salm. It is therefore understandable that he needed the CCB of the 3rd AD. The Stavelot – La Gleize affair had gone on for far too long and the threat had to be eradicated to recover a mass manoeuvre to build a solid barrier to the south.

Ridgway tried to pull off this balancing act knowing that KG Peiper did not have long left. He therefore partly weakened the troops responsible for crushing the cauldron while maintaining the pressure on Stavelot. The CCB moved its trains and Task Force Jordan, while Task Force McGeorge remained to help reduce the pocket of La Gleize the following day, 24 December. Meanwhile, Task Force Lovelady was tasked with completing its mission in Stavelot before being relieved.[19]

The Manhay position held out against the assaults of 2. SS-Panzer Division 'Das Reich'. One of its Panthers is photographed here having been captured after the fighting. (*Nara*)

## The Remaining SS Evacuate the Bridgehead

On 24 December 1944, the clear weather set in for good and so the SS began to constantly scan the now cloudless sky, which they knew heralded the arrival of the American fighter bombers. This change in the weather marked the end of the semi state of grace during which the Luftwaffe's shortcomings in the face of Allied air supremacy had little tactical impact on the situation in the units of the 1. SS-Panzer Division. As we have seen, the consequences of the few bombing raids carried out were nevertheless extremely serious, mainly in terms of supplying the front. Moreover, the air attacks significantly delayed the arrival of 9. SS-Panzer Division at the contact line. The persistent clear weather meant that a decisive offensive capability to the advantage of the Allies could come into play: tactical aviation.

With Peiper needing to get out of the cauldron and cross the countryside in search of a crossing point to rejoin his lines, it was KG Knittel that was to bear the brunt of the battle. As the bridge over the Petit Spay had collapsed and it was impossible to build a movable bridge, Knittel found himself both alone and cut off from the bulk of his division by the Amblève. Several other attacks took place between Stavelot and Petit-Coo, further

As a high-pressure system settled permanently over the Ardennes, the fighter-bombers prepared to go into action. A load of bombs for a P-38 Lightning are seen being prepared at a US Army Air Force base. (*Nara*)

narrowing Knittel's bridgehead. The railway stop at Coo, where a company commander and the rest of his men had been surrounded for several days, was under constant American attack. A wounded man who was brought back to the scene told Preiss that the company would defend it to the last man. The SS position on the river side had become untenable, so a withdrawal had to be made during the night of 24 December to the south bank of

A P-38 pilot in operation over the Ardennes, probably belonging to 429th Fighter Squadron based at Florennes, Belgium. (*Nara*)

the Amblève. 1. SS-Panzer Division was given the new task of occupying the Waimes – Stavelot – Wanne sector, holding on to the latter town.[20]

Exhausted and running out of ammunition, KG Knittel was forced to withdraw to the other side of the river. The decision was even more justified as it was pointless to take the risk of maintaining a bridgehead on the right bank of the Amblève, as Peiper had to return to the German lines. The German pioneers did, however, manage to build a footbridge enabling the SS to cross the river on dry land, although twenty to twenty-five vehicles remained in the pocket.[21]

Around the Petit Spay bridge, the air had become truly unbreathable, and any movement was detected by the formidably effective US artillery observers. With La Gleize in American hands, three artillery battalions concentrated their fire on the isolated areas of Petit Spay. To deal with targets inaccessible to field artillery because of the deepening of the Amblève valley, A Company, 86th Chemical Mortar Battalion, equipped with 4.2-inch mortars, was attached to 30th ID.[22] There was hardly a square metre of the sector safe from shrapnel, and the effectiveness of the conventional artillery was greatly enhanced by the use of Pozit detonators. Although the banks at Pont de Petit Spay were gently sloping, the depth of the river, still swollen by the previous autumn's rain, made it impossible for survivors to cross. Although no ford is indicated on contemporary maps,

The collapse of the Spay bridge had a considerable impact on the fighting at Stavelot. (*Stavelot Library*)

A Sd.Kfz. 251/8 Ausf D from the Knittel medical unit was not spared, despite its clearly visible Red Cross marking. (*Nara*)

Additional support was provided by 4.2-inch mortars from A Company, 86th Chemical Mortar Battalion, which bludgeoned the valley floor. (*Nara*)

The Grille Panzer 38(t) Ausf M were self-propelled infantry support vehicles and were distributed among the various KGs. This one fought in the Trois-Ponts – Stavelot pocket. (*Nara*)

a crossing point had been used to cross the Amblève since time immemorial at the place known as the 'passage des charrettes'. On the night of 23–24 December, the thermometer fell to -7°C and the firm ground made it easier for vehicles to make their way across the meadows bordering the river. This area, known as 'The Seven Mountains', was invisible to artillery observers, which explains why the transit of German forces via this ford was protected from US artillery fire.

At 30th ID HQ, the allocation of missions was adapted to the new tactical situation. A new Task Force (Hickory) was formed, commanded by Lieutenant Colonel Cantey, and comprising all of 2/120th IR, L and I companies and 117th IR: in other words, all the infantry fighting between Trois-Ponts and Stavelot. Lieutenant Colonel Lovelady was responsible for commanding the armour and the isolated roadblock at the Trois-Ponts viaducts. Lieutenant Colonel Cantey's Task Force was to launch its companies at the last pockets of resistance at 9 am, while a US artillery preparation was scheduled for 8:45. Unfortunately, a misunderstanding in the transmission of orders prevented the howitzers from joining in, meaning the riflemen were launched into the assault unprepared. This flaw in the execution of orders proved fatal for many of the US infantrymen. E Company, 120th IR, arrived in sight of its objective, holding under fire the HQ of III/SS-PzGr-Rgt 1, which had set up in the outbuildings of Biester farm. Meanwhile, F Company, 120th IR, and L Company, 117th IR, were trampling on the heights overlooking the road leading from Trois-Ponts to Stavelot through the Coreux and Six Moines woods. SS resistance was stubborn. Worse still, the US artillery was firing too vigorously and F Company received as many shells as the SS ambushers in the forest. G Company, 120th IR, was stopped in its tracks 500 metres from Parfondruy by unidentified fire.[23] In the afternoon of this bloody Sunday, American units, freed from their mission by Peiper's discreet departure, raced towards Trois-Ponts. The second battalion of 119th IR, supported by tanks from C Company and three sections from D Company, part of

The P-47 Thunderbolts of 493rd Fighter Squadron based at Saint-Trond soon entered the fray. (*Nara*)

General Elwood Richard Quesada commanded the 9th Air Force. The appearance of his aircraft over the Ardennes reshuffled the tactical deck. He is seen here inspecting a Stug III Ausf G, destroyed in the sector. (*Nara*)

Lieutenant Colonel George K. Rubel's 740th TB, took part in the slaughter. At Biester farm, around fifty SS soldiers from the company mentioned above by Preiss fired on the column heading towards the Trois-Ponts' roadblock.[24] Surrounded on all sides, the SS fought to the last cartridge. There were no survivors. Rubel's arrival enabled Lovelady's troops holding the roadblock to be released from their mission and to rejoin the CCB of the 3rd AD. The only casualties suffered by Rubel's tankers on Christmas Day were a Sherman and three men who were slightly wounded by friendly fire from the US Air Force.

At the end of the day, trapped between the Croix aux Clous and the junction of the Coo-Parfondruy and Ster roads, the Panzergrenadiere played their last card. By evening, the railway line to Pepinster was in the hands of the GIs. Only Tiger 008, immobilised near Knittel's HQ on the road from Trois-Ponts to Stavelot, was still holding the US troops at bay. The last tanks of Task Force Lovelady were relieved by the Shermans of 743rd TB and returned as a unit towards Manhay.

At around 4 am, taking advantage of the darkness, the last SS troops crossed the Amblève via the monkey bridge for pedestrians and the cart path for vehicles. The last defenders were the crew of Tiger 008, along with Knittel and his staff, but the heavy tank was sabotaged and then abandoned. On Monday, 25 December, Christmas Day, American infantrymen combed the woods for isolated German soldiers. As at La Gleize, the survivors of 1. SS-Panzer Division were able to escape from the trap, but the strike force of the most powerful Kampfgruppe of the Ardennes offensive had finally been defeated.

# Chapter 9

# Peiper Slips Away

## Understated Reports to OKW

Peiper maintained irregular radio contact with his superiors. However, this erratic link did not seem to help him much, at least if the answers he gave to his American interrogators after the war are anything to go by. When asked what orders he had received from his divisional headquarters during this period, he replied, after a cynical sniffle: '*I received a message ordering me to report immediately where my first-aid post for the wounded was, and until I sent a report on my fuel level, I couldn't expect any more!*'[1]

Reports from the headquarters of 1. SS-Panzer Division that went up the chain of command to the OKW were reassuring about the possibility of re-establishing lines of

When they entered La Gleize, the GIs discovered a veritable graveyard of German tanks. The vast majority of Panther tanks from SS-Panzer Regiment 1 lay in the ruins of the village. (*Rights reserved via Lemaire*)

communication with the encircled armoured point. On the morning of 23 December, OB West was informed that the attack to break the encirclement of Peiper had reached Petit-Coo. In the evening, the situation was reported to be even more reassuring in that, after Petit-Coo had been cleared, the attack to break the encirclement continued to advance towards La Gleize. While a bridge was about to be completed at Trois-Ponts, KG Peiper reported that it had succeeded in containing enemy attacks.

The tone changed radically on the night of 23–24 December. Generalfeldmarschall Model went to the headquarters of 6. Panzer-Armee and had the opportunity to speak with all the commanders there. The message he sent to von Rundstedt was far less triumphalist, saying that he was expecting a surprise attack on 24 December towards Bastogne, supported by around 100 tanks. He therefore ordered reinforcements in that direction. Other movements were planned to relieve Dietrich, with LXVII Armee-Korps placed in the bosom of 6. Panzer-Armee to attack in a north-westerly direction to relieve 1. SS-Panzer Division. Meanwhile, 2. SS-Panzer Division was to attack north-eastwards

The 82nd Airborne Division arrived in extremis to block the German armoured point. (*Nara*)

beyond Mormont to widen the base of the attack. Such instructions indicate that Model was concerned about the progress of the assault in the northern sector. However, the following situation report was very optimistic. It stated that all enemy attacks in the Stavelot – La Gleize sector had been contained and that Peiper might even be gaining ground as powerful concentric attacks were reported against these two localities. All day on 24 December, no information concerning KG Peiper was reported and the next day, it was stated that no liaison had been established with Peiper since the previous day.[2] However, the hierarchy of 6. Panzer-Armee could not be unaware of what was really happening.

Hermann Preiss, SS-Gruppenführer und Generalleutnant der Waffen-SS, then in command of I SS-Pz-Korps, was well aware of the pressure being put on KG Peiper from 21 December onwards. He pointed out that Peiper had issued messages indicating he was almost out of ammunition and fuel. Consequently, all available means were deployed by 1. SS-Panzer Division to break the encirclement. He also knew that all attempts over the following two days failed and that Peiper began his retreat on the night of 23–24 December,[3] with information being brought to the attention of 6. Panzer-Armee staff on a daily basis.[4]

## Courage, Let's Go!

On 23 December, the American units did not attack La Gleize with much vigour. The presence of minefields covered by 20-mm anti-aircraft guns and, above all, the threatening presence of Panthers on the edges of the perimeter dampened the ardour of the GIs.[5] Nevertheless, the situation in the pocket remained serious. Ammunition and fuel supplies were virtually exhausted and no food deliveries had arrived since the first day of the attack. The airlift of ammunition and fuel on 22 December did arrive, but only around 10% of the supplies dropped by the three aircraft reached the encircled perimeter – a quantity so small as to have no effect. The church at La Gleize, despite being marked with a red cross, was destroyed by tank and anti-tank fire on the evening of 22 December. After this shelling, American batteries destroyed other buildings on

This captured SPW was used by the paratroopers on numerous occasions after the fighting at Cheneux. (*Nara*)

the morning of 23 December by bombarding them with phosphorus incendiary shells. Early in the morning, Peiper sent a radio message to I SS-Pz-Korps saying: '*Positions considerably worsened. Only meagre ammunition reserves left. Forced to abandon Stoumont and Cheneux during the night. This is our last chance for a breakthrough.*' This message triggered permission to leave the Gleize,[6] but it should be noted, however, that Peiper's message slightly differs from reality: he had abandoned Cheneux and Stoumont twenty-four hours earlier than he admitted to his superiors.

On the afternoon of 23 December, Peiper decided there was nothing left to do but to extract himself from this extremely tight pocket by an infantry sortie, abandoning all heavy equipment, all prisoners of war and all the wounded. According to Peiper, the necessary discussions took place with the commanders of all the battalions at the KG command post set up in the cellar of a farmhouse. Subsequently, an agreement was reached with the captured American officers, specifying that they would assume responsibility for the prisoners of war and all the wounded who were to be left behind

An artillery piece belonging to KG Peiper, captured by 30th ID. (*Nara*)

in the cellars of La Gleize as soon as the sortie was successful. Dr Dittmann, a German doctor and medical officer with III/SS-PzGr-Rgt 2, was left behind to look after the German and American wounded. The agreements were put in writing and signed by both parties, with Peiper signing for the Germans and Major McCown and a captain for the Americans.[7]

Major McCown confirmed that in the late afternoon of 23 December, he was once again called to Peiper's headquarters. The German officer told him that he had been ordered to abandon his position and withdraw eastwards towards the nearest German troops. He added that he knew it would be impossible to save any of his vehicles and that he would have to withdraw on foot. Peiper's immediate concern was for the 150 American prisoners and his own wounded. He still hoped to save his un-transportable men with an exchange plan whereby he would leave all the American prisoners under the command of the most senior officer present, a captain. He told McCown that he had previously left a considerable number of wounded in Stoumont Castle, which had already been captured by the Americans. Peiper proposed in writing that, in exchange for the American prisoners, all the German wounded should be handed over to his division, wherever they were collected.

SS soldier Wolfgang Schleif, who was wounded, was treated in the cellar of the village presbytery and confirmed Peiper's promises about the prisoners. Peiper introduced himself to them and said: *'All of us who could march should retreat and the rest of us who could not should wait to be captured by the Americans, but that we should keep our spirits up, because we would exchange some American prisoners of war that he had kept.'*[8]

The 800 men who were fit to march descended towards Amblève. (*Nara*)

In order for the Americans to comply with his request, McCown was to be held hostage, only to be released when the wounded Germans had also been freed. The US major gave no guarantee that this would happen, as the decision rested with the American High Command. Throughout the night of 23–24 December, plans were drawn up for the exfiltration of La Gleize and at 3 am on 24 December, a column of men set off on foot. Colonel Peiper and McCown took their places just behind the vanguard, with the rest of the regiment, exhausted, following in single file.[9]

## Start of the Nocturnal Odyssey

Peiper infiltrated between the American lines, taking advantage of the entangled front. When he escaped, La Gleize was attacked from the west and north-west by 119th IR, supported by 740th TB. 117th IR attacked from the north-east, while the east of its position was taken by Task Force McGeorge of 3rd AD. The only corridor free of troops was to the south-south-east of La Gleize. The paratroopers of 504th PIR had stopped along the Amblève at Cheneux, where they were struggling to recover from the heavy losses suffered during the fighting on the evening of 21 December. Task Force Lovelady

Peiper's men crossed the Amblève on a railway footbridge that still exists today. (*Hugues Wenkin*)

bordered the Amblève north of Trois-Ponts, where it was engaged facing east with KG Knittel. It was behind Lovelady's positions that Peiper and his men infiltrated on 24 December. McCown accompanied the fleeing SS and his account is almost admiring of the skill with which the SS advanced:

*We crossed the Amblève near La Gleize on a small road bridge just below the railway bridge and headed south, climbing higher and higher on the ridge line. At 5 am we heard the first tank explode and within thirty minutes the whole area previously occupied by KG Peiper was a sea of burning vehicles, the work of the small detachment he had left behind to completely destroy all his equipment. He told me later that there were a few vehicles he hadn't destroyed. I couldn't work out exactly why.*

*The column of infantrymen closed in on a heavily wooded slope of a very high hill. Colonel Peiper, his staff and I, with my two guards, spent the whole of the 24th reconnoitring to find a route to join the other German forces. No food was available at any time after we left La Gleize; the only sustenance I received was four small pieces of dry biscuit and two swigs of brandy given to me by one of the junior officers. Later the German regimental surgeon gave me a piece of sweet, the sugar of which did me a lot of good during the long march that followed. At 5 pm, just before dark, the column resumed its march along the chosen route; we moved into a valley in a single column with a heavily armed strongpoint in front. The noise made by the whole group of 800 men was so low that I think we could have passed within 200 metres of an outpost without being detected. As the point approached the base of the hill, I heard very clearly an American voice shouting, 'Halt! Who's there?' The summons was repeated three times, then the American sentry fired three shots.*

*A moment later, the column was ordered to turn around and head back up the hill. In a few minutes, the whole column was halfway up the hill. A German limped past me. He was probably leading the platoon as he had just been shot in the leg. The colonel spoke to him briefly but did not allow the orderlies to bandage him. He ended up in the column and continued to advance without receiving first aid. The route ran along the side of the hill for half a mile, then turned back into the valley, this time passing undetected through the valley and the paved road that ran along its base. Several American vehicles cut off the column, but at no time was its presence detected.*

*The entire 800 men withdrew into the woods on the other side of the valley in a surprisingly short space of time. I could see then that Colonel Peiper was choosing the direction of his movement over the explosion of American artillery fire as the likely location of his friendly forces. His information on the current front lines of both sides was as meagre as mine, for he had no radio and no other outside contact. He kept consulting his map, proving that he was completely lost. From then on we kept moving up and down the rugged hills, crossing small streams, cutting our way through thick undergrowth and staying away from roads and villages. At around 10 pm, Colonel Peiper, his second in command and his S-3 disappeared from the forward command group. I and my two guards were placed in charge of the regimental surgeon whose familiar Red Cross pack on his back made it easy for me to walk behind. I tried in vain to find out where Colonel Peiper had gone; a friendly enlisted man belonging to Colonel Peiper's HQ told me he was very tired and I believe he and a few selected members of his staff must have holed up in a lonely house for food and rest – to be joined by the main body after locating friendly forces.*

*The change in command of the unit also meant a change in the way the men were dealt with. A young captain in charge of the first company operated very close to me and my knowledge of Latin and the German I had learnt enabled me to understand to some extent virtually all the orders he gave. I heard him tell my guards to shoot me if I showed the slightest intention of escaping, especially when we approached the American lines; whereas Colonel Peiper had given a 'break' for rest every hour or so, the new command gave no 'break' from then on until I escaped. The country we were now passing through was the most rugged we had ever encountered. All the officers were continually exhorting the men to redouble their efforts and to laugh at weakness. I was carrying nothing but my canteen, which was empty, but I know from my own physical reaction how tired men carrying heavy weapons must have been.*[10]

Oskar Siegmund was one of the men who escaped from the cauldron at La Gleize. He explains: '*It started at around 3 am, three men from Skorzeny, who had arrived with us six days earlier at Stavelot, formed the head of the column and they were to annihilate the American posts on the bridge (over the Salm) and this was to be done quietly. We left La Gleize like thieves.*[11]

'We now return one last time to the account of Feldwebel Karl Laun (84. Flak Sturmabteilung), whose account takes a critical look at the SS men he accompanied. Although more poignant than McCown's, the account does not cast a rudimentary veil over the state of disrepair and the hardship of the escape:

*A starry night sky hovered over La Gleize. It was bitterly cold. The flames, still leaping from the ruins, flickered frighteningly. In between, as if to demonstrate that the end was near, the American artillery punctuated the town's death sentence. Since last night, all the shells had hit this small town. The field hospital had to be moved to the relative safety of the cellars. We set off again at 2 am. The Peiper's SS battle group, once so arrogant, was now reclaiming its sad remains. In single file, we crossed the bridge south of the town. Objective: to reach our lines. The Tigers, Panthers, a large number of vehicles and guns were now the Americans' booty, provided they had not already been destroyed by American artillery. I even gave up destroying my 20-mm anti-aircraft guns, although I had received orders to do so.*

*The route took us over cliffs and swampy bayous that often seem to be frozen solid. The Panzerfausts charged us; nobody knew why we were dragging these annoying gadgets with us. Surreptitiously and carefully, these toys were thrown away. A few machine pistols and rifles followed suit.*

*Our password was 'Christmas Present' – and we got it. When we reached the top of the mountain at daybreak, the surprise package was already waiting for us. It took the form of a column of troops marching along a newly constructed forest road. At first we weren't sure whether we were looking at Germans or Americans. But that distinctive American steel helmet soon dispelled any doubts. All discipline was broken as everyone rushed for cover. The danger passed, but the long chain of 700 men was irrevocably broken. I was lucky enough to have my compass with me and I took it upon myself to select the exit route for my small group. The long diversion via Basse-Bodeux seemed safer than the direct route via Trois-Ponts. By midday, we were exhausted and hungry. No one had anything to eat with them; the order was to carry light weapons and nothing but light weapons. It was the burning thirst, caused by the dry cold, that bothered us most. Men plucked the frozen snow from the trees and sucked it. Others, like animals, pounced on every puddle and drank the mud. We still had one more stretch to go before reaching Basse-Bodeux. In groups of twenty men each, we rushed down the road. With our steel helmets in our hands and our camouflage outfits in tatters, we looked more like tramps than soldiers. The sun set sadly, through a curtain of mist, over our follies there below. We stumbled along, but then our troubles began to multiply, as the Jabos hovered overhead and took an interest in us. We sweated profusely in our heavy camouflage suits. I ended up leaning over a murky stream, but my thirst only became more painful. The forest seemed endless. Under the curtain of darkness, we crossed a busy road. Meanwhile, 200 men had gathered again, trying to reach the German lines south of Wanne. Hunger forced me to eat my carefully preserved chocolate bar. But the thirst is becoming unbearable; our lips were chapped and starting to crack. I didn't care how clean the puddles were, but the filthy water was starting to make me nauseous.*

*The men were becoming increasingly exhausted. Here, one fell by the side of the road, there, another broke formation – it was probably best to stay put and spend the rest of the war in a prison camp. When we took a five-minute break, some of the men fell asleep on their feet and didn't wake up when we resumed our march. In the dark, we never saw them again. Both morale and the thermometer seem to be freezing. We stumbled over rocks, got bogged down in the moors, tore ourselves apart in the primeval undergrowth. At last, we reached a good road. We followed it and then found an imposing building. Maybe it was an abbey. But the castle of our dreams suddenly turned into a stronghold, as only 100 metres away we saw American vehicles parked.*

*An American sentry calls out to us, demanding the password. Like a pack of cornered rats, we scattered into the forest. One of the boys from Kommando Greif in Skorzeny was ordered to approach the sentry. An argument ensued between the real and the pseudo-American. And the incredible insolence of Greif's man succeeded! He managed to fool the sentry. But we still took the precaution of making a wide circle around the castle.*

*We reached a railway viaduct; then the Salm, a small river, but at a temperature of 10° below zero (Celsius), two men stumbled and disappeared in the whirlpool of the swollen river. I was freezing when I reached the opposite bank. The welcoming committee was already waiting for us – one of our SS friends. You couldn't recognise his rank in the dark, but he showed his superiority by hurling insults and kicking latecomers. On the other side of the river, these brave gentlemen were very calm and reserved; but now, knowing that the last American sentries were safely behind them, they immediately resumed the arrogance typical of the SS.*[12]

## An American Front Undergoing Restructuring

When they approached the American lines, the SS had no idea where the inevitable encounter with the enemy would take place. In theory, they would approach the enemy's positions from the rear, which would give them a good chance of success. Peiper's intention was to attack by force, which is why he gave priority to carrying individual weapons. Montgomery's decision, however, would enable them to cross the American

Patton's Third Army took longer than expected to reach Bastogne. Its 4th AD met strong resistance from 7. Armee, particularly at Chaumont, where it suffered considerable losses. (*Nara*)

The 7th AD had been holding out valiantly for several days at Saint-Vith when it received the order to withdraw. This AA machine-gun nest had just received the first flakes of snow that fell on the region. (*Nara*)

lines easily. Since the Verdun meeting, the British marshal had been in command of all Allied troops north of the German salient in formation. On 23 December, he was certainly not reassured by developments in the Ardennes and his report to the Imperial General Staff betrayed his fears, particularly with regard to Patton's chances of success:

> *The attack begins today before everything is really ready; but III Corps has been launched all at once to restore the situation at Bastogne where the 101st Airborne Division is surrounded. On the basis of the sketchy information at my disposal I am not happy with the situation on the southern front and feel that the Third US Army will be in contact with the German 7 Army and will be stopped in its advance northwards to hamper the 5. Panzer-Armee. I don't think the Third Army will be strong enough to do what is necessary. If my predictions are correct, I will have to face the 5. and 6. Panzer-Armee without help. I think I can manage that, but it's not going to be fun. The 5. Panzer-Armee is going to have to deal with my VII Corps […] and it's not going to be easy to get past them. I have therefore pointed out that the bridges over the Meuse south of Givet must be held and well secured. The information I have is that they are not and the 12th Army Group is not worried about it, because it considers that the Third Army is going to wipe out the Germans completely.*[13]

The columns of 7th AD withdrew behind the Salm in good order. These M7B1s belonged to a FAAB. (*Nara*)

What can we say about the British's fears, except that they were well-founded? Patton was effectively blocked by 7th Army for another three long days, and it was Montgomery's units that would have to face the entirety of the two German armoured armies. The VII US Corps finally emerged victorious from its confrontation at Dinant and Rochefort, but it would take another week to do so. This situation immobilised its operational reserve in the extreme south of its position, while in the northern part of the front, the situation was far from stabilised. Although KG Peiper had been rendered ineffective, II SS Pz-Korps had entered the battle and was advancing irresistibly towards Manhay, threatening Saint-Vith with encirclement to such an extent that the town had to be evacuated, with the consequent need to abandon Vielsalm as well.[14]

In this sector, therefore, a crucial problem was emerging: the Allies needed to be prepared to hold on to secure positions and therefore shorten the front line in order to restructure and solidify it, at least long enough to absorb the shock. Montgomery's ill-informed detractors might consider his analysis too timid. However, his point of view was confirmed by American analysts, who after the war emphasised the seriousness of the situation at the time. From the Baraque de Fraiture to the Ourthe, the American 'line' was, according to Hugh Cole, difficult to draw. Here and there, elements of 3rd AD and two parachute infantry battalions tried to hold an extension of the American line west of the Baraque de Fraiture, which was only loosely anchored at Lamorménil and Freyneux. At the same time, the exposed American right flank counter-attacked to erase the German penetration, which had advanced as far as the Soy – Hotton road and threatened to engulf the Task Force, which was alone and vulnerable at Amonines, on the west bank of the Aisne. Two untested regimental combat teams from 75th ID were en route to help consolidate 3rd AD's tattered front, but they were unlikely to reach its positions until the evening of the 24th. Throughout the afternoon and evening of the 23rd, the defenders of Saint-Vith poured into the American lines. Aware of the enemy's growing strength south of Manhay, General Ridgway sent troops from 7th AD and the remnants of 106th ID to extend and reinforce the right flank of 82nd Airborne Division. At the same time, he ordered the CCB of 9th AD to assemble as a mobile reserve around Malempré, east of the Manhay road, and to support the American blocking position just north of the Baraque de Fraiture. Ridgway, however, was aware that 7th AD was well below strength and that the rugged, wooded terrain was very difficult to access. The front was not suitable for armoured vehicles and so on 24 December, he asked Hodges to give him an infantry division.

When he visited Ridgway's HQ mid-morning on 23 December, Field Marshal Montgomery immediately realised the American front between the Ourthe and the Salm was full of gaps and was far too wide.[15] In fact, it was the very twisted and tangled nature of the front at this point that enabled Peiper's unit to escape so easily throughout the day on 24 December. As KG Peiper approached the American lines on the night of 24 December, the latter were in full movement towards a position to the rear. The 82nd Airborne Division fell back on a much shorter front running diagonally from Trois-Ponts south-west to Vaux-Chavanne, just before Manhay, while 7th AD CCA withdrew to the low hills north of Manhay and Grandménil.

## Gavin Ignores the Runaways

The fleeing German group did not go unnoticed. On 24 December, General Gavin was perfectly aware of their presence:

> *I had previously been warned by the Corps Commander that we would have to pull out. The orders arrived at 1:30 pm. From a tactical point of view, the withdrawal was justified. However, my men were furious at having to abandon their positions, realising what each hillock, spur and ridge would cost in sweat, pain and blood when it came to reoccupying them. The resistance they were contemplating was tantamount to suicide. I explained to them without managing to convince them, because I saw the red of anger rise to their foreheads because they almost considered that they were being forced to be deserters. The withdrawal to the Trois-Ponts, Erria, Manhay axis was planned for Christmas night. It was very cold, the moonlight was particularly bright, the snow crunched underfoot and the wind whipped up raging swirls of tiny crystals that slapped the cheeks.* [...]

The 75th ID was on its way to reinforce 82nd Airborne Division. This conventional infantry division was not yet seasoned. (*Nara*)

*At 11 pm I decided to join 505th PIR, which was to circle around Trois-Ponts to reach our new front. In Saint-Jacques, I came across a platoon of paratroopers looking for a large German force that had been reported to them. I left for Dairomont to the regiment's Command Post. Indeed, earlier in the evening a driver had spotted heavily armed men heading east through the woods near Basse-Bodeux; some had thrown themselves to the ground, while others were scampering around under cover. Bullets had also hit the jeep of a Signal Corps man checking the telephone lines. Colonel William E. Ekman asked me what he should do: interrupt the withdrawal manoeuvre and comb the wood to neutralise the German group? Or ignore the presence of this enemy and continue the withdrawal? The three platoons he had left on the Salm were beginning to come under heavy pressure from elements of 1. SS Pz-Div. occupying the other bank. I told him to go ahead with the withdrawal: we had identified at least four divisions likely to attack us in the next few hours, so we couldn't afford to divert a regiment to this mopping-up operation: it had to be in place by daybreak on our new line of defence.*[16]

Gavin's account is interesting in more ways than one. First of all, he also recognised the need to stall and therefore validated Montgomery's position. Next, he explains the circumstances that facilitated the exfiltration of KG Peiper, who was also in the process of withdrawing and in a situation that was likely to become critical. What is more, the fleeing German group was not threatening its withdrawal, so was concentrating on its priority: establishing its new position. The situation was unusual, to say the least: a retreat through an enemy line that was also withdrawing. Peiper's men were therefore not going to be troubled and only encountered a very thin cordon of troops on the Salm, when they came up from the rear.

## KG Peiper Manages to Reach its Lines

Major McCown, who was still a prisoner, continues his account of the German withdrawal:

> *We got very close to where the artillery fire was coming in and the point pushed into the American lines three times and turned back. I think the Germans suffered several casualties during these attempts. Finally, the commander decided to go over the ridge and down into the next valley to try and reach their lines. By this time, I was firmly convinced that they didn't know where they were on the map, as the junior officers kept arguing during their conferences. By midnight the condition of the men was such that a halt had to be made and they had to be provided with warmth and food. I heard the captain say that he was going to try to locate a small village where the unit could hole up for the rest of the night. About 1 am I think I heard that a small town on the front line would do. I was not at the front at the time, my guards were holding me close to the position occupied by the covering force between the village and the west, in other words towards the American rear.*
>
> *The outpost had already moved into position before the shooting started not far from where I was standing. My guards and I hit the ground, tracer bullets flew all around us and we could hear MG bullets cutting through the trees nearby. The American unit, which I later learned was a company, moved forward again to clear what they thought was a stray patrol, this time also using mortars. Mortar fire fell all around the German position. I don't know if my guards were hurt or not – shrapnel was spraying from the trees all around us. The American machine gun and rifle fire was far superior to that of the covering force. I could hear orders shouted in German and English, the latter predominating. There was a lot of movement around me in the darkness. I stood still for a while, waiting for one of my guards to give me an order. After a while, I stood up carefully and started moving at right angles to the direction of the American attack, looking carefully behind me to see if anyone was covering or following me. After about 100 metres, I turned around and headed straight for the direction of the American attack. I remember whistling an American tune, but I can't remember which. I hadn't gone more than 200 metres when I was hailed by an American outpost of the 82nd Airborne Division.*[17]

A machine gun nest belonging to 505th PIR. It was through a defensive line dotted with this type of weapon that the SS rushed towards the banks of the Salm. (*Nara*)

In reality, the SS arrived at Rochelinval in the sector held by I Company, 3/505th PIR, which was then in full movement towards its new positions. Sergeant Bill Dunfee explains:

> *By 9 pm, we had all packed up and were waiting for orders to move out. Fortunately, our machine guns were still buried in position covering the shallow areas of the Salm in front of our front. We were in the rear, dozing on our packs, when all hell broke loose. The Germans came up behind us, shooting and shouting like a band of Indians. I couldn't see them to know what they were. The rapid fire of the German machine guns and their pink tracers informed me. They too wanted to get home for Christmas. We immediately got back into our foxholes and started firing. I could estimate that a group the size of my company passed through my sector. Some got to the river, some didn't. I think half got to the river. I think half made it to the other side. Our machine guns were up and chopped them up as they tried to cross the river. When the smoke cleared we realised we were trying to withdraw through an enemy force that was also doing the same. This must not have been unique in military history, but it was new to us.*

A little later, Dunfee collected Major McCown after his escape from German captivity.[18]

Panther Ausf G with a zimmerit turret belonging to 2. Kompagnie, I/SS-Pz-Rgt 1. (*Rights reserved via Lemaire*)

On 24 December, Task Forces Jordan and McGeorge entered a La Gleize free of enemy troops. They were ordered to regroup and move at 3:30 pm towards Stinval, a hamlet north-west of Louveigné. The remnants of KG Peiper left La Gleize at 1:00 am on 24 December and arrived at Wanne at 3:00 am on 25 December. Peiper had been on amphetamines (Pervitin) since the start of the offensive and was suffering from side effects, even suffering from a heart attack during his arduous retreat. According to him, however, it was due to a lack of sleep, after claiming to have been unable to sleep for nine days.[19]

## A Watered-Down Vision of Peiper?

We cannot close this chapter without considering Major McCown's view of the German colonel. He saw him as having a correct attitude towards his adversaries and spoke of him as an idealist who believed in the cause he was defending. He is described as close to his men, friendly and concerned for the wounded. In short, the portrait of a chivalrous fighter. This is striking, to say the least, when compared with the SS' reputation that has gone down in history. Peiper, for his part, seems to have the same sympathy for his interlocutor, declaring at the Dachau trial on 20 June 1946: '*McCown was very interested in the question of how we would treat prisoners of war. I was able to reassure him on the subject and I told him that I was not Genghis Khan, and that that went without saying.* I *spoke with McCown at length on various subjects, and we were both very pleased to learn that the front-line soldiers still spoke the same language.*'[20]

The fact that this report was written shortly before the news of the massacre of prisoners at Baugnez became known, suggests that the image it gives of Peiper is not yet imbued with the war crime of which he was about to be accused.

For the objective historian, it is sometimes difficult to determine a man's culpability. Peiper was not present at the Baugnez massacre, nor did he command the men who massacred the civilians at Parfondruy. McCown presents him as a decent adversary. It is true that, when surrounded in La Gleize, he did no harm to his prisoners, whom he had locked up in the Château de Froidcour. This is to forget the influence that a superior can exert. Tacit pressure can be put on a subordinate to act without explicit instruction. In the first volume, we pointed out that orders were explicitly given to the troops not to take prisoners, but that Peiper did not oppose the executions of any who were. It could be argued that Peiper was tried for his intentions without actually carrying any of them out.

A Wirbelwind was found at La Gleize. It was positioned opposite the town, on the other side of the valley where the forty-seven SPWs were assembled. This position was logical insofar as its function was to protect the contingent from air attack. (*Nara*)

It seems appropriate, therefore, to return to the atmosphere that prevailed in Peiper's unit on this subject. At the trial in Liège, Paul Zwigart, driver of the command SPW in which Peiper and Diefenthal had been seated, described a scene that took place at Cheneux on 18 December. His testimony rules out any lingering doubts about the commander's implicit influence in the war crimes perpetrated by his unit:

*I was driving Diefenthal's armoured car. In addition to myself, Hauptsturmführer Diefenthal and the Regimental Commander, Obersturmbannführer Peiper, were also in the car, as were Unterscharführer Paul Fackelmayer and Rottenführer Hans Assenmacher. The vehicle, like all others of its kind, was open and the occupants' heads protruded over the side walls. Even when you were sitting down, you could look out. If you came under enemy fire, you had to crouch down to take cover. As far as I can remember, at about four o'clock in the afternoon, about a kilometre from where we were attacked by the air force, I saw a Panther tank stopped on the left side of the road.*

*Perhaps 20 metres away, perhaps 30 metres away, perhaps at a greater distance and behind this tank, on the right-hand side of the road, however, were several armoured vehicles from our battalion. I passed these armoured vehicles and stopped level with the Panther on the right-hand side of the road. The order to stop had been given to me by Hauptsturmführer Diefenthal, who was sitting directly behind me. Diefenthal asked the tank commander what was going on. He ordered it to continue on its way. I don't remember what the tank commander's reply was, but Hauptsturmführer Diefenthal and Obersturmbannführer Peiper consulted a map that the former had just taken.*

*While the two men were consulting the map, the deputy commander's car came between our vehicle and the Panther. I should point out that it was about half a length ahead of our vehicle. At about the same time, I think it was when the deputy's vehicle came up to ours, an American jeep, whose driver was certainly unaware that we had already arrived at this point, arrived at high speed, driving in our direction. One of the vehicles next to us, the Panther or the deputy commander's vehicle, opened fire with a machine gun. I can't remember which vehicle opened fire, but it wasn't ours.*

*The jeep, whose driver had certainly been hit, banged into the front of the deputy commander's car. The occupants of all the vehicles, curious to see what was happening, looked outwards. Someone, I think it was Unterscharführer Rinek from the deputy commander's armoured car, it's also possible that there were two or three others as well, in any case all the soldiers not belonging to the crew of our car dismounted and crowded around the jeep; nothing happened at that point and Hauptsturmführer Diefenthal then gave me the following order: 'Zwigart, get that jeep out of the way, we've got no time to lose.' While I was still in my vehicle, I saw two Americans in the jeep who appeared to be wounded or dead.*

*I went over to the jeep and Unterscharführer Rinek – I'm sure it was he who drew my attention to the fact that one of the Americans was still alive and only 'playing' dead. I think it was the driver of the jeep, but I can't say for sure. In any case, one of the two Americans was dead and the other was 'playing dead'. I shouted at the living American to get up and I grabbed him to show him what I wanted. Then the American got out of his jeep and, as far as I could see, he wasn't hurt. I must tell you now – and this is by way of explanation – that at the time I was furious with the Americans because we had just suffered a heavy attack from their air force.*

*For this reason, and also because I knew that my direct superior, Hauptsturmführer Diefenthal, and the regimental commander, Obersturmbannführer Peiper, who was also present, would certainly not mind if I killed this prisoner, I decided to shoot him.*

*During my interrogation, I was asked how I could be sure that Diefenthal and Peiper would agree. I replied that it was because I knew them. I would like to explain this more fully here. I've been in the Waffen-SS long enough to know that even if no formal order has been given to shoot a particular prisoner of war, it's still true that the officers have no problem with it* [underlined by author] *In addition to this, I would say that I knew Obersturmbannführer Peiper as a radical SS man. It was common knowledge in the regiment, before he came to us, that he was Himmler's deputy and right-hand man. On the other hand, there is no need for a lengthy explanation to establish that I had the right to hide behind this agreement, which was considered to have been reached beforehand, by these two senior officers, precisely because this is clear from the circumstances and because the circumstances prove it sufficiently. From the beginning of the incident to the end, both Hauptsturmführer Diefenthal and Obersturmbannführer Peiper watched what was happening and I, as Rottentührer, would certainly not have allowed myself to do anything in front of them which I could have assumed they would not tolerate. I signalled to the American that he should move towards our vehicle. I walked behind him at the distance of half a step. From the moment we discovered he was alive, he had been holding his hands up above his head. In fact, he kept his hands in that position right up until the moment he died. I knew he was an American because I recognised him by his uniform. He was wearing American trousers of a whitish-brown hue and American ankle boots with buckles. On the sleeve, as far as I could remember, he wore one or two stripes like those worn by corporals in the American army. As far as I can remember, he no longer had his steel helmet on his head when he left his vehicle. His gun must also have remained in the jeep, as I'm sure I didn't see any weapons on him.*

*I approached my car with the prisoner and, as far as I remember, I stood on the side of the car where Diefenthal and Fackelmayer were. I said to Fackelmayer, 'Pass me my machine gun, I'm going to shoot this man.' Fackelmayer gave me my machine gun.*

*At the same time, from several cars and several sides at the same time, people were shouting at me loudly and encouraging me: 'Go on, shoot him,' and other similar encouragement. I said, during my verbal interrogation, that it was like being at the Leipzig fair. I was asked to explain the expression I used. I'll give it to you. People on all sides were looking at me with curiosity, the sound of shouts of encouragement and, on top of that, Obersturmbannführer Peiper and the Hauptsturmführer called out to me several times with these words: 'Go, quickly, quickly, we have no time to lose.'*

*I do not want to charge my officers unjustly and I therefore declare under oath that these words 'go, quickly, quickly!' did not mean precisely that I had to hurry to shoot this prisoner or that I had to shoot him quickly, that is not the case. Those words 'go, quickly' meant this: one way or another try to put an end to this affair and do as you please.*

*On the other hand, however, even if I had not received an order to shoot this man, the two officers in my car knew perfectly well that I was going to shoot him and as they said nothing to the contrary, I had to assume that I was doing the right thing. Both Obersturmbannführer Peiper and Hauptsturmführer Diefenthal watched everything. I saw them both looking out of the car. On top of that they saw me as I approached the car with the prisoner and they heard me ask for my machine gun. They saw that this machine gun was being passed to me. An SS officer must have realised what all this meant, even if the whole mass of men present hadn't shouted 'shoot him'.*

*I am quite tall and could see inside the car while standing outside beside it. When I asked for my machine gun, I saw Peiper sitting on the seat opposite me, on the blankets I had prepared for him. There's no doubt about it: Diefenthal and Peiper also knew what I was going to do, but they weren't interested.*

*After I'd received the machine gun, I led the prisoner to the side of the road. My comrades kept shouting at me to 'shoot him'. The forest started immediately beside the road. When I got to about 3 metres from the edge of the forest and the prisoner was walking about 3 paces in front of me, I aimed at his head. I fired a salvo into the head of the man in question (ten to fifteen shots).*

*The American collapsed immediately, dead. I took another quick look at the corpse to see if the prisoner was really dead. There was a huge hole in his head and blood was pouring out. Clearly all my shots had been effective. When I shot the American, he was walking normally, at a man's pace. I confess that in the Zuffenhausen prison camp, I asked Rinek – just in case this murder was discovered – to declare and pretend that this prisoner had been shot during an escape attempt. I also admit now that this American didn't try to escape. Rinek then grabbed the watch of the American who had been shot and, immediately after the shots were fired, he shouted, beaming with joy: 'At least I've got a watch now'. The American had been shot about 10 metres from my car. When I got back to the car, Diefenthal asked me what was in the jeep. I told him 'mines', at which point he shouted at me, saying, 'Get rid of that jeep after all.' He said nothing to me about the murder.*[21]

The practice of shooting prisoners during an operation to avoid wasting time was not unique to the German army or the Waffen-SS. Suffice it to say that on the night of 6 June 1944, the US airborne had received orders to act in a similar way and to shoot prisoners. War sometimes has compelling reasons for ignoring its own laws. The fact that both sides sometimes had to order such exactions in no way excuses the acts tacitly authorised by Peiper. This reality highlights the fact that war remains, and will remain, a lawless zone where anything goes as long as you are not caught, or you are on the losing side.

However, the Waffen-SS was an exception, as this account clearly shows, insofar as behaviour was an unwritten rule applicable almost everywhere. We explained the origins of this mentality at length in the first volume, and will not return to it here. We have deliberately added the adverb 'almost', because in La Gleize's cauldron, the majority of prisoners were treated relatively well. We put forward a hypothesis borrowed from logic to explain this difference in treatment. Peiper knew he was surrounded, and treating his prisoners humanely meant that his wounded, whom they would inevitably have to leave behind, had a chance of escaping. Moreover, as long as he had not rejoined his lines, Peiper would fear American vengeance if he were caught. Peiper's behaviour at La Gleize, which can be described as relatively correct, should not obscure the fact that he played a key role in the behaviour of the social group he led.

## A Sympathetic Debriefing

It was not until almost twenty-four hours after Peiper had returned to his lines that a report from Heeresgruppe B stated that his Kampfgruppe had fought its way back and that the fighting was still going on. The information was given in such a way that the recipient of the message had no idea all his equipment had been lost and that more than two thirds of his men were no longer answering the roll call. Of the 3,000 men involved, only 800 managed to reach the German lines. The entire hierarchy, from the divisional level right up to the army group, deliberately concealed the scale of the failure suffered by 6. Panzer-Armee.

On 27 December, Preiss met Peiper, who gave him a fairly accurate report of the facts. Peiper was not accused of any wrongdoing and Preiss' account of the affair was rather sympathetic towards the SS-Obersturmbannführer, and later provided certain details of his return to the lines:

> *Early in the morning of 25 December 1944, the group reached the river Salm and its commander decided to attempt a breakthrough. As there was no bridge at this point, the Salm had to be crossed partly by fording and partly by swimming. On the east bank of the river, the terrain overhung the stream for around 290 metres. Only when our troops were well advanced did the enemy wake up and open up with heavy machine-gun fire on our troops; SS-Obersturmbannführer Peiper was wounded early on. Some of his men had to support him, but he retained command and managed to get his men through; by 08:00 all were safe in their own lines. Lieutenant Colonel Peiper had made the breakthrough with about 800 men and managed to get out with 770. The group had been fighting under the most difficult conditions for an unbroken period of a week since 17 December. The company was so exhausted that it was only by the use of force that the men could be prevented from falling asleep on the march.*
>
> *In terms of heavy weapons, the KG lost thirty-five tanks, two batteries and around sixty SPWs,*[22] *of which, towards the end, only three tanks, two guns and a few SPWs were usable. In addition, they had lost a considerable number of wheeled vehicles and miscellaneous equipment.*[23]

Peiper's wound was in fact a sprain. Coming from an SS cavalry unit, he had continued to wear riding boots in combat. A choice that posed no problem in mechanised combat, but for a trek through the woods and a ford across a river with slippery stones, wearing such boots is certainly an ordeal for the feet.[24]

Preiss' benevolence towards Peiper was in line with German military tradition since the adoption of Auftragstaktiks, which gave mission-oriented instructions while leaving a great deal to the autonomy of the command in the field and implying a delegation of power. An officer was never reproached for being defeated as long as he had done everything possible to win. For a commander to do otherwise had the effect of discouraging initiative and risk-taking in the eyes of the German officer corps. This was a big difference from what happens today in our Western armies, where every death in the field comes at a political cost to the powers that be. An officer who is unfortunate enough to suffer casualties in an operation sees his career compromised, even if he is not accused of any wrongdoing and is what Michel Goya calls the 'zero-defect phenomenon':

Tiger 104 was used as a training target by paratroopers from 504th PIR resting at Remouchamps. (*Nara*)

a single mistake is now enough to ruin an American officer's career, which does not encourage initiative.[25] In the eyes of modern field officers, such a system kills initiative, the fuel of tactics.[26]

## Peiper's Self-Criticism

Peiper, himself would remain bitter long after the conflict had ended, and his loss of confidence in his superiors was evident in his interrogation:

*It very quickly became apparent that the real aim of the Ardennes counter-offensive was not to reach Antwerp, but simply to disrupt American preparations and delay the winter offensive by two months. This should have been made clear by the High Command before the fighting began. There are certain things I would have liked to have done differently:*

- *a) Introduce a faster refuelling system.*
- *b) No artillery preparation and keep the horse-drawn batteries out of the way.*
- *c) Attack with combat teams and tanks at the same time as infantry. An unsupported infantry attack wastes too much time.*
- *d) Reduce the length of each column: instead of two or three, make it twenty, so it is easier to concentrate on the weak points.*
- *e) Use more infantry on tanks.*
- *f) Take pontoon boat units with each armoured formation.*
- *g) Make each combat team self-sufficient.*
- *h) Put a general on every street corner to regulate traffic.*[27]

## Epilogue

Judged unable to fight, Joachim Peiper was rested as Sturmbannführer Werner Potache took over the reins of the 1. SS-Panzer Regiment and left to fight in the Bastogne sector from 28 December to 12 February 1945.

For his actions during the Battle of the Bulge, Peiper added the swords to his Knight's Cross of the Iron Cross and oak leaves, making him the 119th recipient of this distinction. The notification of the decoration dates from 16 February 1945 and is translated as follows:

*Berlin, 16 February 1945*

*The Führer awarded the Oak Leaf Swords to SS- Obersturmbannführer Joachim Peiper, Commander of the Panzer Regiment of the SS-Pz-Div 'Leibstandarte SS Adolf Hitler'. During the German winter offensive in the west, Peiper commanded the elements of the offensive force that penetrated furthest west. When the unit was surrounded by three enemy divisions, it held these powerful forces in check for six days, then exfiltrated from the encirclement at night, allowing a strong enemy force to be held back and enabling a unit employed further south to advance virtually without a fight.*

As soon as he had recovered, Peiper rejoined his unit in mid-February. On 6 March, 1. SS-Panzer Regiment went back on the offensive with 6. SS-Panzer-Armee,[28] which was still commanded by Sepp Dietrich. The fighting continued until 14 March 1945, when Hitler's exhausted armies could no longer hold their own against the Russian ogre. From then on, the entire German army traded ground for time. After the fighting at Lake Balaton, they retreated to Hungary until the beginning of April 1945.

On 23 March 1945, Joachim Peiper lost an old comrade, Sturmbannführer Werner Poetschke, who was seriously wounded by mortar fire. Peiper moved heaven and earth to evacuate his comrade by plane, but without success. The battalion surgeon, Hauptsturmführer Rudolf Neumayer, took him back to the nearest main dressing station. Poetschke had a double fracture in his leg and categorically refused amputation. The surgeon was adamant that Poetschke could be saved, and Dr Neumayer wrote:

*He was unable to bear the idea of an amputation. He would have done what he had threatened again and again: he said, 'If I can no longer ride in a tank, then life no longer has any meaning for me. I'd rather shoot myself in the head.' He couldn't have survived the unhappy conclusion to this war. He had assured me on several occasions that he would never be in captivity alive. I'm sure he meant it, because he always did what he said he would do.* [29]

On 24 March 1945, Werner Poetschke fell asleep forever. For the survivors, the fight went on, and from 1 April to 8 May, the remnants of SS-Panzer Regiment 1 fought hand-to-hand against the Soviet forces in Austria, before returning to Germany for the surrender.

After the capitulation, Peiper, accompanied by his adjutant, fled and tried to return to his marital home. His wife, Sigi Peiper, had left Berlin under the bombardments to follow the Himmler family to Rottach, a charming town on the shores of Lake Tergensee in Bavaria. Peiper was captured at the end of May 1945 by an American patrol some 30 kilometres from his family and sent to the Nuremberg-Langwasser prison camp. Convicted and prosecuted for war crimes following the investigation into the Malmedy-Baugnez massacre, he ended up in Zuffenhausen prison before being transferred to Schwäbisch Hall civil prison.

His trial, and those of his companions, was held in the former Dachau concentration camp, and lasted from 16 May to 16 July 1946. At the end of the proceedings, Peiper heard the sentence handed down. It was pithy, just these few words: '*Joachim Peiper, the Court, in camera, with at least two thirds of the members present at the time of the vote, has given its approval. It sentences you to death by hanging.*'

The death sentence was set for 20 May 1948. His lawyer lodged an appeal, which was accepted a few hours before the deadline, and so the death sentence was converted to life imprisonment. Peiper spent 1,840 days of anguish in the shadow of the gallows. On 22 December 1956, he was finally released. He was soon back in society, but the powerful IG Metal union pursued him and made life difficult for him. After moving to France, on the night of 13 to 14 July 1976 he was the victim of a raid by former resistance fighters and killed. A charred body was found on the spot, but it was never identified with certainty. At the time, DNA identification did not exist, and only dental prints could be used to authenticate corpses in poor condition. The Munich Forensic Institute was stunned to discover that the head of the body was missing when the coffin was opened. The question remains unanswered: did Herr Peiper choose another life at the age of 61?[30]

# The Violence of a Fiasco

## Equipment Lost by KG Peiper in the Stoumont – La Gleize Pocket

A few days after the fighting, a survey of the equipment abandoned by KG Peiper was carried out. However, during our study we noted a few anomalies, which were due to the rapid removal of maintenance units by the Americans and not to obvious errors. We have therefore drawn up an assessment of these losses using the new information available to us.

These two Panthers were photographed in La Gleize by the US Air Force to assess their impact on the battle. (*Nara*)

The tank meadow at La Gleize photographed after the fighting. The view gives an idea of the scale of the losses suffered by Peiper, particularly its forty-seven SPW tanks, which were captured intact and dynamited by US engineers to prevent them falling back into German hands. This precaution underlines the extent to which, on 24 December 1944, the front had still not been stabilised. (*La Gleize Museum*)

<u>At Neufmoulin Les Forges, Bridge Over the Lienne:</u>

- 3 SPWs including 1 Sd.Kfz. 251/9 Ausf D 'Stummel' intact and reused in the Cheneux attack.

<u>Cheneux</u>

- 4 SPWs and at least 14 anti-aircraft guns of various types.[1] Corporal Graves also points out that the paratroopers recovered 4 undamaged Flak Wagons. Photographic evidence confirm this.
- 1 Panther (Panzer V)
- 2 x 75-mm Pak 40 cannons
- 1 barrel l. FH 105mm
- 1 Maultier
- 1 US-origin ambulance
- 1 motorbike
- 1 Küblewagen
- 2 tracked motorbikes (Kettenkraftrad)

<u>Stoumont Station</u>

- 3 Panthers (215, 232, 211), but missing from this list are Panthers 234 and 231
- 3 SPWs
- 1 French-made ambulance truck

<u>Stoumont</u>

- 2 Panthers (Panther V)
- 3 SPWs
- 1 Flak Panzer IV (Wirbelwind)
- 2 VW Schwimmwagen
- 2 Pak 40 75-mm barrels

<u>La Gleize</u>

- 47 SPWs
- 7 Panzer IVs
- 13 Panthers (Panzer V)
- 6 Tiger IIs
- 6 150mm 'Grille' howitzers
- 3 Panzer spähwagen (Puma)
- 1 Zugmaschine, Flak Wagon, 12 tonnes
- 2 Zugmaschine, Flak Wagon, 3 tonnes
- 4 Russian 120-mm mortars
- 1 Flak Panzer IVs (Wirbelwind)
- 1 Steyr 1500 truck
- 1 VW Schwimmwagen

Panther 124 lost its turret as a result of American sabotage. (*La Gleize Museum*)

- 1 tracked motorbike (Kettenkrad)
- 1 BMW motorbike
- 3 Steyr 1500 A/01 cars
- 1 Pak 40 75-mm barrel
- 1 Flak gun (small static calibre)
- 1 US jeep used by the Germans
- 1 Dodge
- 1 bridge used by the Germans
- 1 Dodge Croix Rouge
- 1 unidentified truck

Only twenty-one Panthers, seven Panzer IVs and six Tiger IIs that left for the assault on 16 December followed the head of 1. SS-Panzer Division 'Leibstandarte Adolf Hitler' beyond Trois-Ponts. They took part in the fighting of KG Peiper and were lost, destroyed, or ran out of fuel or mechanics.

The equipment and manpower situation of 1. SS-Panzer Division as of 1 December showed 633 officers, 4,128 non-commissioned officers, 12,820 troops and 967 Hiwi.[2] The total number of men in the division was 18,548, with a surplus of 2,451 over the normal strength. At that date, the division had 33 Panzer IVs out of the 109 planned and 34 Panthers (Panzer Vs) out of the 79 planned in the theoretical manning table.

These figures do not include attached units such as schwere SS-Panzer Abteilung 501, parachutists and the Luftwaffe anti-aircraft battalion.[3]

The estimated losses of the Leibstandarte for the period from 16 to 25 December 1944 were: 380 killed, 1,150 wounded and 340 missing, dead or prisoners.[4] This means a total of 1,870 men put out of action for the 4 KGs, those of Peiper, Sandig, Hansen and Knittel. This document also shows the total absence of horses.

The breakdown of staff is as follows:[5]

Infantry: 80.4
Armoured vehicles: 3.5
Artillery: 5.6
Pioneers: 3.6
Medical: 2.9
Maintenance: 1.3
Logistics: 1.3
Miscellaneous: 1.4

During the Battle of the Bulge, an American army estimate calculated that 6. Panzer-Armee consumed 255 tonnes of artillery shells and 210 tonnes of shells for tanks and anti-tanks every day.[6] The overall consumption of the Panzer Division Leibstandarte is estimated at 4,800 litres of fuel to cover just 1 kilometre.[7]

## Deploying the Second Line of Defence

In his memoirs, General Gavin talks about an administrative transfer to the front when his unit was sent to the Ardennes. The operation was particularly perilous; in the event of an unfortunate encounter, his men crammed into lorries would not have been able to defend themselves. Despite the incredible combination of circumstances, we cannot simply say that the Americans were lucky. Instead, it was the flexibility of their organisation that helped them out of the predicament. The responsiveness of 291st ECB in particular saved the day in this sector. On the evening of 17 December, a handful of sappers had already delayed the assault on Stavelot in one night. Securing Trois-Ponts and destroying the bridge over the Lienne at Neufmoulin allowed the 82nd Airborne Division to deploy smoothly. The measures taken by Gavin, perfectly adapted to the situation and using the terrain to the full, completed the securing of the second line of defence.

The Germans also disregarded all caution to favour their operational tempo and capture their objective before the Americans recovered from their surprise, but they were beaten at their own game. As the US Army had acquired excellent operational responsiveness, it was able to win the race against time that characterised the opening of the Battle of the Bulge. For more detail on this aspect of the battle, please see the previous volume, *The Breakthrough of Kampfgruppe Peiper in the Battle of the Bulge.*

## Pure Violence

What is perplexing about working with primary sources, as we have done, is the extreme violence of the confrontations over such a long period. Over and above the simplistic idea usually put forward of the fanaticism of the SS, we believe that there were many reasons for this rise to extremes.

The units on both sides fighting in the Stavelot – La Gleize sector were veteran formations, some of which could even be described as elite divisions. Whether SS or American paratroopers, the men fighting in this part of the front were hardened by the intense experience of previous battles. They knew that there was only one way to win: be more lethal, more offensive, more enduring and more cunning than your opponent. '*In the warrior's code / There's no surrender / Though his body says stop / His spirit cries, never*' sang the group Survivor in Burning Heart. Men of war, sometimes in spite of themselves, did not need a song to make them feel that way. We have described enough poignant scenes in this book to convince us of that.

The narrow valleys and thick vegetation of the Ardennes meant that there was little compartmentalisation of the terrain. These topographical factors were further exacerbated by the weather conditions at the time of the fighting, where thick, long-lasting fog meant engagement distances were reduced, sometimes to extremes. To make progress, there was only one possible solution: to go into contact with fire support reduced to its simplest expression, the use of long-range fire being impossible. This was the reality at Cheneux, at Stoumont, with the aggravating effect of the fighting for the Saint-Édouard Sanatorium, which meant hand-to-hand combat from room to room, and in the Stavelot pocket. In this sector of the Ardennes, more than anywhere else on the front, close combat was imposed on the enemy. It was the worst expression of the violence of war. The combat experience was much harsher here than in the armoured rush of the previous days; the period we have described is that of melee combat in the medieval sense of the term. Indeed, Cheneux and the final phase of Agincourt share many psychological similarities.

Veteran units are also formations with strong internal cohesion in which the survival of your brothers in arms is the guarantee of your own survival. This is a reality specific to primary groups they have experienced in other battles. This strong cohesion tends to prolong the moment of final decision, increasing the intensity and duration of combat.

Finally, for the SS, there was the additional explanation of their experience on the Eastern Front, where they faced a particularly tough opponent who was not in the habit of cutting corners. The Leibstandarte's genes were indelibly imprinted with the reality of combat, further enhancing the ferocity of its fighters.

So, we see in the circumstances of the battlefield and the intrinsic characteristics of the units fighting there an explanation for the height of the violence in the Battle of the Bulge.

## The Key Point of the Offensive

In the historiography of the Battle of the Bulge, the influence of Bastogne casts an enormous shadows over the other sectors of the front. The American national novel would have us believe that the battle was won in Bastogne, but nothing could be further from the truth!

Compared with what was happening at the same time in 6. Panzer-Armee's sector, it should be remembered that Bastogne was of secondary importance. In the German plans, Dietrich's army was to break through as far as Antwerp, spearheaded by I SS Pz-Korps. Its failure to do so both at Stavelot and Krinkelt-Rocherath is what caused the offensive to stall.

In December 1944, the senior American officers made no mistakes. Bastogne was a stumbling block while victory was at stake in the northern sector of the front. The stakes were so high against 6. Panzer-Armee that it was imperative to defeat it as quickly as possible, an imposition that made the fighting even more intense. The tactical realities of the confrontation were further amplified by operational requirements. The tip of the spearhead of the Third Reich had to be amputated. The Reich had to be amputated. KG Peiper had to be put out of action, whatever the cost.

# Appendices

## Appendix 1

| Equivalent Ranks | | |
|---|---|---|
| **Waffen-SS** | **British Army** | **US Army** |
| *Reichsführer SS* | *Field Marshal* | *General of the Army* |
| *Oberst-Gruppenführer* | *General* | *General* |
| *Obergruppenführer* | *Lieutenant General* | *Lieutenant General* |
| *General* | | |
| *Gruppenführer* | *Major General* | *Major General* |
| *Brigadeführer* | *Brigadier* | *Brigadier General* |
| *Oberführer* | *Colonel (Senior)* | *Colonel (Senior)* |
| *Standartenführer* | *Colonel* | *Colonel* |
| *Obersturmbannführer* | *Lieutenant Colonel* | *Lieutenant Colonel* |
| *Sturmbannführer* | *Major* | *Major* |
| *Hauptsturmführer* | *Captain* | *Captain* |
| *Obersturmführer* | *Lieutenant* | *First Lieutenant* |
| *Untersturmführer* | *Second Lieutenant* | *Second Lieutenant* |
| *Sturmscharführer* | *Regimental Sergeant Major* | *Sergeant Major* |
| *Stabsscharführer* | *Sergeant Major* | |
| *Hauptscharführer* | *Sergeant Major* | *Master Sergeant* |
| *Oberscharführer* | *Staff Sergeant* | *Technical Sergeant* |
| *Scharführer* | *Sergeant* | *Staff Sergeant* |
| *Unterscharführer* | *Corporal* | *Sergeant* |
| *Rottenführer (Squad Leader)* | *Lance Corporal* | *Corporal* |
| *Sturmmann (Storm Troopen)* | *Senior Private* | *Private First Class* |
| *Oberschütze* | | *Senior Private* |
| *Schütze* | *Private* | *Private* |

# Appendix 2: KG Peiper Order of Battle

| | | |
|---|---|---|
| ***Kampfgruppe Peiper*** | *Obersturmbannführer* | *Joachim Peiper* |
| *1. SS-Panzer Regiment* | *Obersturmbannführer* | *Joachim Peiper* |
| *Deputy* | *Hauptsturmführer* | *Hans Gruhle* |
| *Stabs Kompanie* | *Obersturmführer* | *Rudi Mäule* |
| *Surgeon* | *Obersturmführer* | *Dr Kurt Sickel* |
| ***Panzer Abteilung*** | *Sturmbannführer* | *Werner Poetschke* |
| *Deputy* | *Untersturmführer* | *Arndt Fischer, (killed on 17 December)* |
| | *Untersturmführer* | *Kurt Kammt, (killed on 18 December)* |
| | *Untersturmführer* | *Rolf Reiser* |
| ***Versorgung Kompanie*** | *Hauptsturmführer* | *Ernst Otto* |
| *(Logistics)* | | |
| ***Chirug*** | *Hauptsturmführer* | *Dr Rudolf Neumayer* |
| *Stabs Kompanie* | *Untersturmführer* | *Rolf Buchheim* |
| ***Aufklärung*** | *Hauptsturmführer* | *Paul Ochmann* |
| ***1. Kompanie (Panther)*** | ***Obersturmführer*** | ***Karl Kremser*** |
| 1. Zug | *Untersturmführer* | *Hans Hennecke* |
| 2. Zug | *Untersturmführer* | *Konrad Heubeck* |
| 3. Zug | *Obersturmführer* | *Adolf Thomas* |
| ***2. Kompanie (Panther)*** | *Hauptsturmführer* | *Friedrich Christ* |
| 1. Zug | *Untersturmführer* | *Hubert Kauffmann* |
| 2. Zug | *Hauptscharführer* | *Heinz Knappich* |
| 3. Zug | *Untersturmführer* | *Helmuth Koch* |
| ***6. Kompanie (Panzer IV)*** | *Obersturmführer* | *Benoni Junker* |
| 1. Zug | *Untersturmführer* | *Hans Steininger* |
| 2. Zug | *Untersturmführer* | *Karl-Heinz Asmussen* |
| 3. Zug | *Hauptscharführer* | *August Tonk* |
| ***7. Kompanie (Panzer IV)*** | *Hauptsturmführer* | *Oskar Klingelhoöfer* |
| 1. Zug | *Untersturmführer* | *Heinz Rehagel* |
| 2. Zug | *Untersturmführer* | *Erich Münkemer* |
| 3. Zug | *Obersturmführer* | *Hans Siptrott* |
| ***9. Kompanie (Pioniere)*** | ***Obersturmführer*** | *Erich Rumpf* |
| 1. Zug | *Untersturmführer* | *Günther Hering* |
| 2. Zug | *Untersturmführer* | *Paul Lenk* |
| 3. Zug | *Obersturmführer* | *Werner Kühn* |
| ***10. Flak Kompanie*** | *Obersturmführer* | *Karl-Heinz Vögler* |
| ***III (Gep) Panzergrenadier*** | *Hauptsturmführer* | *Josef Diefenthal* |

| *(Regiment 2)* | | |
|---|---|---|
| *Deputy* | *Untersturmführer* | *Karl Flacke* |
| *Stabs Kompanie* | *Obersturmführer* | *Wolfgang* |
| *Chirug* | *Obersturmführer* | Dr *Willi Dittmann* |
| *9. (Gep) Kompanie* | *Obersturmführer* | *Georg Preuss* |
| 1. Zug | *Oberscharführer* | *Rudi Knobloch* |
| 2. Zug | ? | ? |
| 3. Zug | *Oberscharführer* | *Eduard Maron* |
| *4. Schwere Zug* | *Oberscharführer* | *Rudi Rayer* |
| *12. (Gep) Kompanie* | *Hauptscharführer* | *Jochen Thiele* |
| 1. Zug | *Oberscharführer* | *Paul Pfalzer* |
| 2. Zug | *Unterscharführer* | *Helmut Feldvoss* |
| 3. Zug | *Unterscharführer* | *Toni Motzheim* |
| *13. Kompanie* | *Obersturmführer* | *Koch Gun* |
| 1. Zug | *Oberscharführer* | *Alfred Kleinwächter* |
| 2. Zug | ? | ? |
| 3. Zug | ? | ? |
| 3. Kompanie | | |
| ***Panzerpioniere Battalion 1*** | *Obersturmführer* | *Franz Sievers* |
| 1. Zug | *Untersturmführer* | *August Seitz* |
| 2. Zug | *Oberscharführer* | *Max Beutner* |
| 3. Zug | *Untersturmführer* | *Rudolf Kämpfe* |
| 4. Zug | *Oberscharführer* | *? Kern* |
| ***84. Schwere Flak*** | *Major* | *Von Sacken* |
| ***Abteilung (Luftwaffe)*** | | |
| ***Schwere SS Panzer*** | *Sturmbannführer* | *Heinz von Westernhagen* |
| ***Unit 501 (Tiger II)*** | | |
| *Deputy* | *Untersturmführer* | *Eduard Kalinowsky* |
| *Stabs Kompanie* | *Obersturmführer* | *Paul Vogt* |
| **1. Kompanie *(Tiger II)*** | *Obersturmführer* | *Jürgen Wessels* |
| 1. Zug | *Untersturmführer* | *Rolf Henniges* |
| 2. Zug | *Untersturmführer* | *Heinz Buchner* |
| 3. Zug | *Obersturmführer* | *(Capt) Jürgen Brandt* |
| **2. Kompanie *(Tiger II)*** | *Hauptsturmführer* | *Rolf Möbius* |
| 1. Zug | *Obersturmführer* | *Wilhelm Dollinger* |
| 2. Zug | *Untersturmführer* | *Georg Hantusch* |
| 3. Zug | *Untersturmführer* | *Walter Hahn* |
| **3. Kompanie *(Tiger II)*** | *Hauptsturmführer* | *Heinz Birnschein* |
| 1. Zug | *Untersturmführer* | *Thomas Amselgruber* |
| 2. Zug | *Untersturmführer* | *Winfried Lukasius* |
| 3. Zug | *Hauptscharführer* | *Rolf von Westernhagen* |

| *Initial organisation chart of Kamfgruppe Knittel* | | |
|---|---|---|
| ***Kampfgruppe Knittel*** | *Sturmbannführer* | *Gustav Knittel* |
| ***Stabs Kompanie*** | *Obersturmführer* | *Heinrich Goltz* |
| ***Nachrichten Zug*** | *Oberscharführer* | *Fritz Wiese* |
| *(Transmissions)* | | |
| ***Fahrrad Zug*** | *Untersturmführer* | *Erich Kolaschny* |
| *(Cycling section)* | | |
| *Pionier Zug* | *Untersturmführer* | *Heinrich Dröge* |
| ***Kradschützen Zug*** | *Oberscharführer* | *Théo Gernt* |
| *(Pathfinders)* | | |
| ***1. Kompanie*** | *Untersturmführer* | *? Rentsch* |
| *This company remained in Germany due to a lack of transport* | | |
| ***2. (Gep) Kompanie*** | *Obersturmführer* | *Manfred Coblenz* |
| 1. Zug | *Untersturmführer* | *Wihlem Hilbert* |
| 2. Zug | *Untersturmführer* | *Wilhem Farny* |
| 3. Zug | *Untersturmführer* | *Ludwig Siebert* |
| *4. Schwere Zug* | *Oberscharführer* | *Horst Jacob* |
| ***3. Kompanie*** | *Obersturmführer* | *Hans Leidreiter* |
| 1. Zug | *Untersturmführer* | *Aldolf Hachberger* |
| 2. Zug | *Untersturmführer* | *? Gleseke* |
| 3. Zug | *(Section transferred to Stabs Kompanie)* | |
| 4. *Schwere Zug* | ? | ? |
| *(Equipped with 5 or 6 Panzer Spähwagen)* | | |
| ***4. Schwere Kompanie*** | *Obersturmführer* | *Heinz Wagner* |
| *Kanonen Zug* | *Untersturmführer* | *Horst Kremser* |
| *(Sd.kfz. 251/9 Stummel)* | | |
| *Panzerjäger Zug (Pak 40)* | *Untersturmführer* | *Rolf Telle* |
| *Scwherre IG Zug* | *Untersturmführer* | *Adam Grader* |
| *(15cm SiG33 artillery)* | | |
| *Werfen Granaten Zug* | *Untersturmführer* | *Erich Drenvensted* |
| *(12cm mortar)* | | |
| *Versorgung Kompanie* | *Obersturmführer* | *? Reuss* |
| *(Logistics)* | | |
| *2. Pionier Kompanie* | ? | ? |
| *(SS-Panzer Pionier Battalion 1)* | | |
| *SS-Panzer Battery* | *Obersturmführer* | *Fritz Butschek* |
| *Atillerie Regiment 1* | | |
| *(6 towed 10.5cm howitzers)* | | |

# Notes

**Introdution**

1. *Wacht am Rhein* was the code name for the German offensive in the Ardennes.

**Chapter 1**

1. The Stoumont bridge would have been of no help as it was made of wood and unable to support the weight of the Panthers.
2. This was Knittel's unit, which became infamous for its massacres of civilians in the region, including women and young children.
3. Washington, Nara, Ethint 10, interrogation of Peiper, 7/9/1945.
4. Fontaine S., *Trois-Ponts, décembre 1944, quand les ponts volaient en éclats*, Trois-Ponts, 1992, pp.5–6.
5. Washington, Nara, AAR 743rd Tank Battalion Nov-Dec 1944, p.102.
6. Washington, Nara, 30th Infantry Division After Battle Report, Headquarters 30th Infantry Division, G-3 Section, Period 1–31 December 1944, No date of entry, p.9.
7. Washington, Nara, Interview with Lt. Col. Samuel McDowell, CO of 3rd Battalion, 117th Infantry, and Lt. Andrew Allen Executive Officer of K Company, 117th Infantry, held at 3rd Battalion CP in Roanne on 2 January 1945.
8. Cooke D., Wayne E., *Kampfgruppe Peiper: The Race for the Meuse*, Barnsley, 2005. p.177.
9. Cooke D., Wayne E., op. cit., p.177.
10. Ibid., p.171.
11. See *Stavelot – La Gleize, Le destin des Tiger de Peiper* by the same authors, p.129.
12. Ibid., p.187.
13. Staff company.
14. Brussels, Ministère de la Justice, Archives des Procureurs Généraux, Documents relating to the trial of the Stavelot massacres, Goltz et al., Translation of Manfred Coblenz's written statement of 15 April 1946.
15. Only parachutist Max Zagler has been identified to date. Brussels, Archives des Procureurs Généraux Trial of Stavelot Goltz and others.
16. Brussels, Ministry of Justice, Archives des Procureurs Généraux, Documents relating to the trial of the Stavelot massacres, Goltz et al., Exhibit III/132/1 & 132/2, Witness under oath Ernst Mahl.
17. Transmission section.
18. Cycling section.
19. Brussels, Ministry of Justice, Archives des Procureurs Généraux, Documents relating to the trial of the Stavelot massacres, Goltz et al: List of victims.
20. By studying the events on the ground, the farm is located at 2 Chemin des Haies in Renardmont, Stavelot. A stele commemorates the martyrdom endured by civilians during the winter offensive.
21. Brussels, Ministère de la justice, Archives des Procureurs Généraux, Documents relating to the trial of the Stavelot massacres, Goltz et al., Vol. 10, p.455–456.
22. Testimony of Charles Corbin, https://www.3ad.com, Accessed on 3 October 2023.
23. See *Stavelot – La Gleize, Le destin des Tiger de Peiper*, pp.121–2.
24. By studying the events on the ground, the farm is located at 15 Chemin du Hecheray in Renardmont Ville de Stavelot.

25. Brussels, Ministère de la Justice, Archives des Procureurs Généraux, Documents relating to the trial of the Stavelot massacres, Goltz et al., Translation of Manfred Coblenz's written statement of 15 April 1946.
26. Washington, Nara, Interview held at the CP in Stavelot of 1st Battalion, 117th Infantry, on 3 January, Present were Lt. Col. Robert Frankland, CO; Capt. Clifford Frieman, S-1; Lt. David W. Morgan, S-2; Capt. David K. Easlick, S-3; Capt. John Kent, CO of A Company; Capt. Morris Stoeffer, CO of C Company; Capt. Stanley W. Cooper, CO of A Company.
27. Brussels, Ministry of Justice, Archives des Procureurs Généraux, Documents relating to the trial of the Stavelot massacres, Goltz et al: List of victims.
28. Washington, Library of Congress, Dachau-Trial Vol. 5, pp.1076–81.
29. See *Stavelot – La Gleize, Le destin des Tiger de Peiper*, p.79.

**Chapter 2**

1. Washington, Nara, AAR 30th ID G2, report message n° 90.
2. Interview with Christian Dujardin by Ms Harquemanne on 30 September 2017.
3. Trad: Saint Édouard fortress.
4. Gregoire, G., *Les Panzer de Peiper face à l'US Army*, Stavelot, 1986, p.29.
5. Tiemann, R., *The Leibstandarte,* Vol. IV/2, Winnipeg, 1998, p.87.
6. Gabriel, R., *75 …ans après : La Gleize and Stoumont*, La Gleize, 2020, pp.201–203.
7. Washington, Library of Congress, Atrocity Trial Testimony, Joachim Peiper, p.7.
8. See *Stavelot - La Gleize, Le destin des Tiger de Peiper*, pp.136–7.
9. Ibid.
10. Fontaine. S., *Stoumont Cheneux La Gleize. Stavelot,* No place, 1995, p.21.
11. Agte, P., *Jochen Peiper Commandeur du Panzerregiment de la Leibstandarte*, Paris, 2021, p.397.
12. Washington, Nara, After Action Report of 33rd Armed Regiment for the month of December 1944.
13. Website: http://www.oldhickory30th.com, Accessed on 29 September 2023.
14. Evocation of the Battle of Trois-Ponts by Vandervoort, from the author's personal collection.
15. Washington, Nara, AAR 743rd Tank Battalion.
16. Washington Nara, Interview held at the CP in Stavelot of 1st Battalion, 117th Infantry, on 3 January and on 9 January at the CP near Spa of 823rd TD Battalion.
17. Wijers, J., *Die Ardennen-Offensive: Die Brücken von Stavelot und Trois Ponts Augenzeugen berichten, Zusammengestellt*, p.186. Between the Tiger II positions and the road taken by Lovelady's tanks is a distance of 1,500m, on a clear day the whole US column would have been destroyed without any problem by the powerful 88-mm guns of the German tanks.
18. The house, abandoned by its inhabitants before the arrival of German troops, was completely destroyed by fire and was never rebuilt. The remains of the building are still visible, although more or less hidden by vegetation.
19. 75-mm anti-tank gun.
20. Washington, Nara, AAR 33rd Armored Regiment, month of December 1944.
21. Roberts,A., *Five Star to Victory*, Birmingham, 1949, Chapter IV.
22. Washington, Nara, Interview held at the CP in Stavelot of 1st Battalion, 117th Infantry, on 3 January.

**Chapter 3**

1. Campana, V., *The Operation of the 2nd Battalion 504th Parachute Infantry Regiment 18 December 1944 - 10 January 1945,* Fort Benning, sd, p.10.
2. Tyler, F., *A Fine Sense of Honor: At War with the Men of the 504th Parachute Infantry from Sicily to the Fall of Germany*, Wroclaw, 2019, p.345.
3. Graves, G., *Le sang et la neige*, sd, sl, pp.5–6.
4. Washington, Library of Congress, *Atrocity Trial Testimony Lt Col Peiper,* Chapter IV, pp.7–8.

5. Bastogne, Bastogne War Museum Documentation Centre, After Action Report HQ_82nd Air Borne. G2 report n° 151, In the field, 22 December 1944, pp.1–2.
6. James Gavin's nickname.
7. LoFaro, G., *The Sword of St. Michael: The 82nd Airborne Division in World War II,* New York, 2007, pp.609–10.
8. Stark, M., *Antitank Platoon in Support of Infantry Regiment,* Georgia, Fort Benning, sd, p.3.
9. Ibid., p.13.
10. Carter, R., *Cheneux*, in C.A.M., 1987, pp.16–17.
11. Campana, V., *The Operation of the 504th Parachute Infantry (82nd A B) In the German Counter-Offensive 18 December 1944 - 10 January 1945*, Fort Benning, sd, pp.10–11.
12. All the American reports place this action in Habiemont, although the exact address of the locality is Neufmoulin.
13. German for cigarette butt.
14. MacDonald, C., *Noël, la bataille d'Ardenne,* Brussels, 1989, p.411.
15. The testimonial erroneously specified a 75mm.
16. Stark M., *Antitank Platoon in Support of Infantry Regiment,* Georgia, Fort Benning, undated, pp.14–15.
17. The description of the locations of the German troops is based on a map drawn by paratroopers from 504th PIR and a field study.
18. Stark, M., op. cit., p.15.
19. United States Army, *82nd Airborne Division Artillery*, p.553.
20. Nordyke, P., *More Than Courage: The Combat History of 504th Parachute Infantry Regiment in World War II*, Minneapolis, 2008, p.309.
21. Gavin, J., op. cit., p.223.
22. Washington, Nara, AAR *703rd Tank Destroyer Battalion*, December entry, p.2.
23. Fort Leavenworth, Ike Skelton Library, 504th Parachute Infantry Regiment, unit S3 Journal, p.438.
24. Nordyke, P., op. cit., p.312.
25. Nickname for V1 flying bombs.
26. Graves, G., *Le sang et la neige*, No date, No place, pp.14–15.
27. In US comic strips, 'Knobby' is the trainer of Joe Palooka, a champion boxer.
28. Tyler, F., op. cit., p.346.
29. As is often the case in the region, the ground floor was level with the road, while the cellar gave access down to the orchard. This was where the barracks were located.
30. Gabriel, R., *75ans après de Trois-Ponts à Stoumont,* La Gleize, 2021, p.153.
31. Nordyke, P., op. cit., p.313.
32. Tyler, F., op. cit., p.347.
33. Fort Leavenworth, Ike Skelton Library, AAR 504th Parachute Infantry Regiment, unit S3 Journal, p.439.
34. Carter, R., *Cheneux*, in Périodique C.A.M., n° 1, 1987, pp.18–19.
35. Website: https://www.tracesofwar.com, Narrative of action of the 1st Battalion, 504th Parachute Infantry at Cheneux, Belgium, Accessed 4 August 2023.
36. Carter, R., *Cheneux*, in Périodique C.A.M., n° 1, 1987, pp.20–2.
37. Website: https://www.tracesofwar.com, Narrative of action of the first Battalion, 504th Parachute Infantry at Cheneux, Belgium, Accessed 4 August 2023.
38. Abbreviation for Armour Piercing, Discarding Sabot, piercing shell with detachable sabot, the ancestor of the arrow shell.
39. Washington, Nara, AAR 703rd Tank Destroyer Battalion: The Operation with the 82nd Airborne Division, 20 December - 1 January 1945, 31/1/1945, pp.2–3.
40. Lemp J., Hatfield E., *The Field Artillery Journal*, Washington, April 1945, pp.244–6.
41. Carter, R., *Cheneux*, in Périodique C.A.M., n° 1, 1987, pp.15–23.

42. Nordyke P., op. cit., p.321.
43. Ibid., p.314.

**Chapter 4**

1. Website: https://www.tracesofwar.com, Narrative of action of the first Battalion, 504th Parachute Infantry at Cheneux, Belgium, Accessed 4 August 2023.
2. Ottawa, National Archives of Canada, RG 24, C-3, Vol. 14240, File/ dossier 229, 001141.
3. Ibid.
4. Washington, Nara, Headquarters 504th Parachute Infantry RCT. APO 469, S3 Journal, Sissonne to Remouchamps, December 1944 to January 1945, No entry date, p.4.
5. Tyler, F., op. cit., p.350.
6. In the US Army, Section 1 is responsible for personnel management.
7. Graves, G., op. cit., p.17.
8. Haasler, T., MacDougall, R., Vosters, S., Weber, H., *Duel in the Mist, Vol. II,* Heathfield, 2012, pp.193–5.
9. Washington, Nara, AAR 703rd Tank Destroyer Battalion, The Operation with the 82nd Airborne Division, 20 December - 1 January 1945, No place, 31 January 1945, pp.4–5.
10. Interview with Bill Tucker by Christian Dujardin, July 2009.
11. Ottawa, National Archives of Canada RG 24, C-3, Vol. 14240, File/ dossier 229, 001141.
12. Lafaro, G., *The Sword of St Michael,* Cambridge, 2011, p.448.
13. Graves, G., op., cit., p.17.
14. Haasler, T. and All, *Duel in the Mist,* Vol. II, Heathfield, 2012, pp.122–39.
15. Coles, H., *The Great Battle of the Ardennes, in Belgium and Luxembourg,* Villance en Ardennes, 1994, p.330.
16. Graves, G., op. cit., p.17.
17. Registration of burials.
18. Nordyke, P., op. cit., p.321.
19. Bastogne, Bastogne War Museum Documentation Centre, After Action Report HQ 82nd Airborne. G2 report n° 151, In the field, 22 December 1944, pp.1–2.
20. Graves, G., op. cit., pp.19–22.
21. Fontaine, S., *Stoumont-Cheneux-La Gleize : December 44,* Stavelot, 1995, pp.31–2.
22. Fontaine, S., op. cit., p.20.

**Chapter 5**

1. Washington, Nara, Foreign Military Studies A 877, pp.37–8.
2. It is possible that Vandervoort saw Tiger aircraft, although we lean more towards Jagdpanzer IVs or Panzer IVs.
3. Vandervoort uses the word Clambake, which primarily means a fisherman's pot or, figuratively speaking, a small party.
4. Vandervoort's assertion is totally implausible.
5. Lindzee Prescott, a talented young artist, was the draughtsman and caricaturist for the regimental intelligence service. He had a unique style of distorting perspective and exaggerating proportions to give the illusion of an animated 'German tank', or other caricatures that sprang from his sketches.
6. Probably a Wirbelwind.
7. Evocation of the Battle of Trois-Ponts by Vandervoort, author's personal collection.
8. Washington, Nara, Foreign Military Studies A 877, p.39.
9. Longue,M., *Kampfgruppe Knittel,* Bayeux, 2010, p.93.
10. Washington, Nara, AAR 117th IR.
11. Brussels, Ministère de la Justice, Archives des Procureurs Généraux, Documents relating to the trial of the Stavelot massacres, Goltz et al., Translation of Manfred Coblenz's written statement of 15 April 1946.

12. The transcription of the letter states 461, which seems excessive to us and out of line with the number of days he confided in his father in his other letter.
13. Ibid., appendix to PV 282.
14. Brussels, Ministère de la Justice, Archives des Procureurs Généraux, Documents relating to the trial of the Stavelot massacres, Goltz et al., Translation of Manfred Coblenz's written statement of 15 April 1946.
15. The Petit Spay bridge next to the road linking Trois-Ponts to Stavelot. In clear water, the deck of the old bridge is still visible today.
16. Referring to E Company, 2/505th PIR cfr supra.
17. Preiss is actually referring to assault cannons.
18. Washington, Nara, Foreign Military Studies A 877, pp.39–40.
19. Pergrin, D., *First Across the Rhine: The 291st Engineer Combat Battalion,* Saint-Paul, 2006, p.161.
20. Testimony of Charles Corbin, https://www.3ad.com/history/wwll/memoirs.pages/corbin.pages/parfondruy.htm, consulted on 23 January 2024.
21. Washington, Nara, Foreign Military Studies A 877, p.40.
22. Washington, Nara, Ethint 47, von Rundstedt, *The Ardennes Offensive*, p.1.
23. Washington, Nara, Ethint 34, Buechs, *The Ardennes Offensive*, p.12.
24. Oberbefehshaber West, the German High Command on the Western Front, whose chief was directly subordinate to Hitler. From 5 September 1944 to 9 March 1945, its chief was von Rundstedt. Although he was only marginally involved in the conduct of operations, for a long time the Ardennes offensive was known as the von Rundstedt offensive.
25. Washington, Nara, T311 R31 note dated 15 December 1944 20:30 signed by the Chief of Staff OB West, General Westphal.
26. Washington, Nara, Ethint 21, Krämer, p.5.
27. The Supreme Command of the Wehrmacht (OKW) was the Wehrmacht's highest staff organisation.
28. Washington, Nara, Ethint 21, Krämer, p.5.
29. Weidinger, O., *Division Das Reich. Der Weg der 2. SS-Panzer-Division 'Das Reich'. Band V: 1943–1945. Die Geschichte der Stammdivision der Waffen-SS,* Osnabrück, 1982, p.361.
30. Washington, Nara, Ethint 34, Büchs, p.12.
31. The Pozit detonator is a secret weapon. The detonator is triggered by the Doppler effect. The explosion takes place at an optimum height, where the steel balls are the most lethal.
32. Washington, Nara, G2 report 30th ID Message 8 210105.
33. Washington, Nara, Headquarters United States Army Materiel Command, Fuzes, Proximity, Electrical, 1 July 1963, pp.22–6.
34. Washington, Headquarters United States Army Materiel Command, Fuzes, Proximity, Electrical, 1 July 1963, p.22–26.
35. Dobinson, C., *AA Command Britain's Anti-aircraft Defences of WW II,* London, 2002, p.437.

**Chapter 6**

1. The German name for the Americans.
2. Washington, Library of Congress, Malmedy Trial, Vol. 11, pp.2362–3
3. Haasler, T., MacDougall, R., Vosters, S., Weber H., *Duel in the Mist 2*, Heathfield, 2012, pp.40–1.
4. Gabriel, R., op. cit., pp.203–204.
5. Washington, NARA, AAR 3rd AD, 33rd AR, entry dated 21 February 1944.
6. Ibid.
7. Ibid.
8. Ferris, F., *The 30th Infantry Division, Ardennes 16–25 December 44*, sl, sd, pp.45–6.
9. Knox, D., *Memories Lieutenant Knox, December 44,* https://www.oldhickory30th.com, n.d., Accessed 2 February 2021.
10. Washington, Library of Congress, Malmedy Trial, vol 11, pp.2362–3

11. Gabriel, R., *75 ...ans après: de Trois Ponts à Stoumont,* La Gleize, 2021, pp.274–6.
12. Washington, Nara, Unit Journal 119th Infantry Regiment, December 1944.
13. Washington, Nara, 30th ID, G2 periodic report n° 192, 26/12/1944.
14. Washington, Nara, Foreign Military Studies C 004, pp.12–13.
15. Letter from Oskar Siegmund dated 9 December 1986 to Mr Gosset, Chairman of the CRIBA.
16. Gabriel, R., op. cit., pp.275–6.
17. Ibid.
18. Washington, Nara, 30th Infantry Division, Ardennes 16–25 December 1944, p.47.

**Chapter 7**

1. Washington, Nara, Foreign Military Studies C 004, p.13.
2. The original eyewitness account gives the date as 23 December, but it seems the scene took place on the 22nd.
3. Peiper did not stay at the château, but in the part of the conciergerie inhabited by the gardener, Alphonse Bonmariage.
4. De Harenne, F., *Froidcour & les deux Guerres mondiales*, No place, 2021, p.24.
5. Washington, Nara, 30th ID, G2 periodic report n° 192, 26/12/1944.
6. Washington, Nara, AAR 3rd AD, 33rd AR, entry dated 22/2/1944.
7. Website: http://www.oldhickory30th.com, Accessed on 29 September 2023.
8. Washington; Library of Congress, Malmedy Trial, Vol. 13 pp.2068–71.
9. Ottawa, National Archives of Canada RG 24, C-3, Vol. 14240, File/ dossier 229, 001141.
10. Washington, Nara, Foreign Military Studies C 004, p.14.
11. Washington, Nara, AAR G2, message 94 of 22 December.
12. It is astonishing that the 'decipherers' should have interpreted this as a parachute drop of troops in a region with rugged terrain and dense woodland.
13. Washington, Nara, AAR 3rd AD 33rd AR, entry dated 22/12/1944.
14. Ottawa, National Archives of Canada, RG 24, C-3, Vol. 14240 File/ dossier 229, 001141.
15. Fontaine, S., op. cit., p.43.
16. Letter from Oskar Siegmund dated 9 December 1986 to Mr Gosset, Chairman of the CRIBA.

**Chapter 8**

1. Washington, Nara, AAR 743rd TB.
2. Laby, H., *Ardennes 44 Stavelot*, Herstal, 1999, p.257.
3. Brussels, Archives des Procureurs Généraux Trial of Stavelot Goltz and others, Pro Justitia 2251/17 of 19 February 1947.
4. See *Stavelot – La Gleize, Le destin des Tiger de Peiper*, p.126.
5. There are still two steel beams planted on the banks of the Amblève, marking the spot some 200 metres downstream of the confluence of the Amblève and the Rue de Parfondruy.
6. Biester farm.
7. Wijers, J., *Die Ardennen-Offensive: Die Brücken von Stavelot und Trois Ponts Augenzeugen berichten, Zusammengestellt,* p.253.
8. Website: http://battleofthebulgememories.be/ The Siege at Petit-Coo, consulted on 21 May 2019.
9. Officer in charge of combat tactics.
10. Washington, Nara, AAR G2 30th Infantry Division.
11. The departure of infantrymen from E Company, 120th IR, had to be compensated for by the arrival of I Company, 117th IR, which had taken Renardmont. The hamlets of Renardmont and Parfondruy are only a few hundred metres apart.
12. Uccle, IRM. The nearest station is at the Spa barracks, 12 kilometres away and at the same altitude.
13. Washington, Nara, AAR 117th IR, entry dated 23/12/1944.
14. Website: https://www.unithistories.com/units/30th%20Inf.Div.asp, consulted on 21 June 2019.
15. Wijers, J., op. cit., p.253.

16. Washington, Nara, AAR 117th IR, entry dated 23/12/1944.
17. Stavelot 40 45. Stavelot municipal library, Chauveheid, 10 October 1984, p.76.
18. Washington, Nara, Foreign Military Studies A 924, pp.44–5.
19. Cole, H., op. cit., p.338–9.
20. Washington, Nara, Foreign Military Studies A 877, pp.43–4.
21. Estimate made following aerial reconnaissance. Fort Leavenworth, Ike Skelton Library, R-12434, AAR 30th ID Div artillery, entry dated 25/12/1944.
22. Ibid.
23. Stavelot Municipal Library, AAR 117th/IR.
24. Rubel, H., *Daredevil Tanker: The Story of the 740th Tank Battalion*, Göttingen, 1945, p.70.

**Chapter 9**

1. Washington, Nara, Ethint, p.10.
2. Washington, Nara, RG 242, T311 R31.
3. Freiburg, BA, MSA 877, pp.39–45.
4. Freiburg, BA, MSA 924, p.48.
5. Washington, Nara, AAR, 3rd AD 33rd AR, entry dated 23/2/1944.
6. Washington, Nara, Foreign Military Studies A 877, p.43.
7. Washington, Nara, Foreign Military Studies C 004, p.15.
8. Washington, Library of Congress. Malmedy Trial, Vol XIV, p.217.
9. Washington, Nara, 30th ID, G2 periodic report n° 192, 26/12/1944.
10. Washington, Nara, 30th ID, G2 periodic report n° 192, 26/12/1944.
11. Letter from Oskar Siegmund dated 9 December 1986 to Mr Gosset, Chairman of the CRIBA.
12. Ottawa, National Archives of Canada, RG 24, C-3, Vol. 14240, File/ dossier 229, 001141.
13. Kew, The National Archives, CAB 106/1071. Copies of telegrams between Headquarters 21st Army Group and War Office (16 Dec – 15 Jan), report dated 23/12/1944.
14. Delaval, M., *Saint-Vith During Hitler's Final Blitzkrieg*, Vielsalm, 1984, pp.211–25.
15. Cole, H., *The Ardennes, Battle of the Bulge*, Washington, 1965, pp.526–32.
16. Testimony of General Gavin quoted in Delaval, M., *Saint-Vith au cours de l'ultime Blitzkrieg d'Hitler*, Vielsalm, 1984, pp.239–40.
17. Washington, Nara, 30th ID, G2 periodic report n° 192, 26/12/1944.
18. Nordyke, P., *All American, All the Way,* Saint-Paul, 2005, p.640.
19. Washington, Library of Congress, Malmedy Trial, Vol. 9, p.1962.
20. Washington, Library of Congress, Malmedy Trial, Vol. 9, p.1958–9.
21. Brussels, Ministère de la Justice, Archives des Procureurs Généraux, Documents relating to the trail of the Stavelot massacres, Goltz et al. Translation of the written statement by Paul Zwigart dated 11 February 1946, Dossier 4. p.454–460.
22. The original German version of Preiss' report held by the Bundesarchiv in Freiburg differs quite considerably from the translated version held by the Nara. Preiss' original text clearly states that it refers to SPW Freiburg, Bundesarchiv, Msa 877 p.44. The English version refers to 60 heavy armoured guns. Washington, Nara, Foreign Military Studies A 877, p.46. However, neither version is an exact reflection of the reality of the total number of tanks lost, which is more a reflection of the losses in the cauldron; the number of SPWs seems very close to the total lost during the operation. We set the actual losses at a much higher figure in our conclusions.
23. Washington, Nara, Foreign Military Studies A 877, pp.45–46.
24. Confidence gathered from Rudolf Tiemman by Frank Rockenbrod.
25. Goya, M., *Les armées du Chaos*, Paris, 2008, p.54.
26. Santoni, P., *Le triangle tactique*, Paris, 2019, p.20.
27. Washington, Nara, Ethint., p.10.
28. It had just been given the suffix SS in its designation, which it did not have at the time of the Battle of the Bulge.

29. Agte, P., op. cit., pp.437–8.
30. Arnaud, G., *L'affaire Peiper,* Paris, 1979, Passim. The facts stated by the journalist are sufficiently disturbing to raise the question.

**The Violence of a Fiasco**

1. Cole, H., op. cit., p.330.
2. Hiwi is a contraction of the term *Hilfswilliger,* which literally means 'volunteer helper'. These were auxiliaries, generally of Slavic origin, who were more or less forced to perform mainly logistical tasks.
3. *personale und materiel Lage 1.SS-Panzer Division,* dated December 1944.
4. Bethesda, US Army Concepts Analysis Agency, 7/2/1990, THE ARDENNES CAMPAIGN SIMULATION DATA BASE, p.50.
5. Ibid., p.395.
6. Ibid., p.427.
7. Ibid., p.430.

# Bibliography


**Archives**
Brussels, Ministry of Justice, Archives des Procureurs Généraux.
Documents relating to the Stavelot massacre trial.

**Washington, Library of Congress**
Veterans History Project, interview with Leon Kent (20/7/2003).
Dachau Trials archives.

**Washington, Nara**
Administrative History collection, G4 History, ADM n° 553, December 1944 – January 1945.
Atrocity Trial Testimony Lt Col Peiper.
Ferris, F., Historical Officer, 30th Inf. Div. 16–25 December 1944.
Ethint interviews: 10, 11, 15, 17, 21, 23, 25, 34, 45, 50.
Washington, Center of Military History, Logistics in World War II Final Report of the Army Forces.
Washington Center of Military History, The European Theater of Operations LOGISTICAL SUPPORT OF THE ARMIES, Vol. I & II.
AAR, Headquarters 30th Infantry Division.
AAR 703rd Tank Destroyer Battalion.
AAR 117th IR.
AAR 3rd AD, 33rd AR.
AAR 743rd TB.
Interview with Lt. Col. Samuel McDowell, CO of 3rd Battalion, 117th Infantry, and Lt Andrew Allen Executive Officer of Company K, 117th Infantry.
Foreign Military Studies, MSA 877.
Foreign Military Studies, MSB 347, 733.
Foreign Military Studies, MSC 04 24.
RG407/427A/ box 19014/ folder CI 329A-14.
RG407/427A/ box 19014/ folder CI 329B-14.
Headquarters United States Army Materiel Command, Fuzes, Proximity, Electrical, 1 July 1963.
RG 242, T311, R31.

**Fort Leaveworth, Ike Skelton Library**
Adams, J., *The Operations of A Company, 508th PIR (82nd Airborne-Division) near Rencheux, Belgium, 22–25 December 1944 (personal experience of a Company Commander)*, Fort Benning, 1947–1948.
Cain, F., *The 1111th Engineer Group in the Bulge: The Role of Engineers as Infantry in Airland Battle*, School of Advanced Military Studies US Army Command and General Staff College Fort Leavenworth, Kansas, 1985.
Campana, V., *The Operations of 2nd Battalion, 504th PIR (82nd Airborne-Division) in the German Counter Offensive 18 December 1944 – 16 January 1945 (personal Experience of a Battalion S3)*, Fort Benning, 1946–1947.
Ferris, F., *The German Offensive 16 December Defense of Spa Gas Dump.*

Le Febvre, H., *The Operations of 2nd Battalion, 508th PIR (82nd Airborne-Division) in the Withdrawal and the Recapture of Thier du Mont Ridge, Belgium, 22 December 1944 – 7 January 1945 (Personal Experience of a Battalion Operations Officer)*, Fort Benning, 1948–1949.
Marschall, S., *The Operations of 1st Platoon, Battery C, 80th Airborne Antiaircraft Battalion (82nd Airborne-Division) in the Battle of the Bulge 17 December 1944 – 3 January 1945 (Personal Experience of a Platoon Leader)*, Fort Benning, 1947–1948.
Stark, M., *Antitank Platoon in Support of Infantry Regiment,* Georgia, Fort Benning, sd.
Carlisle Barracks Pennsylvania. US Army College. USAWC Strategy research project from the Red Ball Express.
HEADQUARTERS 12TH ARMY GROUP (FINAL AFTER ACTION REPORT), VOL II.
847-9, AAR 612th TD Battalion.
8833 TD AAR 823rd TD Battalion.
847-59 AAR 825th TD Battalion.
8743 TD AAR 743rd Tank Battalion & S3 Journal-History November – December 1944.
AAR Unit Journal 119th IR, December 1944.
AAR 504th Parachute Infantry Regiment, unit S3 Journal.
N17500-1033-2, MSB 151.
N-17840, War Experiences of Commanders of German Panzer Units, General Sepp Dietrich and Colonel Joachim Peiper.

**Kew National Archives**
Kew, National Archives, CAB 106/1071.

**Ottawa, National Archives**
RG 24, C-3, Vol. 14240, File/ dossier 229.

**Freiburg, Bundesarchiv**
MSA 873, 877, 924.

**Brussels, Archives of the College of Procurators General**
Trial of Stavelot Goltz and others.

**Bastogne War Museum, Fonds Criba**
After Action Report, Headquarters 823rd TD Battalion.
After Action Report, Headquarters 30th Infantry-Division.

**Memoires**
Gavin, J., *On to Berlin,* New York, 1978.
Ridgway, M., *Soldier: The Memoirs of Matthew B. Ridgway,* New York, 1956.
Rubel, G., *Daredevil: The Story of the 740th Tank Battalion*, Göttingen, 1945.

**Works**
Coll, *Stavelot 40–45*, Chauveheid, 1984.
Coll, Bethesda, US Army Concepts Analysis Agency, 7/2/1990, THE ARDENNES CAMPAIGN SIMULATION DATA BASE.
Agte, P., *Jochen Peiper, Commander of the Panzerregiment of the Leibstandarte*, Paris, 2021.
War Crimes Commission, *Stavelot,* Liège, 1945.
Arnaud, G., *L'affaire Peiper,* Paris, 1979.
Cailloux, L., *Ardennes 1944, Pearl Harbor in Europe*, Première partie, Liège, 1969.
Cain, F., *The 1111th Engineer Group in the Bulge: The Role of Engineers as Infantry in AirLand Battle, Fort Leavenworth,* 1985.

Carter, R., *Cheneux*, in periodical C.A.M., 1987.
Celis, P., *Fighters Defending the Ardennes*, sd, sl.
Cole, H., *La grande bataille des Ardennes en Belgique et au Luxembourg*, Villance-en-Ardennes, 1994.
Cooke, D. and Evans, W., *Kampfgruppe Peiper at the Battle of the Bulge,* Mechanicsburgs, 2005.
Cook. D. and Wayne E., *Kampfgruppe Peiper: The Race for the Meuse*, Barnsley, 2005.
Cuppens, G., *Massacre à Malmedy*, Bayeux, 1989.
De Harenne, F., *Froidcour et les deux guerres mondiales,* Froidcour, 2021.
Delaval, M., *Saint-Vith During Hitler's Last Blitzkrieg,* Vielsalm, 1984.
De Meyer S., Haasler T., MacDougall R., Vosters S., Weber H. *Duel in the Mist*, Newcastle, 2007.
Dobinson, C., *AA Command Britain's Anti-Aircraft Defences of WW II,* London, 2002.
Ferris, F., *The 30th Infantry Division, Ardennes 16–25 December 44*, sl, sd.
Fontaine, S., *Trois-Ponts, décembre 1944, quand les ponts volaient en éclats*, Trois-Ponts, 1992.
Fontaine, S., *Stoumont Cheneux La Gleize Stavelot,* No place, 1995.
Gregoire, G., *Les Panzer de Peiper face à l'US Army*, Stavelot, 1986.
Gabriel, R., *75 Years On: La Gleize and Stoumont,* La Gleize, 2020.
Götzel, H., *Generaloberst Kurt Student und seine Fallschirmjäger, die Erinnerungen des Generaloberst Kurt Student*; Friedberg, sd, 1980.
Goya, M., *Les armées du Chaos*, Paris, 2008.
Graves, G., *Le sang et la neige*, sd, sl.
Heptia, T.H., *History of the Bierset Base,* Bierset, 1990.
Hewitt R., *Work Horse of the Western Front*, Washington, 1946.
Jentz, T., *Germany's Panther Tank*, Atglen, 1995.
Laby. H., *Ardennes 44 Stavelot,* Faimes, 1999.
Liddel-Hart, B.H., *Les généraux allemands parlent,* Paris, 1949.
LoFaro, G., *The Sword of St. Michael: The 82nd Airborne Division in World War II,* New York, 2007.
Longue, M., *Massacres en Ardennes*, Brussels, 2006.
Mac Donald, C., *The Battle of Ardennes*, Brussels, 1989.
Merriam, R., *Dark December,* New York – Chicago, 1947.
Meyer, K., *Soldier of the Reich*, Bayeux, 1996.
Nordyke, P., *More Than Courage, The Combat History of the 504th Parachute Infantry Regiment in World War II*, Minneapolis, 2008.
Pergrin, D., *First Across the Rhine*, Saint-Paul, 2006.
Reynolds, M., *The Devil's Adjutant,* Staplehurst, 1995.
Reynolds, M., *The Devil's Warrant Officer*, Erpe, 2000.
Roberts, A., *Five Star to Victory*, Birmingham, 1949.
Rogister, H., *Décembre 1944 : Bataille des Ardennes de Baugner à Stavelot,* CRIBA, Liège, 2009.
Santoni, P., *Le triangle tactique,* Paris, 2019.
Tiemann, R., *The Leibstandarte Vol IV part 2*, Winnipeg, 1998.
Tyler, F., *A Fine Sense of Honor: At War with the Men of the 504th Parachute Infantry from Sicily to the Fall of Germany*, Wroclaw, 2019.
Weidinger, O., *Division Das Reich: Der Weg der 2. SS-Panzer-Division 'Das Reich'. Band V: 1943–1945. Die Geschichte der Stammdivision der Waffen-SS,* Osnabrück, 1982.
Wijers, H., *The Battle of the Bulge: The Losheim Gap/Holding the Line*, Mechanicsburg, 2009.
Wijers, H., *Die Ardennen-Offensive,* Vol. 4, sl, sd.

**Webography**

https://www.criba.be.
Brussels, Belgium, Royal Meteorological Institute, Spa Station.
https://www.3ad.com
http://www.oldhickory30th.com
http://battleofthebulgememories.be
https://www.unithistories.com/
https://www.tracesofwar.com